MEN
WITHOUT
FACES

BOOKS BY LOUIS FRANCIS BUDENZ

•

THIS IS MY STORY

MEN WITHOUT FACES

MEN
WITHOUT
FACES

The Communist Conspiracy
in the U. S. A.

By LOUIS FRANCIS BUDENZ

HARPER & BROTHERS · NEW YORK

MEN WITHOUT FACES

To

J. M. J.

CONTENTS

PREFACE

On October 2, 1935, the *Daily Worker* publicly announced that I had joined the Communist party. I had signed my application for membership the previous August, but had been kept waiting until Earl Browder's return from Moscow, when the decision was made whether I should function openly or as a concealed Communist. Several of the Red leaders thought that I should take advantage of my wide acquaintance in the labor movement to act as an undercover member of the party. I did not favor this, and Browder and the Communist International representative, Gerhart Eisler, agreed with me.

The immediate reason I became a Communist party member was the adoption of the People's Front policy at the Seventh Congress of the Communist International, held in Moscow in the summer of 1935. I had previously read Lenin and other Communist authorities, and had accepted the Communist viewpoint some years prior to this time; but my experiences in the labor movement, which had been rather extensive, had led me to insist that the Communists' labor tactics and subservience to Moscow were wrong. I favored what I called the "American approach." However, when Georgi Dimitrov, speaking for Stalin at the Seventh Congress, stated that the Communists in each country should have due regard for their respective national traditions, I became converted to the necessity of joining the party.

I became a Communist with my eyes open. For a number of years I had alternately criticized the Communist party and worked with it in united fronts. Upon joining, I agreed to the oath of fealty to Stalin, and in the public statement in the *Daily Worker* I acknowledged Stalin's leadership. I then believed that the Soviet dictatorship, when established over the world, would lead to emancipation of the workers and to a "higher stage of democracy."

This decision of 1935 had been in the making for twenty years. A fourth-generation Indianian, I had grown up in a Catholic household with a father of German ancestry and a mother of Irish descent. When very young, I became aware of discrimination against the Negro people and workers who lived in our vicinity. Studying every available book I could get hold of on these matters, I resolved to do something to remedy such abuses. During my high-school days, my attendance at the conventions of the United Mine Workers of America, which were then held regularly in Indianapolis, convinced me still further of the urgency of taking a stand on the side of labor. In order to help my work with and for labor, I took a degree in law and became immediately afterward editor of *The Carpenter*, the organ of the United Brotherhood of Carpenters and Joiners, then the largest union in the American Federation of Labor.

From then on, the story was one of increasing labor activity. By the twenties I was in New York as editor of *Labor Age*, a monthly magazine devoted to industrial unionism. It had on its board national officers of most of the unions which later formed the Congress of Industrial Organizations. Organization work accompanied my editorial work, and resulted in my direction of strikes in Kenosha, Wisconsin; Nazareth, Pennsylvania; Paterson, New Jersey; and the Auto-Lite contest in Toledo, Ohio. Concentrating especially on getting injunctions and yellow-dog contracts nullified, I was arrested twenty-one times and acquitted twenty-one times in the course of these organizational drives.

Throughout this period I was studying the Communist "classics," especially the works of Lenin. *State and Revolution* particularly impressed me, with its promise that the Soviet dictatorship would voluntarily end in the anarchistlike Communist society. It was quite easy by then for me to view Marxism-Leninism sympathetically, since I had broken with the Catholic Church in 1914. Actually excommunicated at that time for marrying a divorced

Catholic, I had been increasingly impatient with the Church for not more rapidly facilitating reform. It was only after long years of sweat and strain that I was to learn that impatience is not a virtue.

Shortly after joining the party, I was appointed labor editor of the *Daily Worker* because of the belief of Jack Stachel and other leading Reds that I could help considerably in infiltrating the new CIO. In that capacity, I quickly learned that the party in this country was completely controlled by aliens hidden from the public view. The discovery was a distinct shock; but for a long time I excused the czarlike rule exercised by Moscow's foreign agents on the ground that it was necessary in the fight against Hitlerism. Many other revelations that "workers' emancipation" had become a cloak for world slavery I likewise explained away on the grounds that these measures would lead in time to the withering away of the state and the establishment of the free Communist society.

It was only after ten years of active Red leadership, when I could no longer evade the incontestable fact that the Soviet dictatorship was bent on world conquest by armed minority bands in each country, and could lead only to world slavery, that I broke with the party.

The decision to break was not made overnight. I had to think carefully about what I actually believed. It was difficult to admit publicly that I had been mistaken ten years before when I joined the party, and that thirty years before the Church had been correct and I had been wrong. My reluctance to make this admission undoubtedly contributed to the delay. But, among many other considerations, I had to recognize that the Church had foreseen the evils in the Communist camp which I had become acquainted with by experience. It had also understood clearly that the gravest danger of all nations was their failure to grasp the true nature of Communism.

Out of my experiences of ten years in Communist leadership, I hope in this book to make the American people understand the extent and character of the Communist conspiracy for world conquest.

I hope to demonstrate that the Soviet dictatorship and its fifth column in this country constitute a clear and present danger to the existence of the United States.

I want to show beyond question that the Communist party is not a political party in the American or democratic sense, but solely a fifth column of the Kremlin.

Finally, I shall try to make clear, once and for all, from the repeated pledges of the Kremlin itself, that the Soviet dictatorship will not rest until it has achieved its objective of the "World October," the world Soviet dictatorship.

L. F. B.

Fordham University
Easter Week, 1950

MEN
WITHOUT
FACES

The House

on Thirteenth Street

I MANAGED the *Daily Worker* from a guarded, locked, sound-proof room. It was guarded, locked and soundproof because as managing editor I did more than get out a daily New York newspaper. I was an active participant in the whole network of conspiracy of which the *Daily Worker* is a part.

The only men and women permitted to enter the room were those who were successfully serving Stalin in America. Some of them were directing espionage against the United States. Others were working secretly—and effectively—to influence the opinions of people who counted in American life. Not infrequently a select comrade did both. More than a few of our visitors were from the Red underground, and as abruptly as they had come, would disappear into it again. Occasionally, either through unwelcome accident or design, one or another of these hidden comrades was snatched suddenly from his oblivion by the bright searchlight of American newspaper headlines. Still others, sometimes seen in the *Daily Worker* and registered there as the Kremlin's faithful servants, lived openly as non-Communists. A long list of these loyal and concealed Communists, men and women who occupy distinguished positions in business, professional and public life, was given to me orally by Politburo members and committed to memory. Never was this list of names

permitted to appear on paper. Today, now that I have left the
Communist party, it gives me a distinctly queer feeling to see and
hear these people, who I know have sworn fealty to Stalin,
fervently defended by unsuspecting and patriotic Americans.

The *Daily Worker* is the daily official organ of the Communist
party of the United States, and the years that I functioned as
its editor were those very years in which the Reds sank their
roots most effectively into many key places in American life.
Their gain was not so much in numbers (although they made
headway there too, to some degree) as in "influence," that mysterious factor to which the Communist leaders refer so frequently
in their official reports. To gain this "influence," the Communists
infiltrate key government posts, undermine the patriotism of well-
meaning people in strategic or confidential positions, and win over
those whose words, spoken and written, have an effect on American public opinion. With the recognition of the Soviet government by the United States in November, 1933, this process was
enormously accelerated. Checked partially during the Hitler-
Stalin alliance, it went all out in the course of the Second World
War. Precisely what was achieved, and how it was achieved, I
shall try to show later.

Every morning as I entered my office I stepped from American
to alien soil. The *Daily Worker* is located in the narrow loft
building that houses the national offices of the Communist
party at 50 East Thirteenth Street in New York City. To guard
what goes on within, the building has been deliberately surrounded with an atmosphere of concealment and conspiracy. It
is difficult to obtain entrance, except upon the word of a leading
comrade. Everyone who does business there is watched carefully
from the moment he enters until he leaves, a rule which was
observed even during the days of the party's alleged honeymoon
with the Roosevelt administration and "bourgeois democracy."

The Red newspaper offices are on the eighth floor, the last
stop before the famed (or ill-famed) Ninth Floor which figures

so prominently in all trial testimony concerning the Communist party and its subversions. That floor houses the Politburo—the party bosses who exercise a bureaucratic control over the entire party apparatus in this country, and who are in turn controlled by the Communist International bosses appointed by Stalin. At the managing editor's desk, I was in constant communication by special telephone with these "upper regions," as the journalistic comrades, partly in jest and largely in awe, called the headquarters above.

Down from the Ninth Floor came several times each day at least two of these party bosses—to direct, harangue, command, in accordance with the latest directive received through "the channels from abroad." Members of the Politburo though they were, their own fate hung on a nod from Moscow or on some possible change in the party line which might render them no longer useful. This uncertainty of the future and of their master's favor added to the frantic eagerness with which they sought to execute every order given them.

Politburo is the name given to the body of six to twelve men who dictate the course of the party to the district organizers and other party representatives throughout the country. Although the title was changed twice—first to the Political Committee and then to the National Board—to accord with American usage and make the party sound native in character, the name Politburo continues in general use among the comrades. The present party chief, William Z. Foster, burst out with it in his printed speech in the September, 1945, issue of *Political Affairs,* when he denounced Browder. It is taken of course from the powerful Politburo of Moscow, the oligarchy which rules the Soviet government and the Reds in all parts of the globe. But the Politburo here has only the shadow of power; its members are completely puppets of the Kremlin's personal representatives in America.

Through these men or through their agents, or from others engaged in the far-flung apparatus, conspiratorial information flowed every hour to the *Daily Worker* managing editor's desk.

For example, in 1944—some months before Stalin welcomed Roosevelt and Churchill at Yalta—the "must" order from Moscow to its agents in America was that this country should be "re-educated" on Poland and China. The idea of setting up Red governments in both those key nations was to be forwarded at all costs and foisted upon the American public. The order was brought to the attention of the Political Committee upstairs through a memorandum from Gerhart Eisler, Stalin's chief agent here, and expounded at a secret meeting of the National Committee of the Communist party by Earl Browder, the party leader. The same information was passed on to me. A Red Poland and a Red China would aid democracy. Mao Tse-tung, leader of the Chinese Communists, was no tool of the Soviets but merely a mild agrarian reformer. This was the bill of goods that was to be sold to the unsuspecting Americans.

The Politburo's instructions, relayed to the party leaders throughout the country, were reflected almost at once in declarations by men termed experts, who looked with favor on the Chinese Reds and on Moscow's designs in Poland. Men and women who could not be accused of communism, save at the expense to the accuser of his reputation for veracity, came forward in newspapers, magazines and on the platform to further Moscow's ambitions. And at the *Daily Worker* managing editor's desk the ways and means by which these people had been induced to say these things so injurious to their native land and to the world's future were known. Who among these experts were the Kremlin's agents was also known.

It was one of the most fantastic hoaxes ever attempted—and it was successful. How completely America was hoodwinked by the inspired propaganda about Mao, for instance, is made painfully evident in his statement of July, 1949. In it he scorns any friendly relations with this country and places himself solidly on the side of Soviet Russia in the "anti-imperialist camp." He is for smashing the "foreign reactionaries" opposed to Moscow and therefore to a Red China.

As managing editor of the Red newspaper and as a member of the National Committee of the Communist party, I had a large part in this campaign. Every waking moment was devoted to attending the secret meetings of the Politburo, the caucuses of other groups ordered by that body, and to conferring personally with influential people on the subject. From such experience I gained a thorough knowledge of the ramifications of the Soviet fifth column in the United States. Increasingly I became impressed with its strength, its resourcefulness, its utter unscrupulousness.

The aim of this fifth column, and of the dictatorship manipulating it, is the violent destruction of the American Republic. It plans the conquest of the United States by setting up a world proletarian dictatorship guided and ruled by Joseph Stalin. As comfortable as it may have been in the past to evade that ugly reality, it can be evaded no longer. The fanatical hope, if you can call it that, which gives drive to these conspirators is the belief in "The World October." This promised extension to the entire globe of the October Russian revolution which set up the Soviet dictatorship is the dynamo of the Communist movement. That whispered promise is on the lips of every obscure comrade; it is proudly proclaimed in every important speech and every fundamental book by every leader of the Soviet state.

In the first pamphlet on communism that I was given to study on entering the party, this pledge to wipe out the American government by fire and sword was stated in the most bloodthirsty terms. The pamphlet was written by the late Moissaye Olgin, officially heralded as among the most revered of Red leaders.

This pledge is made again even in Georgi Dimitrov's famous statement on "The United Front" in 1935, when in Stalin's name he was supposedly wooing the "democratic" nations: "The proletariat is the real master, tomorrow's master of the world," said Dimitrov, "and it must enter upon its historical rights, take into its hands the reins of government in every country, all over the world." And how will it do that? "If we and the proletariat of the whole world firmly follow the path indicated by Lenin and Stalin, the bourgeoisie will perish in spite of everything." The bourgeoisie will perish because the path of Lenin and Stalin is the violent overthrow of all governments like that of the United States. These words were distributed by the tens of thousands by the Communist party of the United States, and studied zealously by all loyal Reds.

In March, 1949, the Communist party leaders issued from the House on Thirteenth Street a declaration which President Truman promptly and correctly labeled the work of traitors. It placed the chairman and general secretary of the Communist party, William Z. Foster and Eugene Dennis, squarely on record in favor of aiding Soviet armies should they invade American soil. It did so, of course, indirectly, in that Aesopian language which Lenin has recommended to the Reds—by applauding Maurice Thorez of France and Palmieri Togliatti of Italy for asserting that they would welcome the Soviet military forces on the soil of their countries, "when in pursuit of an aggressor." Since any nation opposed to Soviet expansion is *ipso facto* an "aggressor," the pledged aid to Soviet imperialistic conquest implied in these words was quite plain.

The amazing thing about this Foster-Dennis statement wasn't that it was made, but that some of the supposedly well-informed and leading figures in the United States were amazed at it. It is precisely what the Soviet dictatorship and its agents on Thirteenth Street and other places have been saying throughout the existence of the Communist conspiracy. It is what Lenin set as the goal of the Bolshevik dictatorship at the very dawn of Soviet power. In his masterpiece, *State and Revolution*, the violent smashing of the civil apparatus, the judiciary and military of the "bourgeois" states is set down as the chief aim of the Soviet regime. And in order that there should be no misunderstanding, Lenin asks the question: "Does this apply to the United States of America?" and answers that it emphatically does so apply. In other works, notably *The Proletarian Revolution and the Renegade Kautsky*, Lenin repeats and underscores this aim. These are fundamental textbooks which every Marxist-Leninist, every comrade in the House on Thirteenth Street and everyone following them must study as guides to action.

This is likewise what Joseph Stalin wrote carefully and with consideration in his two outstanding volumes, *Foundations of Leninism* and *The History of the Communist Party of the Soviet Union (Bolsheviks)*. In the Communist world, these books are not mere studies of social developments. They are the Korans of the living Red legions, pointing the way to the winning of the earthly paradise, the Communist Society. They are required reading for Communists throughout the world, the subject of discussion and study and the basis of all Red plans for action. They are for sale at every Red bookstore.

The same goal was again affirmed in the celebrated "Program of the Communist International," adopted at the Sixth World Congress of 1928; it was reasserted at the Seventh World Congress in Moscow in 1935; it has been proclaimed the objective of the Communist party of the United States in official resolutions and other documents which could be piled ceiling-high on any stage or platform.

It is disconcerting, then, to hear and read the extensive speculations of certain men in public life about what Soviet Russia means to do and what its fifth columns plan. The Reds have said so clearly what their reason for existence is, and have so scrupulously and relentlessly pursued the path set out for them, that such speculations would be absurd were they not so tragic.

There is no greater tribute to the effectiveness of the Soviet fifth column in this country than the obvious fact that it has befogged the American mind regarding its ruthless resolves to wipe out American independence. Nothing is so clear-cut as its continual insistence within its own ranks that violent attack upon the government here is highly essential. But so skilled are its propagandists—disguised as non-Communists in the radio, newspaper and moving-picture world—that they have made Americans believe every revelation of Red espionage is the result of hysteria. They have done a fairly adequate job of making America ashamed of defending its own freedoms.

Perhaps the greatest reason for this marked success of the Reds is the extensive lack of understanding in America of just what the Communists are and just how they work. And that is what I want to show in this book; that is why I am writing it.

Take, for example, the phrase "Aesopian language" used by Lenin to describe the conspiratorial style in which Communists must write. That phrase has now become well known as a result of its disclosure at the trial of the eleven Communist leaders. When I first explained on the witness stand that the Communists wrote everything in "Aesopian language" in order to convey a treasonable message to the comrades without revealing it to others, most Americans, apparently, learned that fact with surprise. No one had ever stressed it or even mentioned it—until then. Yet the expression appears prominently in the preface to Lenin's great work, *Imperialism,* and every party member is familiar with its derivation—the slave language resorted to by Aesop to permit him to comment on his masters without being successfully pinned down as disrespectful. As used by the Reds, the average American would call it double talk.

The revelation that Communists use this elaborate method of conveying seditious messages did make America open its eyes for a moment. Yet it is questionable whether anything happened beyond that; whether in the light of this knowledge many Americans began to examine Communist expressions any more closely.

For instance, there has recently been a heated discussion of "cosmopolitanism" in the Soviet press. It has led to anti-Semitic assaults upon many Jewish writers in the columns of Russian papers. What is this "cosmopolitanism"? Despite much discussion of it, it has remained largely a mystery. Nevertheless, even a quick study of the Soviet publications translated into English for the American comrades would have enlightened anyone. In the *New Times* of Mos-

cow, April 6, 1949, we have cosmopolitanism explained in detail.
(So vital is this matter that the Communist party here reprinted
this piece in its official theoretical organ, *Political Affairs*, for July,
1949.)

Cosmopolitanism, as analyzed in the *New Times,* is "internationalism" which does not base itself on Soviet patriotism. In other
words, it is opposed to "proletarian internationalism," which devotes
itself to advancing Soviet domination of the world through the
coming world proletarian dictatorship. The entire thought is neatly
developed, so that anyone who talks of "international relations"
and wishes to say a good word for the United States is denounced
as a cosmopolitan, a term which even in Marx's day denoted a
villain.

According to this (Soviet) theory, "Today the world is divided
into two camps—the anti-democratic camp of imperialism, headed
by the United States, and the anti-imperialist camp of Socialism
and democracy, headed by the Soviet Union and the People's
democracies." The first camp cannot promote anything but oppres-
sion, economic and political enslavement and other evils. Its "internationalism" and any friendly relations based on such an idea are
false and deceptive. The second camp is the source of all peace,
liberty and independence. The "proletarian internationalism"
which promotes that camp's domination of the world is the real
internationalism.

There is only one genuine patriotism, then—*loyalty to Soviet
Russia;* and only one internationalism—*loyalty to Soviet Russia.*
It's all very simple, but the Soviet agencies keep it complicated
and confused for the outside world.

The Soviet fifth column, moving and living on the instructions
which flow into the House on Thirteenth Street, can be likened
in organizational form to a tree. Its roots are the men and women
of the deep underground, the political tourists, as they are called,
sent here by Moscow to direct the life of the Communist party.
Among those roots was Gerhart Eisler, long a representative of

the Communist international machine in a number of countries. Another man there was J. V. Peters, whose names run from Israel Bornstein to Alexander Stevens, and who directed the enrollment of party members for espionage over a period of years. Such men are the direct mouthpieces of Moscow; they transmit instructions to the puppet party leaders of native origin. There are several scores of them.

The trunk of the tree is the "open party," which functions none too openly at that from its national headquarters. Among those found in the trunk are William Z. Foster, eagerly striving for the honor of being Stalin's gauleiter in America, Eugene Dennis of many false names and many subversive missions, and Earl Browder when he was at the party's head. They of the trunk are the means of contact which the men of the roots have with those concealed in the branches. And these last are the men and women who swear that they are not Communists—or refuse to answer the question about membership when brought before a Congressional committee—and who operate as non-Communists on an extensive scale. They are frequently defended by the responsible press, treated as people of the highest integrity, and move in circles where they play hob with American opinion. If there is proof of the "political light-mindedness of Americans," to which the comrades on Thirteenth Street often refer, it is to be found in the failure to label properly the Kremlin agents of this category. A little research would reveal their constant Red associations and the wide range of their pro-Stalin acts.

In religious literature the devil is said never to be so triumphant as when he persuades men that he does not exist. It is much the same here. The Soviet fifth columnists are never more effective in advancing Stalin's objective of world conquest than when they get Americans to believe they are nonexistent. And the reports which flowed into Thirteenth Street when I was there indicated that considerable progress was being made in this respect. The comrades were encouraged and spurred on to new subversive work.

The frequent happy outcome of Soviet projects never fails to fire the fanaticism of Stalin's legion here. In particular do the constant setbacks suffered by the United States—the most powerful nation on earth—add to the comrades' firm belief that the Soviet State and the Communist Society are inevitable and confirm their basic premise that the great scientist Stalin can make no mistake and that his cause will be endlessly triumphant. I have often sat in on meetings where, in the midst of a studied atmosphere of "scientific discussion," an almost mystical joy was registered at the defeat of American plans.

I recall particularly a conversation with Robert Minor, the cartoonist and Communist leader, and Max Bedacht, another noted Red, in 1933, when I was drawing near to party allegiance, though not to join until two years later. Minor and Bedacht, standing in the narrow corridor which served as an entrance to the Thirteenth Street building, spoke almost mystically of the coming "seizure of power in the United States and the smashing by violence of the Roosevelt war-and-hunger government." That was what I was reading in the *Daily Worker* almost every day, in fiery editorials promising the imminent destruction of the American "Wall Street" government. It was much more vivid, though, when heard from the lips of men one knew. The work ahead was bloody, they agreed, but their justification and their reward were "the glories of Communist discipline in the forming of character," in "the making of a new kind of man."

It is this promise of the "creation of the perfected man"—the new type of human being who begins with the Bolshevik—that steels them, too, against the disgrace or defection of so many of their leading comrades. Their certainty is a godsend to the comrades' morale. Under the ruthless Stalin machine, these men and women are expendable. The Soviet dictatorship proceeds on the theory that only those who can serve constantly are of value. Many a Red leader in this country has found serious disgrace awaiting him toward the end of a life devoted to the Kremlin. Minor and

Bedacht were to experience some such fate. Minor, the son of a Texas judge, who surrendered a distinguished place in the journalistic world to advance communism, was ignominiously demoted in 1945 as being too close to Earl Browder. Both he and Browder had said and done only the things ordered by the Kremlin in pursuance of the Teheran accord of 1943, under which Stalin, Roosevelt and Churchill guaranteed "generations of peace" among their three nations. But Minor and Browder were of no further use, at least immediately, under the "cold war" program instituted by Moscow in 1945. They were treated as outcasts, though Minor was permitted to crawl before his masters and eventually make his peace.

The Swiss barber Max Bedacht had an even harsher fate meted out to him. Having come to this country in his young manhood, he had graduated quickly from the tonsorial parlor to the editorship of several small German-language Socialist papers. In time he became a charter member of the Communist party, a member for more than twenty-five years of its Central (later National) Committee, and was honored as general secretary of the party during the interim between Stalin's expulsion of Benjamin Gitlow and appointment of Browder. By 1933 he was general secretary of the International Workers Order, the large insurance front of the Communists and their source of contact with many other organizations. It was during that period that I was invited to attend one of several official parties arranged by the Ninth Floor in honor of his fiftieth birthday. He was hailed by the party leaders on that occasion as "a symbol of the revolution," and as one whom all the comrades should emulate.

When Foster and Dennis succeeded Browder in command of the American party in 1945, some thought that Bedacht might come into a higher position. Instead, he was first retired and then expelled as an enemy of the party. Without protest, he disappeared into the shadows, as so many who receive such treatment decide to do. His sole chance of rehabilitation in the party now, despite his long years of service, would be to enlist in its espionage division, taking advantage of his status as an "ex-Red" to glean valuable information.

Another friend of Foster, who was expected to rise with him in 1945 but who fell instead, was William Francis Dunne, the rough-and-ready intellectual from Butte, Montana. Former commissar for Stalin in Outer Mongolia, vigorous spokesman for the Central Committee during the period just before 1935, Dunne had nursed Foster's bruised feelings against Browder. They both hated the "quiet man from Kansas," as the songster Earl Robinson once called Browder. But Moscow is the determining force, not the local chiefs, and Dunne received a thumbs-down decree from abroad. He was expelled after I left, because he would not toe the line. So it went, too, with Harrison George, editor of the Communist daily on the Pacific Coast, the *People's World*, and a charter member of the party. Though his own son Victor Baron (named after his mother Rose Baron) had been killed in Brazil on the Kremlin's business, George was expelled as an enemy of the party after I had left. Vern Smith, veteran party journalist and former correspondent for the *Daily Worker* in Moscow, received a like sentence at about the same time.

Thus do the ghosts of many leaders who were hailed and then condemned walk through the records of the Communist parties of all nations. Some unthinking journalists poke fun at the Reds for their arbitrary expulsion of those who have long served their cause. It is no laughing matter, and such jests indicate the lack of knowledge that still prevails regarding the role that discipline plays in the Communist party. Through these expulsions there is hammered into shape a "steeled" group which is subject completely to the Kremlin's will and has relinquished all independence of thought to those who give the orders from the Red holy of holies. So well has this iron discipline functioned that a comparatively small number of Communists, aided it is true from abroad, have been able to becloud American thought to a serious degree.

In the klieg lights which are turned on espionage cases (and they have been exposed only in small part), we are likely to forget that it is the Communists' hidden influence on American opinion that has been most devastating. I can speak with full authority on that matter, having been deeply engaged in directing and executing Moscow's orders for molding American thinking.

Repeatedly from the House on Thirteenth Street orders went out to form this committee and that, to set up groups of citizens with patriotic names and allegedly patriotic objectives. Then these committees, headed by steeled Communists from the "branches," would roll up huge numbers of letters and telegrams from all sections of the land—with a view to influencing Congressmen and securing the passage or defeat of some particular piece of legislation. Thousands of loyal Americans, in the name of "civil liberties," "rights," "fascist abuse of labor," are thus inveigled by the Communists into support of moves and measures which build up the enemies of all liberty. And the end is not yet; even now, as I hope to make clear, new committees under new names are pounding on the doors of Congress and the courts. Each of their insistent demands aids the Communists in undermining the nation.

The energy that marks such campaigning is engendered by the *Daily Worker* through devices which again arouse the laughter of the unthinking. Anyone who picks up that paper today will be arrested by the foul abuse which characterizes its columns and which is hurled at all those with whom the Reds disagree. So extreme are these vilifications that a casual reader will find it hard to believe that anything could be gained by such foulness, which must offend a great many people. Nevertheless much is gained by it. Through this excessive appeal to hatred, the Red newspaper whips up its readers (who live on a philosophy of hate) to induce others to get busy. In working on others, the faithful *Daily Worker* readers do not use the same phrases, as a rule;

that would be ineffective. But the spleen developed in them by what they have read is transmitted in action to those they meet in shop, neighborhood or community. The device is one that wins —if used in a steeled army of agents for a foreign power, and among a trusting population such as ours.

There is indeed one immense anticlimax at the end of this savagery, self-sacrifice and plotting. While Red machinations do shake seriously the security of our nation, they also serve to forward a colossal paradox: the success of a failure. Founded on the promise of higher living standards for the masses, Soviet Russia is conquering and prostrating countries with a higher standard than its own. The "movement" that boldly asserts that it is dedicated to the emancipation of the working people is bringing about the enslavement of mankind. Ostensibly opposed to monopolies and monopoly capitalism, it creates the most gigantic monopoly of all—the State dictatorship. Out of the Soviet "experiment" (as evidence which came freely to the *Daily Worker* desk disclosed) a far-flung slave empire is being erected.

It is slavery in a physical, intellectual and spiritual sense that the Soviet regime is furthering. It is a slavery that extends even to the party faithful in America and to the *Daily Worker* desk and controls the comings and goings of all those who work through Thirteenth Street. There they watch for every new word from Moscow, in order to be able to defend the Kremlin and its new position. They hold many meetings, within and without the building, to learn the meaning of the slightest new tone or phrase in a statement by Stalin or Molotov, *Pravda* or *Izvestia.* Moscow is their Mecca, to which they turn morning, noon and night for instruction, orders and inspiration.

This fanatical preoccupation with carrying out orders, this willingness to use any lie or trick to execute them, has played a large part in the victories of the Soviet fifth column in the United States over the American people. Those victories are pronounced, and in danger of becoming permanent. Nation after nation has fallen under Soviet control, and America has been unable to rescue them. The world has been kept unstable, uncertain and therefore, from the American viewpoint, unsafe. And the vacillations of American opinion, fostered by the operations of the Communist fifth column, have contributed to this outcome.

Another big reason for these Red gains is the ability of the Communists to take advantage of the many and often contradictory voices raised in democratic discussion. Such discussion would help to rout communism, if it were always predicated on reality. Many "authorities" write on things Communist, however, without knowing too much about such matters, having had no experience with the Red apparatus. They caricature the Soviet fifth column and give to the average American a comic-page concept of a Communist and how he acts. The party's rigid control by Moscow, for instance, is frequently overlooked completely by some of these wise men in their exceedingly foolish books and articles on the Kremlin's tools. When those who do know by actual experience, the ex-Communists who have held responsible party positions, begin to tell their stories (and they can tell only a portion of what they know in order to obtain credence at all), there are many critics who raise their eyebrows. They question the validity of charges not based on printed instructions or party cards—as though conspirators make it their business to use such devices freely to aid their quicker detection.

Another mistaken supposition is that every Communist working in the non-Communist world carries around with him some indelible "mark of the beast," and that his slinking manner and furtive eye reveal him readily to the average American. "The nice-appearing man who is acting like a Communist in my local union or lawyer's group or neighborhood organization can't possibly be one: he doesn't look like a Red!" is a too-general assumption. The truth of the matter is that the Red agent is chosen specifically to accord in appearance with the group which he is penetrating. In the State Department he can wear morning clothes, is thoroughly familiar with protocol and is more State Department than the State Department. In the Department of Justice she is one of the brightest of Barnard students, with parents who are far from Red in outlook.

In the present critical hour is it not to the point for the American citizen to make a declaration of independence from his too-prevalent naïveté? This study of the House on Thirteenth Street, as seen from the *Daily Worker* desk, is designed to help America to that end. I have therefore adopted a unique method in the preparation of this book. My previous book, *This Is My Story,* served as the base for the trial of the eleven Communist leaders, though that was not its aim. It is the only work on communism in America to have been subjected to drastic cross-examination in five successive court cases and to have stood up successfully under such fire. But this account of *Men Without Faces* will have an additional guarantee. The extensive data which is at my disposal from my long experience in the Communist camp has been carefully winnowed out, and not one statement on Communist plans shall appear in this book (though all are based on my personal experiences) which is not supported by documentary evidence. This procedure will cut through for good, I hope, much of the haziness which pervades the debate over the men who do the bidding of Moscow.

It is essential to any understanding of the Red mind to comprehend that one is dealing with people obsessed by a fixed idea—the "infallibility of Stalin." This distinguishes them from others in American life, so far as motivation goes. It makes understandable their willingness to serve as tools for the destruction of their nation. It gives us the tale of "men without faces" and "faces without names" which we are about to recount, men who labor like moles in the political underground—and whose pictures, incidentally, are never permitted to be published.

Throughout my service as managing editor, I worked under strict orders from the Ninth Floor not to print pictures of most of the leading comrades. Men like Alexander Bittelman, Jack Stachel, John Williamson, Eugene Dennis, Gerhart Eisler, J. V. Peters, even Alexander Trachtenberg who was so well known to celebrities in the writing and moving-picture field, were not to have their faces shown in the paper which they so vigorously aided. The exclusion of these photographs was to be my personal political responsibility, as Browder told me solemnly when he broke the news that I was to take over the management of the paper. It was just before he went to jail, although the rule was in force throughout the ten years of my participation in party editorial work.

Every time there was a party conference or convention, I examined carefully the photographs which were taken by the *Daily Worker* photographer, the only news cameraman allowed to be present. If any comrade appeared whose name was on the long list of those I was to keep out of the paper, I ordered the photo destroyed. In serious cases I personally watched the operation, the burning of the film. The prohibition applied to nine tenths of the district organizers and to scores of active party workers who were also engaged in secret courier duties.

They were "men without faces," indeed. To them were added the faces without names, the men and women who were introduced merely as "a friend," which was the common name for a Soviet secret-police agent or a comrade working deep in the NKVD underground with those police.

I remember well my own friendly relations with one of these people, a Soviet spy in Canada, a writer for a Communist weekly, who to most comrades was only a face. This was the genial Rudy Baker, who later wrote under the name of Ralph Bowman for the *New Masses* to cover up his extensive espionage activities in this country. His original name was Heinz Zimmerman, and I had learned all about him from the late Jack Johnstone, veteran member of the Communist National Committee in America. Jack had regaled us a number of evenings at my home with stories of his underground work in Canada with Baker.

Without warning, as though out of a void, Baker would appear suddenly at the *Daily Worker* to obtain information which he could piece into the facts he was gathering. Frequently he asked me to arrange meetings for him with certain people in influential posts in Washington. Always he was pleasant, almost jovial. Seeking to penetrate American defense plans, he assumed as protective coloring a most casual attitude.

So skillfully did Baker conceal the work he was doing from most fellow Communists whom he met that he became known generally in the 40's as a gentleman farmer near Peekskill. He was even able to persuade people who had left the party that his interest in communism was merely intellectual—more or less Bohemian. In this manner, he obtained information valuable for his purposes. He was one of the several key Communist agents who have used the Polish ship *Batory* as a means of flight from this country during the past few years. Baker fled just as his activities among certain atomic scientists were about to be divulged.

Late at night, when the *Daily Worker* building in general was quiet save for the noises connected with putting the newspaper to bed, I have been interrupted by a message from some comrade en route secretly from Mexico to Canada—reporting again of progress toward Soviet domination of the Western Hemisphere.

In those night hours spent in getting out the late morning edition, often the telephone operator (trained in a special school for underground work) would say: "A comrade from abroad to see you. His credentials seem satisfactory." And I would climb up from the seventh floor, where the linotypes were, back to the eighth, to see him. I can recall the tired face of a young New York businessman who had carried in his shoe past the American border guards a request from the leader of the Mexican Communist party for $5,000 to start a revolt in a Latin-American country. He had combined sedition with a business trip. I can still see the smiling and youthful features of a sailor who brought to me personally from the Chinese Communists literature which could be used to assure our active comrades that "we are revolutionaries, not reform-ists." With that communication was another for the Ninth Floor, rearranging courier service through the Pacific via the party office in San Francisco. The *Daily Worker* and I were the receiving station for much courier service in the never-ceasing network of espionage against the United States, a network which reached across two oceans.

Each of these comrades was inspired by the thought that the Cominform is now driving again into the Reds everywhere: The Communists, guided by Comrade Stalin, will advance in all countries. "They will be victorious throughout the world under the militant banner of Marx-Engels-Lenin-Stalin."

I can still hear the broken accents of Morris Childs, a big figure in the underground apparatus, giving that incentive to a roomful of young men and women out in Chicago. They were in training for secret work, and this belief in complete victory for Stalin was their reward for obscure labors in sedition.

When I left the Communist movement in 1945, I predicted in a statement to the American press that "the masters of the Kremlin were about to unleash a creeping blitzkrieg across Europe and Asia, directed at the United States." That declaration was then greeted with considerable skepticism. Today that "creeping blitzkrieg" is a reality—a grave threat to America's future freedom. Since 1945, Eastern Europe has succumbed and a considerable area of Asia has surrendered to the advancing Red power.

The extent of American setbacks is to be witnessed in the burial of the "Four Freedoms," which was the battle hymn of the recent war. The dockers' strike in Canada and England, the *New York Times* tells us in a sober summary, ended with the Communists in control; they will be able to shatter Europe's economy on a bigger scale when it serves their purpose. In Hawaii we had a pre-view of the paralysis that can be caused in the Pacific when the 1949 strike of Harry Bridges' longshoremen's union brought to a dead halt all water transportation in that area. The demands were those all unions could support, but they were distorted by the fact of Bridges' position as head of the maritime division of the Communist-controlled World Federation of Trade Unions. The Communist victory over the Chinese people is being followed (as Moscow predicted would be the case) by disturbance in Japan. Even with the marked gain for America in the Atlantic Pact and the Marshall Plan, the existence of subversive elements in the Atlantic community presents serious shadows of future danger. The High Commissioner of Atomic Energy in France, for instance, is Joliot-Curie, the scientist and a devout Stalinist. In the United States, the fifth column's custom of relying on perjury and false passports has received a new breath of life in the Supreme Court's decisions in the Christoffel and Eisler cases.

And still a large-sized skepticism remains. A Maginot mind may prove fatal to this nation. Impressed by our physical strength, we may forget the poison of fifth-column influences, although it is a lesson the country should have learned after being so tragically misled about the nature of the Chinese Reds. The comrades in the House on Thirteenth Street have cause for satisfaction. Their works are bearing good fruit—for the invincible Stalin.

(II)

Not a Party

SEPTEMBER 1, 1949, marked the thirtieth anniversary of the Communist party of the United States. Three decades is time enough to make a record, and the record of this party is summed up in the book that the 1948 Red convention ordered its members to study vigorously for the entire year preceding the birthday celebration.

The title and author of the book, which the convention called the "classic of our time," was Stalin's *History of the Communist Party of the Soviet Union (Bolsheviks)*.

The spectacle of an allegedly American and democratic party selecting as its leading guide the work of a foreign dictator is sufficiently characteristic. It says quite definitely that this party is *not* a political party in the American and democratic sense.

This fact becomes even more evident when it is understood that the book specifically urges the violent smashing of all "imperialistic" governments, of which the United States is the outstanding example. The central consideration of the book is the establishment of the dictatorship of the proletariat in every country. It is always read with a companion volume, Stalin's other great apologia, *Foundations of Leninism,* in which Stalin follows and embellishes Lenin's declaration in *State and Revolution* that "the smashing, the destruction" of the state machinery in the United States and England is essential for a "real people's revolution."

To put the whole business frankly, the Communist party members, in studying Stalin's works, are preparing themselves to destroy by violence the United States government created by the Constitution.

Any organization that had based its structure and its activities on Hitler's *Mein Kampf*, when the Führer was the Nazi dictator, would obviously not have been considered a legitimate party. The group founding its labors on Stalin's two-volumed *Mein Kampf* is in a similar category. By its own banner, the Communist party of the United States proclaims itself Soviet Russia's fifth column and nothing else.

Further study of the characteristics of the party, based on my own experiences on Thirteenth Street, confirm this fact beyond any doubt or dispute.

Out of those experiences this indictment can be drawn on the basis of cold, hard documentary evidence:

1. Throughout the entire thirty years of its history, never has the Communist party here been out of step with Moscow. Always it has reflected the difficulties or triumphs of the Soviet dictatorship and the "line" laid down by the Kremlin.

During my ten years as an editor of the *Daily Worker* and its subsidiary, *The Midwest Daily Record*, I had occasion to study the files of the paper throughout its lifetime. With almost startling fidelity, the party and its paper echoed at any given moment the current Soviet attitude toward America and the rest of the world.

2. For a number of years—at least fifteen—the party was openly subsidized by the Soviet government through the Runag News Agency. This subsidy was halted by Attorney General Francis Biddle.

3. An overwhelming majority—we can say, 90 per cent—of the Communist party leaders have been trained in the Lenin School (for foreign service) in Moscow. This school is similar to those created by Hitler in the Third Reich to train agents for work outside the Reich's borders.

4. The Communist party conducts its affairs with a complete absence of democratic discussion or procedure. The use of parlia-

mentary law in Communist national or state committee meetings or conventions is forbidden. The Reds learn parliamentary law, but merely so they can use it to capture or disrupt the groups they are infiltrating. Communist sessions resemble a teacher instructing pupils, save that the Red pupils have no chance except to agree with the instructor, "the party leader."

5. Under the iron hand of "party discipline" alien tourists direct every party move. Behind the "open party," thus steered by these mysterious strangers, there is the illegal or conspiratorial apparatus, stamping the whole setup at once by its correct name.

Recently, rereading the resolution of the August, 1948, convention ordering the comrades to restudy Stalin's *History*, I recalled the hectic days of 1939 and 1940 when the red-covered volume was first pressed upon the party members. It was the period of the Stalin-Hitler pact, and of course the Communist party here was doing all in its power to shut off any military supplies to Britain. The book was pushed then for the same reason that it is being pushed now—to work up the comrades' hatred of our government.

Published first in Russian in October, 1938, Stalin's *History* was issued in its American edition and English translation by International Publishers the following year. I can remember Alexander Trachtenberg, the shrewd, dark and slightly stoop-shouldered commissar of culture for Moscow in our midst, dropping into a chair beside me on the Ninth Floor one day in 1939. I had come in from Chicago to make a report. He was showing signs of happy excitement. "At last," he said, "I have received the English translation of Stalin's famous *History* as approved by the Marx-Lenin Institute in Moscow. Its publication will be a big event, one of the biggest in party history."

So it proved indeed. Thirteenth Street mobilized to the hilt. Messages on little onionskin papers went out to many hidden mail drops (at that time the party was operating illegally, by its own decree), instructing the leaders to make Stalin's book "the property in full of the party." The *Daily Worker* took up the story. Every leader of the party went around with the red-bound book under his arm. Those who could function publicly or semipublicly were ordered to teach it wherever they could, and special arrangements for this purpose were made.

A moving picture of my own experiences as a "teacher" would show me with the book in my hands before a small cell of university professors in Chicago, again with a crowd of miners in the Springfield, Illinois, area, once more before a group of lawyers and other professional workers in New Rochelle, New York, on one occasion at a secret meeting of scientific workers held just out of New York City, and finally talking to little clumps of Negroes in both South Chicago and Manhattan.

The order to carry Stalin's message to the party had come directly from the Comintern and its representatives here. From his hiding place, the overactive J. V. Peters, then disguised as Alexander Stevens, sent repeated and heated instructions to the "legal comrades" to push the *History* even more vigorously. Similar and almost hysterical directives came from Jack Stachel. He had gone underground near the Mexican border, for he too was hiding from the American law-enforcement authorities and the public. However, he was always keenly aware of what Moscow wanted.

Now in 1949 and '50 pressure of the same kind is again being put on the comrades by the Cominform. In its October 1, 1948, issue, the Cominform's semimonthly paper alerted Communists everywhere with an edition devoted exclusively to Stalin's *History*. Accompanying a huge picture of the Leader, banner headlines proclaimed his work as "the powerful ideological weapon of the International Communist movement"; the guide to action "for the conquest of power" in all lands.

In a full-page article telling how the book will aid the Reds internationally, the leading Soviet theoretician P. Yudin, declared that it commits the Communist parties of all countries to the violent overthrow of capitalism and consequently of such governments as that of the United States.

Thus tipped off through the Cominform, *New Times* and other agencies, the Communists here immediately took up the cry. When we multiply this incident by every major move of the party, we can appreciate the completeness of Moscow's control.

Clearly an agency thus controlled is not a democratic political party.

Nevertheless, it is on this point that the Reds have had one of their greatest successes in creating confusion. "The Communist party is a legal political party!" That was our slogan on Thirteenth Street when I was there; and we pushed it vociferously for all it was worth, and more. With the help of concealed Communist party agents in various professional groups representing college and university professors, scientific workers, lawyers, and public-school teachers, we raised an uproar that threw over the party's subversive plottings a mantle of legality. The party agents even employed this argument to justify their control of unions. Whenever patriotic workers objected to this subversive control, the Reds would reply: "We are members of a legal political party" or "we are not Communists, but suppose we were; is there anything wrong with that? Isn't the Communist party a legal political party?" That argument was supposed to be a clincher; opposition was frequently silenced, and indeed many non-Communists were induced to go around and peddle the idea until it became widespread.

So strong has this contention proved to be that the American Association of University Professors in its 1949 convention declared anew in favor of Communists as teachers "as long as the Communist party remains a legal political party." The professors do not even add that they know, as intelligent people, that one Communist professor can develop a number of Judith Coplons, students who will use their intellectual alertness to betray their country. A Communist, the professors should know, *cannot* take a platonic attitude toward his beliefs. Anyone who entertains such an opinion of the Reds has been badly misled. The Red must always be dynamic in his adherence, translating into action the views to which he adheres.

I regret that the university professors could not have sat in, as I did, on the Politburo discussions of the cases of Professor Granville Hicks and Instructor Morris Schappes. We had long touted Hicks as the intellectual companion of our then great leader, Browder. In public speeches throughout the country, we had, under instructions, referred to him as a leading example of the trend of intellectual Americans toward communism. He had written such pro-Red books as *John Reed—the Making of a Revolutionary*. For five years he was on the editorial staff of the *New Masses*, a Communist weekly, while occupying an important post at Harvard University. Because of his comparatively high standing in the academic world and in the Communist ranks, he was ordered abruptly in 1939 to come out publicly for the Hitler-Stalin pact, and in effect for the support of Hitler against Britain. The Politburo, in taking up his case, was particularly determined that he should take a strikingly abject stand, to indicate his subjection to the party. That he refused to do so, writing a letter to Browder in opposition to such a stand, may be considered to his credit. His expulsion from the party is a reminder of the fate of any professor who dares put his judgment above that of Stalin and the party.

I was also present when Morris Schappes, well-known Red schoolteacher, appeared before the Politburo in connection with the testimony he was to give before the Rapp-Coudert Committee of the New York State legislature. The party's New York State Bureau had ordered Schappes to swear falsely on the stand that he was not and never had been a member of the Communist party. This was a dangerous proceeding for him, since many Communists knew of him in active Red work. He had been a prominent member, for instance, of the secret trade union commission of the party in New York. Schappes thought it would serve his future usefulness to the party if he could discover some way to avoid the risk of perjury, but when he presented this idea to the Politburo, it was sharply rejected. He was told that if he admitted secret membership, the next question would be: "Who are your associates?" Schappes followed orders like a faithful Red, committed perjury, was convicted, sentenced, and served his time in jail.

Then there is, quite recently, the expulsion of Dr. Bella Dodd to illustrate how a teacher and professional worker who is a Communist must surrender her entire character and will to the party. One of the Reds' ablest representatives among the New York teachers for many years, she led a large group of them in the pro-Red stand which caused them to be expelled from the American Federation of Teachers, to form the Teachers' Union and then go into the CIO for refuge. Although she denied her Communist party membership in the early stages of her career, she eventually left the Teachers' Union to become the legislative representative of the Communist party in New York State. She also became openly a leading member of the New York State Committee of the party and a member of the National Committee. But during the discussion on the demotion of Browder, her lack of warmth in advocating the cold-war policy was noted by the special control commission, the official semisecret group that guarded the comrades' integrity. I learned of that black mark against her when I was called before the commission to discuss the integrity of certain other comrades. It was not surprising, then, to hear that in 1949, when the party needed exhibits of white chauvinism to stir the comrades into action, they chose Dr. Dodd as their victim. She was accused of not acting properly in the case of a Puerto Rican family, whose landlord she had represented in her newly established practice of law. Although her whole record was against such an assumption, she was found guilty and expelled. In its statement on her expulsion, the New York Committee threatened her with attack on personal as well as political grounds.

Ironically, the man behind the Communists' loud insistence that they are members of a "legal political party" and should therefore be left undisturbed to execute their fifth column plots was the Russian-born alien Alexander Bittelman. Slight, wiry, nervous, keen in intellect, Bittelman is one of the most devoted and intelligent of that corps of political tourists sent into the United States to direct the party.

Bittelman, who has never troubled to become a citizen and who cannot vote for the "legal political party" though he helps control it, forged the tactic of the "legal" party from his hideout in Miami, Florida. That was during the period of the Hitler-Stalin pact—a period of self-imposed illegality for many of the leading comrades. So many of them had committed offenses against the United States (or were in this country illegally for the "legal political party") that there was a general migration underground. The Ninth Floor was largely denuded, only the white-haired Robert Minor, the stumbling Roy Hudson, the newly active Elizabeth Gurley Flynn, William Z. Foster occasionally, myself and a few others roaming through its quiet hall and cubbyhole rooms. The party was run through secret conferences, held in apartments and out-of-the-way places, and through notes that arrived mysteriously from the undercover leaders. Through such notes, delivered by Red couriers, Bittelman hammered at Minor to raise higher the cry of the "legal political party."

This is a clever contention, by no means unknown to the Reds in other lands, for it poses a difficult problem for a democratic nation. Garbing itself in the attire of a regular political party, the Communist organization raises on behalf of its own legality the cry of those "civil liberties" which it officially declares it intends to abolish. The matter would be less confusing if the Red missionaries in the guise of liberals, radio commentators and trade unionists were not so successful in preventing Americans from learning the truth about their conspiratorial setup. The whole fictitious character of this "political party" claim could be easily exposed if it were established (as it can be) from Red documents and acts that the so-called Communist party is and has always been nothing other than one division of a dictator's army with which he hopes to conquer the world.

The party has characterized itself as this by stating that it is "a party of a new type, a Marxist-Leninist party." This description appears in the party's latest official statement at the Fourteenth Annual Convention (1948). It is to be found in countless official Red documents over the past decade. Significantly, it is the term popularized by Stalin in his *History*.

When I was operating on Thirteenth Street, there was no phrase that sounded more frequently in my ears. Bittelman went nervously from conference to conference among the comrades on the various floors—repeating it, insisting upon its use in inner-party lectures to branches and sections, and on making it the paramount consideration in "mastering Marxism-Leninism." Bittelman's word on a matter of that kind was law; for his was a direct commission from Moscow to assure the "ideological clarity" of the party here. His function, recognized throughout the building and beyond, was to keep the comrades straight on "theory" in accordance with Moscow's wishes. Therefore, when Bittelman said over and over again that a "party of the new type" must be emphasized, everyone else reiterated that assertion wherever they went and whenever they spoke.

"What does this mean, this party of a new type?" Bittelman would ask in his shrill voice, and then would answer: "It means a disciplined party, whose sole goal is the overthrow of its own country's imperialism, the abolition of capitalism and the government apparatus by organized force. It calls for comrades who are disciplined, who are steeled to meet any emergency, who must be prepared for organized violence, for street fighting, for breaking down the morale of the soldiery."

Then, hammering one fist against his open palm, he would go on, earnestly: "It requires more than that. It makes it imperative that we understand that there is a peculiar Communist morality, as Lenin has said, a morality derived from the interests of the class struggle of the proletariat. That morality calls for the employment of illegitimate and illegal methods when required, for the concealment of facts, for swearing in a manner that will protect the party and not in accord with bourgeois concepts of truth. These are the considerations bound up in the term 'a party of a new type.' "

An interpolation might be in order here, for this whole matter of Communist morality is—not surprisingly—much misunderstood by Americans in general. This was pointed up recently by the Hiss-Chambers trial. The Reds are organized experts in lying—but the lies in which the Red engages are those that will aid the cause and the party. In such circumstances, according to the peculiar ethics of the Communist, it is right, not wrong, to lie. The Communist will not hesitate to spread scandalous falsehoods about a man or woman who has been declared to be an enemy of the party. He will do all in his power to get non-Communists to accept and spread the same malicious slanders. On the witness stand, he will resort to perjury, if necessary, to protect the interests of his party. But this is done under party orders and for party purposes, and is regarded as a cardinal feature of Communist morality.

It is not a question of being a pathological liar. In his ordinary relations of life the Communist may be quite truthful. In his reports to the party he is compelled to tell the truth, and no more accurate statements can be found than those made by Communists to party headquarters.

The greatest danger is that many people, finding those whom they think or know to be Communists truthful in ordinary matters, are taken in by these same Communists on political matters.

In all this, as Bittelman always said in concluding his talks, the comrade is only proving himself a fit member of "a party prepared for the seizure of power whenever the revolutionary situation arises."

Rounding it all out, Bittelman would inspire the comrades with an appropriate set of quotations from Stalin on the subject.

Quotations from Stalin were not hard to find. The chief conclusion in his study of the Bolshevik party in the Soviet Union is that ". . . the victory of the proletarian revolution . . . is impossible without a revolutionary party of the proletariat. . . ." and "only a party of the new type, a Marxist-Leninist party . . . a party capable of preparing the proletariat for decisive battles against the bourgeoisie . . . can be such a party."

How does a "party of the new type" guide itself? By "Marxist-Leninist theory," of course, replies Stalin, which "is not a dogma but a guide to action." And who determines modern and living Marxist-Leninist theory? Why, the new autocrat of all the Russias, of course, Comrade Stalin. As he himself solemnly declares on page 358 of his *History*: "Stalin and the other disciples of Lenin" are the only Marxists capable of interpreting Communist beliefs.

It is Stalin, then, the "chief disciple of Lenin . . . the Lenin of our day," as he has been officially proclaimed by the Soviet Politburo members, who determines the thought and action of the Red parties everywhere. For those "other disciples" of Lenin to whom Stalin modestly refers are solely those Communists who have continued to agree with the leader. Any who did otherwise have been thoroughly liquidated in Soviet Russia and driven from the Communist ranks throughout the world.

Bittelman made this historic fact a political virtue for the Communist party of the United States when in 1937 he wrote his *Milestones in the History of the Communist Party*—one of the "golden books" of Thirteenth Street. The party here is guided by the Communist International in Moscow, Bittelman told the comrades in this booklet. And the Communist International, the Comintern, he added, has for its dominant purpose the establishment of a world Soviet dictatorship.

But is this Comintern, which guides the "American" party, in itself guided by the Communist party of Soviet Russia and by its leader, Stalin? Yes, replied Bittelman to the comrades and "Yes" replied the comrades to each other. "The leading role of the Communist party of the Soviet Union in the Comintern needs neither explanation nor apology. A party that has opened up the epoch of the world revolution, and that is successfully building a classless society on one-sixth of the globe, is cheerfully recognized and followed as the leading party of the world Communist movement. And by the same token, the leaders of that Party—first Lenin and now Stalin—are proudly followed as the leaders of the proletariat and of all oppressed in every country in the world."

Bittelman proudly acknowledges that the Comintern, ruled by the Communists of Russia and their leader Stalin, does indeed interfere in the affairs of the "American" party repeatedly. That interference, he submits, is "fortunate" because it speeds the day when Stalin's banner shall fly over America. And the proof of it is, writes this political tourist and citizen of Soviet Russia who has been telling the American Communists what to do for years, that Stalin says so himself!

"And when a revolutionary crisis develops in America," wrote Stalin as quoted by his tourist-agent Bittelman, "that will be the beginning of the end of world capitalism as a whole." Therefore, the chief obligation of the Communists here is to speed the American "revolutionary crisis," by shutting down foreign markets and paralyzing production through political strikes.

"For that end," continues Stalin (that is, the "end" of overthrowing the present American form of government), "the American Communist Party must be improved and Bolshevized." And Bittelman dutifully cites these orders from the Kremlin's overlord as commands for the American Reds to obey. The Ninth Floor, whipped into a frenzy by the sharp demands from the leader and guide at each new "turn," calls meetings, harangues the comrades, compels new studies, orders new subversive acts.

Even in 1937—when the Reds were seeking to make the White House and America as a whole believe that they were a supertype of patriot—this "Bolshevization" command by Stalin through Bittelman convulsed the party. I was in the midst of the countless con-

ferences and the endless activities necessary to fulfill Stalin's order
that the comrades be "steeled" and "ready for revolution."

No amount of "Aesopian" language can conceal the raw reality,
namely, that a group of people so completely under foreign-dic-
tatorship control is not a legitimate political party. It is an arm of
the conspiracy directed by that foreign power; in other words, an
alien fifth column.

Steve Nelson, part of whose lurid past as a secret agent of the
Soviet underground was brought to light before the Congressional
Committee on Un-American Activities in 1948, is a living exhibit
of the fifth-column character of the Communist party and of the
manner of men who steal quietly back and forth from outlying
areas into the House on Thirteenth Street on the Kremlin's business. The Committee on Un-American Activities, on the basis of
documentary evidence before it, characterized him as "a leading
functionary in the Moscow-controlled Communist underground."

The allegation against him was that he had passed secret data
on atomic bomb production (obtained from a scientist) to Vassili
Zublin of the Soviet Embassy in Washington. This had taken place
in the grounds of the San Francisco Hospital while Nelson was
under observation by Federal agents. In the subsequent investiga-
tions and hearings, a record of false passports was also brought out
against him, together with his formation of a cell to penetrate a
laboratory engaged in atomic-energy processes on the West Coast.

Eleven years before these disclosures—in late 1936 or early in
1937—I discovered that Nelson was something more than a casual
comrade. He came to my attention first when he was section organizer for the Communists in the anthracite region of Pennsylvania. He had been a candidate for office on the Red ticket in
Luzerne County, and therefore represented the "open party" there.
As labor editor of the *Daily Worker*, I used to get reports from him
by mail on conditions in the anthracite region from the party point
of view; we also used to confer hurriedly at National Committee
meetings in New York on stories which would help his work in

that area. It was at one of these meetings that I learned inadvertently from Joseph North (later editor of the *New Masses*) that Nelson had a wider range of assignments than appeared on the surface. The same could be said of North and myself, for that matter, since I was at that time meeting twice a week with members of the Soviet secret police on the Trotsky case, and North had underground work of his own.

Nelson had asked me to wait at the end of a National Committee session, and I was standing at the back of the hall when I found North also waiting for him. North was then editor of the Sunday edition of the *Daily Worker* and I was associated with him at the editorial board meetings every day. We had become quite friendly and he had confided to me his determination to go to Spain, to report the Civil War there. He had even raised a portion of his passage money so that he could get the quicker approval of the Political Committee. He now opened up on the subject in connection with Nelson.

"We're going to Spain, both of us," North said, with quiet elation, "and it's unlikely that he'll want to talk to you today. We're seeing Mills right after this session and also the Russian comrade in charge of instructions concerning secret work in Spain."

So it proved to be. Nelson had to excuse himself to "see Mills" (A. W. Mills who organized and helped drill the men who went to Spain). Immediately thereafter I learned that Nelson was in charge of training volunteers for the Abraham Lincoln Brigade, that he was given a "key post," and that it had to do with "contacts for the Soviet secret police in the Spanish Republican forces." My informant was the best authority there could be in such matters, J. V. Peters, the liaison officer between the Soviet secret police and the Communist International staff representatives in this country.

Before departing (as Fleischinger) for Europe Nelson had asked me to forward to him copies of Bittelman's *Milestones*, which was soon to come out. He would use the booklet, he said, to inspire the men who would be under his command.

We hastened to round up and forward to him copies of that part of *Milestones* in which Bittelman emphasizes the Stalin cult, and upon his return from Spain, at the first National Committee meeting he attended, Nelson thanked me in his peculiarly harsh, surly way for having got these copies to him. "We hardened the comrades in many a tight spot by reminding them, through these pages, that Stalin was invincible," he stated.

It was another illustration of the influence exerted by Stalin worship.

During the Spanish Civil War, Nelson rose to the rank of lieutenant colonel, and I heard much about his courage and his ruthlessness in stamping out Trotskyites for the secret police. "Stamping out" is not a figure of speech; it was one of his duties to locate "nests of Trotskyites" in the anti-Franco ranks and have them killed. When he came back in late 1937, he was given "preeminence as a member of the National Committee," an unusual procedure to distinguish men who have performed exceedingly valuable Red deeds.

The suggestion for conferring this honor was made by Earl Browder at the National Committee meeting in New York. Then the undisputed head of the Communist machine, Browder spoke in glowing terms of Nelson's "great services, great heroism and exceedingly diligent work in uprooting anti-party elements in the Republican ranks."

Nelson's biography is one of long association with the Red underground. Born Steve Mesarosh at Chaglich, Yugoslavia, in 1903, at seventeen he gained admission to the United States as Joseph Fleischinger, that being the name of his mother's brother-in-law. Subsequently arrested with his mother and sisters for false entry, he was permitted by the government to legalize his entrance by reapplying under his correct name. This success in defeating a violation of American passport regulations seems to have encouraged him in other violations. In 1925 he joined the Communist party, but in 1928, when he became a citizen of the United States, he swore that he had no connection with such an organization.

Three years later he had become so distinguished in the Communist party as to earn appointment to a course of study at the Lenin School or Institute in Moscow, where the Soviet dictatorship trains its fifth-column agents for foreign service.

To get to Moscow for this purpose, Nelson filed a passport application with the Department of State in 1931 in which he requested permission "to visit Germany to study building construction." He falsified his passport by stating that he was of Swedish descent, that his father's name was Otto (which was untrue) and that the applicant had been born at Rankin, Pennsylvania, on December 25, 1903. His falsification was not discovered until after the statute of limitations had expired, which is generally the case with Red violations of the passport laws.

Throughout his entire period of attendance at the Lenin School, Nelson was in close touch with the Soviet secret police, according to the testimony of a fellow student, the Negro ex-Communist William Nowell. Probably as a result, he was assigned to work with the Communist International apparatus in China where he served under Arthur Ewert, a famous Comintern representative who was later imprisoned in Brazil for participation in the armed attack upon that country's government in 1935.

Back in the United States by 1934, Nelson again resorted to a false passport when he went to Spain a few years later. This time he used his first alias, Joseph Fleischinger. Once more the statute of limitations prevented prosecution for perjury.

It can be understood why we at the *Daily Worker* were instructed not to use Nelson's picture in our columns unless by special permission of the Ninth Floor and during certain "safe" periods. This rule continued even after he made his "heroic record" in Spain and was pre-empted by the National Committee. Nothing was a more constant reminder of the conspiratorial nature of the work done on Thirteenth Street than this constant compulsion to keep from the public eye the faces of most of our "heroes." But since so many of them had sworn falsely on passport applications or had been guilty of other frauds against the United States, such reproduction even of small group pictures in which they appeared was strictly prohibited. Whenever any were taken, they were submitted to at least three inspections before publication was allowed. The force of this iron rule is not weakened by the fact that since the Communist leaders have been exposed by indictment, the party has permitted their photographs to appear in non-Communist publications in order to help their case.

However, up to the recent past, the most thorough search of the so-called capitalist press will fail to turn up any photograph of Stachel, Eisler, Peters, Bittelman, Golos, or of any of the inner circle—the real rulers of the party. No newspaperman was ever permitted inside a party convention, except the representatives of the Red press; and the men of party importance, except such public figures as Browder and Foster, never spoke from a public platform. In addition, Communists in newspaper offices were instructed to make certain that city desks and morgues "lost" any chance photographs of leaders whose undercover character was to be preserved. Even from the Hearst morgue in New York, a picture censored by the party was stolen and destroyed. Beyond that, it is interesting to know that Hearst mats were regularly purloined for use by the *Daily Worker.*

During the trying days of June, 1945, when Browder was demoted by orders from Moscow, Nelson struck up a new comradely acquaintance with me. "Who is this guy Browder anyway?" he asked abruptly one day as we came out of the long and long-winded National Committee sessions which were then unanimously condemning Browder. "I never had one good talk with him; he was always too busy to see me in any private conference. Who is he anyway?"

This comment, made in Nelson's usual hard-boiled manner,

caught me by surprise, since Browder had spoken so glowingly of him when he was added to the National Committee. I told him of that, for he had not been present at the meeting.

Shrugging his shoulders, Nelson replied: "Oh, he had to do that. The guy was under orders from the secret police to give me the post. He wasn't enthusiastic." And that appears to be true. Bittelman shortly after verified Nelson's assertion.

The record of Steve Mesarosh, alias Nelson, alias Louis Evans, alias Joseph Fleischinger, alias Hugo, is proof of the fifth-column nature of the Communist party of the United States. He carried this record to its logical conclusion when, questioned by the Committee on Un-American Activities about where his loyalty would be in case of war between Soviet Russia and the United States, he replied: "I refuse to answer that question," on the ground it might incriminate him.

Over the House on Thirteenth Street hangs constantly the consciousness of the duty—the urgent duty—to know and carry out the requirements of the "line." Any comrade on any one of the nine floors who shows signs of having even a reservation on any current "line" is speedily ostracized, subjected first to whispered attack, and finally tarred with open abuse and expulsion. I have seen this happen many times; and it was my own constant responsibility to detect any signs of weakness in the *Daily Worker* staff and among those with whom I associated.

The representative of the Control Commission—either the late Jacob Golos, who was then chairman, or the secretary Charles (also known as Clarence) Dirba—constantly visited me secretly to check on the comrades around me. I would take them to a locked room at the north end of the building, which was set aside for just such "confidential communications." Little sandy-haired Golos and tall, lanky, bespectacled Dirba were quite unlike in general physical characteristics. But they were similar indeed in their tiptoe walk, their stealthy manner and their quiet speech.

Often, when I was managing editor, a whispered word would

come to me in the midst of some editorial conference: "Comrade Golos wishes to see you." There was always a dead hush among the editorial board members as I, asking to be excused, stalked out of the meeting to see Golos. The eyes of each comrade present followed me, and certainly more than one thought: "What is he reporting now to the Control Commission?"

Sometimes, as with Nat Honig, I was even asked to check on comrades three thousand miles away. At the time this happened, in the late '30's, Honig was doing party work on the West Coast and was known as William Z. Foster's good friend. Nevertheless, I received instructions from Jack Stachel and Dirba as early as 1937 to check on all communications that members of the *Daily Worker* staff received from Honig. I was told that when Honig was living in Moscow, on an assignment from the party here to the Communist International, he had shown too close friendship for Louis Fischer, who was a pro-Soviet American correspondent at that time but who later changed his mind about the Moscow dictatorship. Now, Stachel and Dirba said, Honig was showing signs of Trotskyite tendencies. Hence the watch upon him. Some of his personal correspondence was obtained from *Daily Worker* staff members and turned in to the Ninth Floor. Later, while editing the Communist paper in Chicago, I was again warned on Honig, this time by Morris Childs, who conveyed the Control Commission's requests to me in that area. I was not surprised, then, to learn in 1939 that Honig and his wife had been expelled from the party for not agreeing with the Hitler-Stalin pact—this despite the reputation the party had previously built up for him as the man who had saved Foster's life, when Foster was suffering from serious heart disease, by bringing him from Russia to America.

One of the final assignments upon which I acted for the Control Commission at the *Daily Worker* itself was to check on the Communist conduct of Harry Raymond, at that time City Hall reporter for the paper. I was told that Raymond was in doubtful political company, both at City Hall and in his too close friendship with

William F. Dunne, the American Red who had formerly been commissar for Stalin in Outer Mongolia but who for some years had been skirting expulsion. In accordance with the Control Commission's order, I selected two comrades to cultivate Raymond and report on his "tendencies." I was obliged to warn them carefully (as I had been told to do) that Raymond would try to conceal any antiparty sentiments under a show of personal devotion to William Z. Foster. When I left the party, this surveillance was still being continued. Dunne was expelled shortly thereafter; Raymond is still in the party.

Early in my experience at the *Daily Worker*, I learned the startling efficacy of the words "Control Commission" and "Golos" when I saw the effect they had on the generally self-possessed Harry Gannes, the well-known foreign editor of the paper. It was in 1936, during some office trouble involving the so-called James Casey, then managing editor, who was later expelled for Trotskyism. Harassed for weeks by the Politburo and by the continuous surveillance of the Control Commission, Casey, in desperation one night, had destroyed a ten-page editorial on China, which I had written after consultation with Bittelman. Had it not been for the officeboy of the paper, who we then learned was an agent of the Control Commission, Casey might never have been identified as the culprit. But that vigilant young Red produced from Casey's own office evidence of how the editorial had been torn up, and Casey was found guilty of an antiparty act.

Before this discovery was made, however, and while the affair was still a great mystery, the paper's editorial board had met. Bittelman, acting as the liaison officer of the Politburo to the *Daily Worker*, declared that he would call in the Control Commission through its chairman, Jacob Golos. The suggestion threw Harry Gannes into a frenzy of fear. He raised his voice in pleading protest, in a way I had never heard him talk before, and actually shook violently in his fright. When I asked him later why he had been so terrified, since he could not possibly be guilty, he said that didn't make any difference—the Control Commission would find someone guilty, and that someone would be anyone it served the party's purpose to find guilty.

The method of procedure within the party is an eternal reminder of the tie with Moscow. Each comrade, in performing his daily "task," moves and has his being according to directives from above. Moissaye Olgin, in his *Why Communism?*—the pamphlet which serves as a guide for daily party work, though it has long since ceased to have public distribution—states categorically that this is the hard-and-fast rule of the party. J. V. Peters in his famous *Manual of Organization*, which was another key reference book for action, in outlining the party's course to bring about a violent overthrow of the government, stresses the same point. This strange way of doing business is called "democratic centralism," although Foster admitted in September, 1945, that it was all centralism and not in any way democratic. Constant confirmation in practice shows that Foster was right.

Let's look at one of my own experiences, one of many hundreds. It is cited because it indicates that in 1944 Soviet tactics were already forecasting the "cold war."

In December of that year a report came that the British and Greek Communist "EAM guerrillas" had clashed. Upon learning this I rushed to the office, for it hinted a busy day. Sure enough, a consultation on the "Greek crisis" was in progress on the Ninth Floor. Jack Stachel and Gene Dennis were there, with the courier, Felix Kuzman, in attendance. That spelled special directives from and through Gerhart Eisler.

The big question was: How far should we go in denouncing the British "attack on the Greek patriots"? After all, we had been shouting that the Teheran agreement the year before meant what it said in guaranteeing "generations of peace." To attack Churchill in all-out fashion would be to differ publicly with one of the men whom we were hailing as "architects" of peace. Nevertheless that's what we were told to do. The "Greek crisis" was to be the instrument for bringing pressure on the British statesman so that he would yield to the Soviet dictator on Poland and Yugoslavia at the next meeting of the Big Three.

For our part, in America, we were to begin a hot campaign against the British. Accordingly, Dennis prepared the directives that appeared in the next *Political Affairs* under the title, "The Crisis Is in Britain—Not Only in Greece!" The *Daily Worker* shelled Churchill with every editorial gun at its disposal—even threatening that President Roosevelt would not be able to see his way clear to help Churchill under such circumstances!

Taking their cue from these pages, the comrades in disguise immediately assailed Churchill in unions, church groups, community organizations, political clubs—and made Greece the occasion for pressing for his acquiescence to the arrangement at Yalta in February, 1945, which prepared the way for Poland's subjugation to the Reds.

There was no democratic discussion among even the Red high command here on this matter; it was purely a question of executing a "directive" sent from abroad. And that is the continuous story within the party, which in turn educates an "aroused American public opinion" or strives hard to do so. In this case, its effort was crowned with success.

Since Communists here act in unison with the Reds in every other country on the globe, while we were engaged in this blackmailing operation, the Reds in other lands were doing the same thing. Strikes, demonstrations and other disturbances were threatened, to protest the "British massacre of the People's Greece."

"Democratic centralism" prevails at National Committee meetings to the same degree as in the daily "tasks." Usually a member is notified of these sessions by a little onionskin paper containing a typewritten notice of the place of meeting, given as a rule only twelve hours before it opens. Each member has a numbered card which he presents as he goes in.

The "discussion" is begun with the extensive report of the

general secretary, the "leader," outlining in detail the party policy
for the next period of time. This consumes from two to four hours.
Thereafter each member of the National Committee arises and
expresses complete agreement with the report. The chorus of approval continues for three days without letup, the district organizers
who direct the work in the various states joining in the unanimous
assent. Their statements are in the main an outline of how the new
"line" can be carried out in their states—how organizations can be
penetrated and leading citizens possibly beguiled into a pro-party
position.

The conclusion comes with a summary by the leader. This
summary and his original report are unanimously adopted as the
basis for work.

The district organizers then go back to their states to repeat the
same performance. They read the report of the national leader,
which is greeted with unanimous approval by the section organizers
and other active local Reds. These people bring it down to the
sections and thence to the branches, with unanimous *Ja* votes
greeting the reports all the way.

Such a procedure is another mark of the fifth column.

During the Hitler-Stalin pact period, the American people became enough aware of the disruptive activities of the Communists
to hit out at this foreign control. The outcome was the Voorhis
Act, which passed Congress in 1940 and provided for the registration of all foreign agents. The party leaders knew that this legislation was aimed directly at their organization, though they pretended (the usual Red device) that all labor was endangered by the
act. Nothing could be more absurd, but the party's hysterical warn-
ings on this score were no more unjustified than the hopes of the
Voorhis Act authors that the party would be curbed thereby.

The House on Thirteenth Street was momentarily perturbed
when the act was adopted, but it soon recovered. Getting together
its staff of legal advisors, headed then by the late Joseph Brodsky,
the party found a quick way out. On November 16 and 17, 1940,

it held a special National Convention in New York City and voted to "disaffiliate" from the Communist International, though still retaining the name of Communist party. The vote was of course unanimous. The party's constitution was amended accordingly.

I was a member of the National Committee to which Browder reported on this step before it was taken. He emphasized then that it was being done for legal and protective reasons only, and that our "internationalism" and "learning from the model party, the Communist party of the Soviet Union," would remain as strong as ever.

And Bittelman, the voice of Moscow, pledged in his editorials in *The Communist* that despite the Voorhis Act, "we shall always try to learn from Comrade Stalin and transmit our knowledge to the masses. . . ."

The comrades in Akron or San Francisco, studying *The Communist* eagerly and often for its Aesopian interpretation of events, were not to be left uninformed.

The party, Bittelman told them through his pages, would perform "the tasks of a Marxist-Leninist party in the situation created by the Voorhis Act," continuing to promote "working class internationalism, inspired as never before by the example of the great leadership of Comrade Stalin."

That was clear enough. It told every Communist who read it that the Voorhis Act would in reality be only a piece of paper so far as the party was concerned.

We pounded away on it for months—in the pages of the party's theoretical organ and in the countless "educational" discussions conducted in the various units and other divisions of the party. Shortly before the special convention had opened, I had attended a conference on the Ninth Floor, to consider how to spread the maximum understanding among the comrades that the legal move of "disaffiliation" meant nothing. Under the direction of the Soviet espionage agent J. V. Peters (who sent in voluminous notes from underground through the intellectual V. J. Jerome), it was decided to run two articles on the matter in the November, 1940, and January, 1941, issues of *The Communist*.

"The path of Lenin and Stalin leads to victory" was the theme of the first article on "the increasing turning [of the people] with yearning and hope toward the Soviet Union." It was intended to inflame the comrades with an even greater loyalty to the Kremlin's master, with a deeper sense of his invincibility, so that they might then inflame others with the same spirit.

Max Weiss, the secretary of the Young Communist League, wrote the second article: "The great sacrifice which the Communist Party of the United States made in disaffiliating with the Communist International in order to remove itself from the provisions of the Voorhis Act was a sacrifice made in the interests of furthering the Leninist struggle for proletarian internationalism."

There was much more to the same effect. To the normal American this verbiage seemed like a monotonous incantation. But to the comrade, painfully poring over each word and phrase to find the hidden meaning, it gave a dynamic message. It was all a long song of fealty to "the Soviet Union today, led by Stalin, Lenin's comrade-in-arms," to cite another Weiss quote.

It was a song of triumph, too; for the party, while thus repeating its old command of allegiance to Stalin, was able to continue its legal existence as a conspiratorial agency. The Voorhis Act failed to cut off the fifth column from Moscow.

Once more the "non-Communist" comrades, enlightened and inspired by these articles and by the *Daily Worker* editorials, launched a big campaign among their unions, professional organizations and community groups. Since they were not known as Reds, they were particularly persuasive in showing that the Communist party "has given up its international connections, and is now a purely American party."

"The accusation of 'orders from Moscow' is an ironic joke, a serious one, for it is bound to get us in trouble some day with that rising and powerful Russian nation," I heard a distinguished pro-

fessor say to a group of professional men in a Chicago hotel. I
had been invited out there as an observer, but my official or political
position had not been mentioned and I had not been recognized as
a Communist.

"The stupidity of the Congressional committee making such
unfounded accusations is not only irresponsible; it is dangerously
near to being fatal for America," the informed gentleman continued. Most of the men present nodded knowingly and laughed
at the suggestion that there might be any connection between such
"nuts" as the American Reds and a great man like Stalin. They
did not know, and would not have believed, that the Communist
antics here followed a pattern cut in Moscow. And that the con-
tortions were not so insane as they looked; that they had indeed
deceived badly most of the American nation.

In the crusade to prove that the American Communist party
was not controlled by Moscow, the comrades made haste to quote
Stalin himself. Talking to delegations of foreign workers in 1934,
Stalin had said—and these were the sentences generally quoted—
"There are no Communists in the world who would agree to work
'under orders' from outside against their own conviction and will
and contrary to the requirements of the situation. Even if there
were such Communists, they would not be worth a cent. Communists bravely fight against a host of enemies. The virtue of the
Communist, among other things, lies in that he is able to defend
his convictions."

Fine words and impressive until analyzed. The big catch in this
assertion, which was widely and solemnly repeated all over America
by the Reds, is that it is precisely the fact that he *is* constantly receiving orders that makes the Communist so effective. The pain
and trouble of having to think out a policy in a basic way is saved
him; all his energies can be devoted to executing the line as handed
on to him by the Moscow representative and ultimately by his
local leader. In the House on Thirteenth Street, every man can be
compared to a soldier in an invading army; he is bitterly hostile to

the government he is confronting, but his hostility to it is expressed
not on his own initiative but by carrying out the commands given
him. Frequently he is required even to simulate affection for the
country he is seeking to undermine, in order to creep forward to
a political killing or to the capture of a political outpost.

Whatever he does, the general strategy is not his in any sense.
Not only is it provided ready-made, but it is supplemented by publication after publication which he must read, and which aid him
to express himself in thought and act. The directives in *New
Times*, coming every week direct from Moscow to the active comrades and distributed officially to every member of the *Daily
Worker* staff, are of immense help. So also is the organ of the
Cominform, and the translations of *The Bolshevik, Pravda, Izvestia*,
and many other Soviet publications, all explaining and occasionally
expanding the "line." The ingenuity of the comrades is concentrated solely on doing the various things this "line" calls for.

As a method of operation, this represents the highest possible
efficiency in sedition.

These considerations recall the afternoon in late August, 1935,
that I crossed Union Square, walked down University Place and
entered the House on Thirteenth Street for the first time as a prospective Red. I went there to file my application card with Clarence
Hathaway, who was then editor of the *Daily Worker*. The first request Hathaway made of me was to read an article about to appear
in the paper, written by the party theoretician, Bittelman.

"It's a review of Browder's latest book, *Communism in the
United States*," said Hathaway, "but it's more important than that.
It tells what we think and mean to do."

I read the review as soon as I got the chance. In it Bittelman
paid a warm tribute of allegiance to the Communist International,
"headed by Comrade Stalin," and the direction it gave the Communist party of the United States. Particularly striking was this
expression: "In brief, Browder shows how the Soviet Union is the
only fatherland of the workers and the toilers the world over."

An organization ever under the thumb of a foreign dictator, accepting subsidies from him, agreeing always with him, idolizing him, directed by his agents, refusing to permit any democratic life within its ranks—that is not a legitimate political party. That is a fifth column. And that is Stalin's creature, the Communist party, U. S. A.

(III)

Stalin's Political Tourists

ON MY first visit to the Ninth Floor, in 1933, I discovered something of the influence wielded by one of Stalin's chief political
representatives in the United States. Though the man was dead,
and I was then not yet a member of the party, I was made vividly
aware of the strength of his Kremlin-stamped directives. His name
was Sergei Ivanovitch Gussev, and he had just died in Moscow,
after having controlled the Communists in America for almost ten
years.

From 1925 on, for a considerable period, he had been Stalin's
personal agent among the American Reds. Under the name of
P. Green, he had directed the crushing of Stalin's foes and had
made the party completely subservient to the Moscow dictator. By
1932, his work well done, Gussev had returned to the Soviet capital
to attend the Twelfth Plenum of the Executive Committee of the
Comintern (the ECCI). At that meeting, he had delivered a report
on "the main tasks of the Anglo-American sections of the Communist International," ordering a "turn" in the party's practices in
the U.S. The four tasks assigned to the party here were to popu-
larize as issues the defense of the Soviet Union, the Red conquest
of China, social insurance and self-determination in the Black
Belt. This last was the phrase used by the Communists to characterize their plan for a separate Negro republic, to be carved out
of several southern states and established through an armed up-
rising. The entire plan was devised to create dissension, and is a
distinct disservice to the Negro people. Indeed, both of the domes-

tic demands in the Gussev program were to be raised primarily to
gain influence for the party among special groups, that they might
more effectively advance Soviet Russian and Chinese Red ambitions.

It was this report that showed me the power of Stalin's personal
representatives over American Reds and in the American scene.
Jack Stachel quoted it to me at some length on that first visit of
mine to the upper regions on Thirteenth Street, endeavoring to
prove, with Gussev's words, that the Communists were adopting
new and vigorous measures in the "struggle for the proletarian
dictatorship." That struggle, according to Gussev, was about to
shake the world. But in many countries one element necessary to
the struggle was lacking—"wide contact with the masses." Gussev
specifically ordered the Reds here to arrange such contacts; hence,
said Stachel, they were now seeking new allies and relationships.

The Gussev report, with its command to "go to the masses,"
became famous in American Red history; it was a big moment for
the Communists here. First published in 1933, it was the beginning
of a new twist in American Red tactics which was to give them a
golden opportunity to infiltrate Washington and other key places
on a large scale. It prepared the way for important alliances for the
Party within American political life, and was the prelude to the
Teheran, Yalta and Potsdam agreements which helped to build
up Soviet power. It also opened the road for infiltration by the
Communist fifth columnists into many nooks and crannies of
American activities, from which, incidentally, they have by no
means been seriously dislodged.

As one of the earliest moves in carrying out Gussev's orders, the
party leaders called an extraordinary conference, out of which came
an open letter to the comrades, stressing the need of "building a
mass Party," and concentrating strength in the decisive industrial
centers. To attract a wide membership of any real permanency, the
party was compelled to adopt outwardly a more characteristically
"American expression" of its views. By thus concealing its real

nature, it gained increasingly the adherence of those professional and intellectual workers who as we shall see were to prove so valuable in the penetration of important posts.

As *Political Affairs* so proudly reported on the thirtieth anniversary of the party in September, 1949, the Gussev order also opened the way for the subsequent infiltration of the CIO in the steel, automobile and similar industries. But it did more than that. For a number of years it also made possible Communist control of the American Newspaper Guild, whose national office is, however, now out of Red hands. It gave the party an entering wedge into lawyers', artists', writers', and other professional groups of many kinds. The number of these people, indeed, reached such a considerable size by 1937 that the party began to take more open and official cognizance of them as party members. In a now famous article, William Z. Foster instructed them that it was their duty to be conscious of their Communist membership and Marxist responsibility at all times.

In short, the Gussev report inaugurated a new era for the comrades in America, an era in which they began to use a new language that eventually enabled them to look more like Americans, sound more like Americans and superficially to act more like Americans—and by that fact to penetrate various democratic organizations more freely and effectively than ever before.

I was one of the people attracted by the party's New Look and new language, though at the time this all began, when I first visited the Ninth Floor, I was still a non-Communist, as I have said, and was to remain one for two more years.

To get up to the sacred heights of the Ninth Floor in this nonparty capacity was something of a feat. I realized to some extent that my exceptional position was due only to the fact that the party leaders were feeling around for ways to carry out Gussev's orders to "get more contacts with the masses." I could have no real idea until later how much I had been made an exception to the general rule against admitting outsiders to the upper region.

The Ninth Floor, as a matter of fact, is carefully safeguarded from unwanted visitors. As a rule one can get to it only from the Twelfth Street entrance to the building. There is a large elevator at the main entrance on Thirteenth Street, but it is designedly used a great deal for freight. When in passenger service, it seldom travels to the top; its last stop is the eighth floor, the *Daily Worker*, and the stairs on that floor going upward are carefully shut off by a huge locked iron door.

Only once a fortnight or so did that elevator make the full journey up the shaft, and then it was freighted with important conspirators. As I was up there on my own business in later years, I saw many surprising faces—surprising, that is, in that the public would not have expected them to be seen in any such place— getting off at the Ninth Floor. That was the "road" taken by Frederick Vanderbilt Field and his partner in the anti-China conspiracy, Philip Jaffe, in those days of the late '30's when Field swore he was not a Red. He was then known in the world outside Thirteenth Street as a wealthy young man, and an officer of the Institute of Pacific Relations, who there hobnobbed with bigwigs from the State Department. For instance, among the gentlemen with whom Field was on good terms in the IPR was Dr. Philip Jessup, later to become famous as the author of our White Paper on China. Up on the Ninth Floor, and in my hearing, Mr. Field used to report on how men connected with the State Department, or considered to be experts on foreign affairs, had been persuaded to denounce Nationalist China as "feudal" and laud Red China as "democratic." Up there, too, I have run into State Senator Stanley Nowack of Michigan, at a time when he was denying all relationship with the Communist party but when I knew him to be taking orders from the party leaders. To the Ninth Floor came likewise political leaders in several states, such as State Representative Kathryn Fogg of Washington, who among others admitted under oath in 1948 that she had long been a Communist. That is the way Sam Carr or Kogen or Cohen, national organizer of the Communist party in Canada, slipped into conferences with shadowy figures like Peters and Eisler, when he did not want it known that he was in the United States. That is the route followed by Latin-American Reds (who often entered the country under false passports) arriving for secret deliberations with the leadership of the Communist party here.

If you try to get to the Ninth Floor from the apparently public or Twelfth Street side, you can get no farther than the outer vestibule without a sharp challenge. No one, unless he is a trusted and leading comrade from some other floor, can go freely through the locked door leading to the main corridor. Even prominent editors, to my own knowledge, have attempted it without success. Non-Communists (or even comrades from other parts of the country) who do finally get into the inner corridor do so only after severe scrutiny and on the word of one of the leaders within.

These are wise precautions for a conspiracy to take. From the barred and guarded precincts of the Ninth Floor, Gussev-trained agents have worked successfully for Stalin and against America. From there Gussev's successor, E. Edwards (better known under his correct name of Gerhart Eisler), directed the San Francisco general strike and skillfully laid the foundations for the Reds' entry into governmental circles and organs of opinion-making. Through that barred corridor have entered the scores of Moscow-trained alien political tourists who form the core of the party here, and from its narrow confines they have emerged to control the party in such far-distant states as Washington and such nearby cities as Washington, D. C.

Some of these underground members were men and women who disdained citizenship, probably on orders from Moscow. Others were immigrants who had entered under some legal cloud or criminal circumstance, and whom Moscow therefore felt could be counted on to be loyal to the Soviet regime rather than to this nation. Still others obtained citizenship as a temporary device that would enable them to function more effectively against the government until such time as they were ready to depart.

It was the studied policy of the Comintern to make aliens the supervisors of native Reds, as Jacob Golos explained to me one day when we were talking in his office in the Flatiron Building.

"An American might be a Comintern man in such countries as China and the Philippines," Golos said, in the careful manner of a man still unfamiliar with the language. "That was the case with Browder and with Steve Nelson and Bill Dunne. He will never yield to any homesickness for those lands, nor will he think of his family there in a moment of weakness. For they won't be there; they'll be in his native country, America. And at the same time," he continued, "for this country the C.I. man and the C.I. agents under him will always be non-Americans—and noncitizens if at all possible."

Golos, himself an alien, was an authority on the subject, for his World Tourists agency was for years one of the chief means by which the Soviet dictatorship moved its spies and other agents into this country and out again. It was a "false-passport factory" of no small dimensions, as the records of the Department of Justice and of the Federal courts prove beyond doubt.

As we looked out of the window in the point of the "flatiron" onto the crowds below, I became aware that he was moved by some inner excitement. "We are doing things for Stalin," he told me, "which these poor people do not understand." He might have added, "nor do they suspect."

Among the foreign-born tourists to whom the Moscow-controlled string was attached, not the least was Boleslaw Gebert, a veteran espionage agent and Communist party official. In the early '30's he was district organizer for the Chicago area, one of the most responsible posts in the American Communist party. During the great CIO drives, he was moved into the Detroit-Pittsburgh regions to direct infiltration of the automobile and steel industries. Simultaneously, to my knowledge, he engaged in espionage for the Soviet government, reporting immediately to Eisler, the notorious Peters, and to other persons whom I do not know. That his residence here, though it lasted a number of years, was temporary in character is demonstrated by what Gebert has since done. As soon as Red Poland was set up, Gebert was called back to that country (his native country) and became one of the top officials of the government's chief internal tool, the Polish Federation of Trade Unions.

Red rule in the Polish FTU was forced down the throats of the workers by a Red fifth column unable to win the support of more than 2 per cent of the Polish people until it employed force. The complaints in the Communist international discussions had made the American Reds conscious of the numerical weakness of the Polish Communist party and of the hatred with which it was regarded by the majority of the Poles, who considered it correctly an outpost of Russian aggression.

In 1949, Gebert blossomed forth as the official in charge of the trade departments of the Communist-controlled World Federation of Trade Unions, entrusted with the task of creating disruptions in the economy of the democratic countries. Early in 1950, he returned to the United States under diplomatic immunity as the representative of the WFTU on the economic and social council of the UN, under an arrangement whereby the WFTU is one of the nine nongovernmental agencies granted consultative status on that body. And thus, the Soviet agent, whom the United States government tried to deport in 1933, is back with us again.

"Bill" Gebert, as he called himself over here, was one of the Communists whom I came to know best—a tall, heavily built, blond-haired man with a marked accent. He turned up in many localities and in many types of work, generally of an underground character. He was an apt pupil of Sergei Ivanovitch Gussev, whose name he mentioned with deep reverence.

When I first met him on the Ninth Floor in 1933, he was denouncing the "Roosevelt–Wall Street government," saying in his clipped, heavily foreign speech, "Only the overthrow of capitalism can establish peace," and pointing to the Soviet dictatorship as the hope for the American masses.

He was at that moment redictating excerpts from his article in the *Daily Worker* of July 9, 1933, in which he had called on the comrades to "demonstrate on August first against Roosevelt's Imperialist War Program." The excerpts were for a leaflet to be distributed, I believe, in the Middle West, emphasizing that Stalin's dictatorship was the only hope for peace.

Stachel interrupted him to introduce me, saying that Gebert was one of the "wise men" of the party who had come in to attend the extraordinary national conference to strengthen work in the trade unions.

Gebert laughed in his peculiar clucking, almost hiccuping way. "If I am a wise man," he retorted, "then I prophesy that the extraordinary conference is a big affair. It will be a big noise in time. It will be heard from."

As a prophet, he was a success. The extraordinary conference, which got out the famous Open Letter to the party members, not only broke the ground for the expansion of Communist influence in the United States, as I have said, but also opened up espionage possibilities for the Reds throughout the nation. For, having once established themselves in communities and in the new unions being formed by the CIO—developments which the party's new American look made possible—the Reds were able to move with ease in circles where information vital to the Soviet government could be obtained. Take as one small example the case of Julius Emspak, known to the leading Reds as "Comrade Juniper." Before the period made possible by the open letter, Emspak was an insignificant and unknown Communist. Solely through the new tactics, developed after 1933 and brought into full bloom after 1936, Emspak became general secretary of a union of 500,000 Americans, located in an industry strategic from the viewpoint of national defense. This union, the United Electrical, Radio, and Machine Workers Union, was expelled from the CIO in 1949 because of its devotion to Red ideas. The story of how Emspak, first planted in a shop by the Communists, emerged into office in a small union which sprang out of the Red-controlled Steel and Metal Workers Industrial Union and then became a leader of the UE is told in the chapter "Red Web in Labor."

Is it not clear that as a prominent union leader in a vital industry Emspak was in a splendid position to obtain information for the Communist party? I know that he did obtain such information; that he secretly attended certain meetings of the National Committee of the Communist party; that he took part in discussions on how to shut down American industry on behalf of Hitler during the Hitler-Stalin pact. More than that, when he became a member of the President's Labor Advisory Committee, during World War II, he made constant reports to the Ninth Floor on information he gained at the national capital.

The extraordinary conference, which produced such extraordinary results in a few years, was in no small measure Gebert's handiwork. The party had not made the "turn" as fast as Moscow wanted, just as twelve years later it did not act on the celebrated Duclos article against Browder as rapidly as Moscow thought desirable. Consequently, a political tourist had been dispatched to America to prod the fumbling comrades. He was the creator of the "extraordinary conference," and he drew heavily upon Gebert's aid in the matter. This political tourist, the "architect" of the open letter, was the then unknown (to America) and quite underground Gerhart Eisler, or E. Edwards, as he was then called.

How do I know this, when I was not then in the party? Because in later years, when the open letter was referred to in discussion, which happened frequently enough, its "architect" was mentioned. Stachel, Peters, Browder, Foster, Gebert, have all in turn—and on several occasions—paid this tribute to Stalin's man Edwards-Eisler.

It is unfortunate that American agencies of public opinion paid so little heed to the inner workings of the Communist party. Americans might otherwise have understood better exactly what was implied by the extraordinary conference and the open letter—terms which have been so much Greek to them, if indeed they were familiar with them at all. The events they represent had much to do with the average American's fate; they advanced the possibility of Soviet Russia's defeat of his country.

Today it is equally unfortunate that even well-informed Americans are not fully aware of the party's present inner working and inner discussions. They would know better how to checkmate the new campaigns being launched in the name of democracy to create sedition among the youth, the Negroes and Mexican-Americans—campaigns that seize upon justified grievances and twist them into causes for Soviet subversion. They would appreciate that Paul Robeson's recent outbreaks against America are not only expressions of his personal resentment; they fit in with a much larger plot to create dissension and division in the United States. The current Red publications and inner-party discussions prove that decisively and, as a matter of fact, it is all set down in print, for any person to read.

The decisions of the extraordinary conference of 1933 "to go to the masses" and to establish concentration districts among the basic industries were preliminaries to wider influence and to direct subversive assaults upon the U. S. The Communists' goal was to have such a grip on the basic industries as to be able to paralyze America by political strikes and thus bring about her downfall. That was the general program set forth at the Sixth Congress of the Communist International, and studied and repeated endlessly in Communist conferences and educational meetings ever since. As worked out in detail by Eisler and Gebert, the scheme was to concentrate organizational efforts in those geographical areas—like Chicago, Detroit, Pittsburgh—which contain the industries that America depends on for its very life. By first entrenching themselves in the big industries and then gradually extending their activity out through the auxiliary sections of the community, to ensure additional support, they planned to be in a strategic position to shut down essential production in time of a crisis.

Gebert's aid to Eisler in working out the "concentration district" idea was not forgotten. Two years later, when the Congress of Industrial Organizations began its organization drive in steel, Gebert was put in charge of the party's participation. The CIO development offered the party immense possibilities for getting a real foothold in organized labor which it had never had before; Gebert's assignment was therefore a notable one.

As infiltration of the CIO progressed, the IWO, the party's insurance front established in 1930, was to prove an excellent channel for the purpose. Gebert was in familiar company with the IWO, for he had been associated with it since its birth, active always in its Polish section. Later he was to be vice-president and then president of the Polonia Society, its national Polish division.

This gave him a good base from which to proceed. Although he was not too successful in capturing entire steel locals, Gebert set up an undercover network of Red agents in the steel fields. Their responsibility in any Soviet war upon America will be to attempt to get control of the steel organizations and to create chaos in our major war industry. The Communists know from long experience that if one of their cells is permitted to remain in any factory or locality, it can expand rapidly in an emergency. It comes forward first with what appear to be justified demands, and constantly seeks to translate them into revolutionary actions. Measured by this standard, there are still enough Red agents in the steel industry, planted by Gebert, to affect seriously this country's defenses in war.

Then it was into the automobile center of Detroit that Gebert was sent. In his alien hands was placed the grand strategy of getting control of the giant auto union. This was a measure that the party considered of the utmost importance; for in case of the Soviet-American war that Gebert prophesied was inevitable, to shut down our aircraft and tractor factories would be to strike a big blow for Moscow. In the automobile and aircraft industries, Gebert made more progress in some ways than in steel. For a time he was a mighty power in the United Automobile, Aircraft, and Agricultural Implements Workers Union, and was constantly consulted by certain of its national officers. He succeeded in establishing strong cells in the Ford local, in the Packard local, and in other divisions of the organization. However, with the victory of Walter Reuther, much of the public result of Gebert's work has been erased. But the strong cells remain, awaiting the possibility of expansion should war or depression come.

Gebert was a typical Bolshevik, always looking for the imminent destruction of "American imperialism." Whenever I ran into him, as I did often, he was inspiring himself for the humdrum tasks of penetrating unions by quoting the revolutionary promises of Lenin and Stalin and the hair-raising *Daily Worker* editorials of the 1933-1934 period.

Even in late 1937, when the Reds were hammering away at the People's Front idea, I found him at a similar exercise. I had just gone out to Chicago to become editor of the Communist *Midwest Daily Record* and was staying with my family in a hotel there until we could get permanent quarters. In the lobby I ran into Gebert, down from Detroit.

When our meal was over we went out for an evening walk on Michigan Boulevard. Referring to a recent article in the *Daily Worker* which had mentioned "permanent employment" as though it could be won by the People's Front, Gebert went on to stress that such an achievement was possible only under socialism. "As Marx has shown," Gebert said with grim fervor.

Then, to my amazement, he quoted in full the conclusion of an editorial in the *Daily Worker* of more than four years before—July 5, 1933—which reminded the working class that the Soviet Union was its natural home and that in case of war against Soviet Russia "the working class must be prepared to rally to the defense of its Fatherland."

"Why, that editorial appeared about the time I first met you on the Ninth Floor," I said.

"Yes," he responded, "I wrote it for the *Daily* then, as Comrade Edwards ordered it prepared. That's something we have to keep before us always—that the Soviet Union is the only fatherland the workers of this or any other country have. Just as a Christian renews his baptismal vows," he continued, with a smile.

Expanding, Gebert then told me something he had been leading up to all the while. "The comrades in Chicago are not supposed to know I'm here," he finally said, looking at me sidewise. "It's not a woman," he went on, laughing, "though it might be that, too. But it's something much more serious: it's the business of getting our Slav comrades to work undercover for the defense of the Soviet Union."

By then I was well acquainted with the meaning of that expression. It was espionage work that Gebert was doing in Chicago; and he told me he came down "almost every week for a day or two" to attend to it. "You can forget my special assignment," he said, as we parted after a prolonged jog along Chicago's attractive lake front. I assured him it would be lost in my memory.

Not long before I left the party, in 1945, I learned from Gebert the wide extent of his espionage work. We met in his office in the national headquarters of the International Workers Order, on lower Fifth Avenue, New York, where as president of the Polonia he was directing Red control of the American Slav Congress.

So well informed was the party of the fact that the United States was yielding on its promise of free elections to the Polish people that even then, Gebert was making ready for his return to Poland. News of these behind-the-scenes developments in Washington was coming in constantly from the party's agents in the government and from the powerful "Washington cell," which co-operated with them. These undercover Communists in the national capital had carried out their instructions skillfully, and according to Gebert their reports showed that a great deal of progress was being made in breaking down any militant attitude against a possible Red Poland. He mentioned in passing the recent visit to the Ninth Floor of a lawyer well known nationally, who had brought good news about the policy on Poland that was taking shape in the State Department. Now confident that the Soviet conquest of eastern Europe would take place without serious opposition from this country, Gebert said airily that I might soon learn of his departure for "home."

"But I won't have gone back empty-handed," he said with satisfaction. "I have helped the Soviet Union's defense while I was here. In the Slav field and at Detroit, too, we got valuable advance data on American imperialism's latest aircraft plans." He mentioned military planes.

He suggested that after he left perhaps I could help some of the leading Slav comrades continue this form of activity. Though I said nothing on that, he took it for granted that I would help, and added that I would hear from him before his departure.

As we talked we both were thoroughly conscious that our big mission just then was to obtain American acquiescence to a Red Poland and the Communist conquest of China. That twofold objective had been dinned into the ears of all the leading comrades for more than a year. It was to forward this objective that Browder had scuttled the Communist party and formed the Communist Political Association in 1944, just one year previously. In the National Committee meetings at which he proposed the change, he had specifically told us that Moscow wanted it made in order to persuade America that Communism was no longer a threat. This fear allayed, he pointed out, it would be easier to win from Washington concessions on Soviet expansion in Europe and Asia.

Every wind that blew from the Kremlin brought the same instructions. *War and the Working Class*, in its Number 6 issue of 1945, sent from the Soviet capital for our direction, told us that the only possible stand on Poland was for the Provisional Government set up by the Reds. We were instructed to raise the cry that the

Provisional Government had "always stood for broad national unity," although we knew that this was the usual "United Front" device, designed in this instance to crush the major Polish party under Stanislaw Mikolajczyk. Our assurance that this would be achieved and that the strength and presence of the Red Army would ensure the domination of eastern Europe, as the *Red Star* predicted in April, 1945, has been borne out by history.

In the light of this firm expectation, Gebert said something in the course of our talk that is worth remembering: "When we gain the upper hand completely in Poland and other European countries, and set up fully the People's Democracies, we shall have plenty of outlets for information in America. Every consulate under our banner shall be dedicated to defense of the Soviet Union, and that will ease the road of the party here in its aid to that defense. Where we now have one man with diplomatic immunity we shall have at least a dozen."

That wasn't new. I had heard it many times in the previous year in our discussions on why we should concentrate on winning American opinion for a Red Poland and Red China. But its reiteration at that moment, as Gebert was planning to leave, gave it a garb of reality which it had not fully possessed before. His was not idle chatter; he wanted me prepared to work in co-operation with the consulates should I be called upon to do so.

Gebert had obtained men to do such espionage work in the past. Two of them I know, and I will present their names to any governmental body meeting in executive session. Both were men prominent in their local communities, their Communist allegiance being either totally unknown or much in doubt with people outside the party. It was this ability to move about without suspicion in large industrial centers, to talk to workers and to businessmen and technicians, that made them so valuable for secret operations.

That was my last interview with Gebert, since I left the party in the early fall. As for Gebert, two years later, in August, 1947, he stepped on the Polish ship *Batory*, just as his fellow-tourist Eisler was to do after him, and without any passport or State Department consent, sailed off to what had become Red Poland.

Gebert's work furnishes an excellent example of the technique by which the so-called open-party work is merged with infiltration of non-Communist bodies and with espionage. Here is seen the emphasis on combining "legal" with "illegal" work that every Red learns from Lenin's writings. While dealing with people openly on party matters and union affairs, Gebert was constantly receiving information and establishing contacts for undercover activity.

Through his contacts with the international office of the Automobile Workers Union, for example, he obtained considerable information on the new types of planes, information which he then adapted to undercover work. I stood with him, talking, before the Bell Aircraft Corporation at Buffalo in 1941, when the auto workers' convention delegates threw a picket line about the plant, and was struck with the detailed information he had about what Bell was doing. In the Communist caucuses at the auto workers' conventions, he showed himself equally well informed on the wider field of aircraft. And on such occasions he was always collecting the latest data on new planes from the Reds who were then among the union officials. I can remember him on a number of occasions in earnest conversation with two men in the union's educational department—asking them questions about the speed, size and type of the newest military aircraft.

The methods of operation followed by the Communists at the union conventions made it possible for a shrewd Red agent, which Gebert was, to pick up military secrets with some readiness. The Politburo always assigned a leading comrade to attend every large labor convention that was held. Usually, his presence in the convention city was unknown to anyone except the Communist delegates. In some more or less obscure hotel, they would confer with him; when occasion warranted, secret caucuses of the Red delegates to the convention would be held at his call and under his control. Generally, the Detroit representative of the *Daily Worker*, who was assigned to many types of underground work, would quietly see each one of the Red delegates on the convention floor and instruct them verbally to attend a caucus in a specified hotel room.

The general purpose of these caucuses was to direct Communist penetration of the union, and to give the comrades their orders regarding the policies and candidates in the convention. But these conferences—either private or group—gave Gebert an excellent opportunity to collect technical data. Piecing together information obtained bit by bit from men who frequently did not realize the full import of what they were doing, Gebert would forward it to his "contact" who was associated with the Soviet consulate in New York.

I have mentioned "the wider field of aircraft" because with World War II the expansion of the aircraft industry was accompanied by union organization of that industry. The United Automobile Workers changed its name to The United Automobile, Aircraft, and Agricultural Implement Workers Union, CIO, in recognition of its extended jurisdiction. This permitted Gebert logically to ask questions concerning aircraft which formerly he had asked about other war materials manufactured in those centers.

In late 1941 Gebert's old comrade Eisler returned to the United States with news which gave Gebert an even greater area in which to operate. For he brought instructions to speed the creation of an All-Slav Congress, designed to glorify Soviet Russia in the anti-Hitler war. The order to form the Congress had arrived in America ahead of Eisler, but he emphasized the urgency of making such a body permanent for future Soviet purposes. It was to be a copy of the All-Slav congress held in Moscow the previous August.

The full story of the American Slav Congress can wait until subsequent pages disclose the big Red campaigns to deceive America. The Congress was designated as subversive by Attorney General Clark, and a competent survey of its seditious work has been prepared by the Committee on Un-American Activities. The Congress provided Gebert, its chief creator, with new men both as espionage agents and as outright propagandists for Soviet aggression in Slav countries.

In contrast to the professional anonymity sought by most political tourists was the spotlight which played around the person of Eisler, alias Edwards, alias Berger and many other assumed names. As it was, that publicity came about in an unexpected and unplanned way, even so far as I was concerned. Had the year of silence which I imposed upon myself when I left the Communist party not ended on October 11, 1946, Eisler might have been on the high seas when my mention of him occurred. That twelve months of no writing and no public statements was decided upon at Notre Dame, in order to give me time to reorganize myself and to help me act in a responsible manner. Then, in ending that period, I did bring Eisler into the picture on the occasion of my second talk, October 13, 1946.

Even then, when I broke the silence by my reference on the Detroit radio to the representative of the Communist International who issued orders to the party here, I did not give his name. I was more interested in letting my fellow citizens know the fact than in exposing the man. Clever newspaper work by Frederick Woltman, with the remarkable memory that he has, led him to the deduction that the man I had mentioned was Eisler and that his assumed name was Hans Berger. Then, of course, I could not deny it.

In 1947, Eisler went to trial twice for the least serious of his offenses against the United States. The more flagrant had been ruled out by our statute of limitations, which is particularly generous to alien seditionists who can hide out in other countries while the statute of limitations is expiring. But he was convicted twice by juries in the District of Columbia. The first of his offenses was contempt of Congress, for which he received a one-year sentence in a Federal penitentiary. The second was visa frauds, in violation of several sections of the United States Code. For that, his sentence was from one to three years. But Eisler showed his contempt for the United States courts—which I had often heard him express—

by escaping on the Polish ship *Batory* while his appeal was pending before the United States Supreme Court.

Nevertheless, his work still marches on. It was living down on Foley Square, at the United States Court House, in the tactics adopted by the defense in the trial of the eleven Communist leaders. We can note that Eisler did not embark upon his flight on the *Batory* until he had attended the trial for a number of days, sitting in the front row, and had given the Politburo the benefit of his observations and directions.

The entire Communist strategy for this trial was mapped out by Eisler in a memorandum to the Politburo during the trial of the alleged Nazi agents at the nation's capital in 1944. Lawrence Dennis, the intellectual Fascist, who was prominent among that group, was particularly admired by the Communist leaders. While shouting for his blood in public because that was then the thing to do, they paid a number of compliments to his ability in the course of their discussions of the trial.

Eisler asserted, after studying the case, and the Politburo agreed and so decided, that should the Communists ever be defendants in a "mass trial," they would comport themselves in much the same way. "To disrupt and expose American bourgeois justice," Eisler declared, "would be of immense service to the Soviet Union." The Soviet agent did not reckon with the patient persistence of Federal District Attornies John I. X. McGohen, and Judge Harold R. Medina.

It was from Eisler that I learned definitely of the proconsular power exercised by the Communist International representatives as channels of communication with the leader. As a non-Communist in the early '30's I had of course known little of how Gussev operated; there was nothing in my American experiences to give me a clue to that.

It must be remembered that Gussev's original job in America had been to make certain that Stalin, rather than his rivals Trotsky and Bukharin, would control the party here. As time went on, and

Stalin's power increased throughout the Communist world, Gussev assumed the position and the full responsibility of the chief Comintern representative in America. He laid down the pattern which was followed by all his successors, in particular by his most notable one, Eisler. Nothing illustrates the continuity of Stalin's control better than the series of episodes connected with these two men. Gussev's labors for Stalin bore their fruit under Eisler.

If earlier I had not completely realized the extent and source of Gussev's power, after 1935, seeing Eisler in action behind the Red scenes and hearing him (first as Edwards and later as Berger) tell me and other leading Communists what to do, I no longer had any doubt that the party here was counseled by Stalin's agent on Stalin's behalf, and, more than that, that he exercised autocratic powers over those who were supposedly the leaders of the party.

Some readers may exclaim at my naïveté. Why was I not more alert, before entering the party, to the remote control exercised by the Comintern representative? There is little doubt that I shall have to plead guilty to a considerable degree, especially since I was so close to the Communists before I joined them and could read in the *Daily Worker* their effusive expressions of devotion to Stalin. In that paper I could also read on September 1, 1933, Edwards' printed orders to the party leaders to carry out the line of the "open letter" with more zeal and vigor. There were the words of sharp command, asking how it was that this step was not taken and that measure not followed out. The conclusion was a threat of Kremlin discipline for those who forgot where their responsibilities lay.

But naïve as I was, and proved to be for a long time, I was no more naïve—and this is no consolation—than many responsible American citizens who have swallowed whole almost every fabrication that the party has produced. A greater measure of their gullibility is their continued acceptance of excuses and explanations that do not excuse or explain, throughout the period of the cold war, from 1945 to the present day.

This self-deception of Americans concerning the Reds was never better illustrated than in Eisler's case. Even after he had fled from his two convictions in American courts, an outstanding New York newspaper ran a sketch of him which leaned strongly to his own representation that he was a poor Nazi refugee who had been on his way to Latin America in 1941 but had become sidetracked. His arrival at Ellis Island was passed off as a mistake. Nothing was said in the article about Eisler's having entered and left America on several previous occasions with false passports, deliberately forged, in which he swore that he was one Sam Liptzin. (Liptzin was actually a naturalized American citizen, and one of the most prominent of the comrades connected with the Communist *Daily Freiheit.*) For forging the names of alleged witnesses to the Eisler passports, the Communist Leon Josephson did spend a few months in jail, but the whole significance of a Soviet agent's flaunting American citizenship laws as Eisler had done was lost on the newspaper writer as well as on Americans as a whole.

Little was written either in that article or elsewhere about Eisler's having been a Comintern agent in China just before he came to the United States in 1933. Nor was any reference made to the accusation by his sister, Ruth Fischer, that he had been one of Stalin's chief finger men and had caused the murder of many of his comrades in the Far East.

That Eisler was not a genuine refugee can be ascertained by any man of average intelligence from the fact that he is now a member of the (Red) People's Council of Eastern Germany, of whom there are only 35 in all. It is confirmed by his appointment to a chair in the University of Leipzig, and in the elaborate arrangements made by two Soviet satellites, Poland and Czechoslovakia, to facilitate his escape from American justice. Further, he has lately become Propaganda Minister for the Red-ruled regime in East Germany.

When I first dealt with Eisler upon my entrance into the party in 1935, he ruled from the Ninth Floor under the name of Edwards. Not one out of a hundred American Reds knew who

"Edwards" was, as is frequently the case in such a conspiratorial setup. He appeared on no public platform; was not to be seen at any public Communist event except strictly on the sidelines. He was, however, anything but retiring when presiding on the Ninth Floor. Nervous in manner, sometimes shrill when impatient, he ordered party leaders about with a sharpness and even brutality of manner that suited well the Gauleiter of a ruthless dictatorship. Through such methods, he molded the party into a competent conspiratorial agency. He "made the party come of age," as Browder once said of him at a dinner given to the newly elected National Committee in 1936.

During his Edwards period, from 1933 to 1936, he supervised the development of the tactics for penetrating the CIO (with the proper caution on John L. Lewis which will appear later), infiltrating American agencies of every sort, and expanding the espionage system. But his masterpiece was the deception the Communists practiced on President Roosevelt by backing him for re-election while continuing with their plans to overthrow by violence the government of which Mr. Roosevelt was the head.

This was the famous People's Front policy; and it relied strongly on the use of professional workers in strategic posts and on concealed Communists in important labor positions—men and women who mingled with governors, newspaper editors, scientists, and who were at home in Congressional circles. Polished and able, such people were effective in spreading the pro-Soviet point of view among the groups that most mattered.

I recall the unrestrained joy on the Ninth Floor the day it was learned that President Roosevelt was to commute the sentence of Earl Browder. It was not so much the fact of the commutation itself that caused this pleasure as the fact that the President had done it in the name of "national unity." It was precisely the necessity of getting this phrase into any order for Browder's release that Eisler had insisted upon and that had formed the subject of several tense Politburo discussions when I was present. It was felt that the

President's use of this phrase would give the Communists a new status.

Eisler's strategy in regard to F.D.R. in 1936 (given to him by Moscow) is the key to the permanent Communist plan for infiltration of American agencies; it explains the Communists' super-confidence in the achievement of the Soviet conquest of this nation. We can therefore afford to get a good view of it.

One afternoon in the late spring of 1936, I was called into a Politburo meeting being held in the large office just off Browder's on the Ninth Floor. There I heard Eisler report on what he termed "Gussev's gift" to the party. I can remember with what earnestness he insisted that America could be taken in. Support to F.D.R. in the coming Presidential campaign was to be given in an "indirect way," by assailing the Liberty League—"the Morgan–du Pont group"—as the greater evil, as men determined "to shift the burdens of the crisis ever further onto the backs of the toiling masses." Thus the Reds would be able to ally themselves to many people in key positions in the government. At the same time, explained Eisler, they would be strengthening their own stand for the Soviet overthrow of "American imperialism." And accordingly he proceeded to outline the platform and resolutions later adopted in the June, 1936, National Convention—the famous Ninth Convention of the party.

While urging the necessity of "defeating Landon and his stooge Lemke," these resolutions emphasized that the fundamental aim was "a Soviet government and Socialism." Again they declared, lest it be misunderstood, that the Reds were fighting for "a Soviet America," and to clinch the matter concluded thus: "While carrying on the daily practical and political tasks as outlined above, the Communists must systematically educate the masses to the Marxist-Leninist position on war as embodied in the thesis of the Sixth World Congress of the Communist International and in the resolution of its Seventh Congress."

There was Aesopian language for you! The Sixth World Congress had set out in detail the program for "turning the imperialist war into civil war" and for the violent smashing of the United States government as set up under the Constitution. The Seventh Congress had endorsed that program. Thus the party planned to use the wider associations it would form by getting on the Roosevelt band wagon to promote the violent destruction of the United States government. It was as simple as that, but many authors and politicians did not see it.

And yet these resolutions were available for study to anyone, since they were prepared and sold in printed form. And the *Program of the Communist International*, outlining this plan for destroying the government, was then being distributed by the party in thousands of copies. There was one phrase which Eisler insisted upon inserting into the resolutions, which burns into our consciousness today: "Collaboration between the United States and the U.S.S.R. would constitute the surest guarantee of peace in the Pacific and in the world, the safest guarantee of keeping this country out of war."

I can hear him yet, explaining this phrase to the comrades in that small conclave of the Politburo which preceded the 1936 convention: "This U.S.A.-U.S.S.R. collaboration, we understand, comrades, would eventually make the Pacific a Soviet lake. That would give the Soviet fatherland the power to defend itself against American imperialism, after having won the original aid of the United States against Japanese imperialism."

Subsequent history indicates painfully that Eisler knew whereof he spoke. These contributions were, he then said, his "last words to the party," and in a short while he was in the Civil War zone in Spain. Playing an apparently obscure role, which deceived even the former managing editor of the Socialist *New Leader*, Liston Oak, he was actually in a key post—working with the Soviet secret police as he had in China.

When last I received his orders in the '40's, he was known as Hans Berger, and ruled from the Communist underground. Never was he to be seen on Thirteenth Street. But there was frequently to be heard mention of his assumed name—"Comrade Berger thinks this," "Comrade Berger reports that," "Comrade Berger instructs"—at Politburo meetings, at closed *Daily Worker* editorial-board conferences. It was as though a ghost were directing the party discussions and decisions. Through competent couriers he sent crisp instructions to the party leaders every day. Sometimes a note would come to me from Berger, sharp, Germanic in style, always to the point. The Joint Anti-Fascist Refugee Committee was the center from which he operated, and Felix Kuzman of that organization was one of his chief couriers.

His was a double life, politically. At the Joint Anti-Fascist Refugee Committee, he went by his own name of Eisler; this was also his practice in writing for the German-American paper which the Communists, at his suggestion, began to issue. Down on Thirteenth Street, his powerful orders came over the name and by the authority of "Berger." Even at the Joint Anti-Fascist Refugee Committee, where his alleged status as a refugee supplied a legitimate reason for his presence, he maintained an obscure position. It was an ideal setup for the representative of the Comintern under the conditions that surrounded his entry into the country. He had sworn that he was not a Communist on his last trip, just as he had sworn falsely on other occasions that he was Sam Liptzin.

The Joint Anti-Fascist Refugee Committee, from which he received funds as Eisler, was ostensibly an open and aboveboard organization. But its roots reached so far into the concealed foreign Communist colony that its directors have preferred to face jail sentences rather than tell Congress what appears in the Committee's records.

The trained Communist—even if he had not been in direct contact with this mysterious stranger as I was—would have recognized Hans Berger's authoritative position from the vital articles he wrote for *The Communist*, which was then the title of the official theoretical organ of the party. In work that is conspiratorial to the core, where free discussion is forbidden, the articles a comrade writes in the theoretical organ give a clue to his status. Measured by this standard, Berger was obviously of the highest rank.

When exposed as the Comintern representative in 1946, Eisler leaned heavily upon his claim that he was merely a "Nazi refugee." His Berger articles, identified by me before the Congressional Committee on Un-American Activities, demonstrated the falsity of that claim.

What were the facts? In the last part of 1941, Eisler sought entry at Ellis Island on the plea that he had been headed for Latin America when he heard he could not be admitted. Swearing falsely that he was not a Communist, he was held at Ellis Island and then admitted. In late 1941 I was informed by the Ninth Floor that one Hans Berger was detained or had just been released from Ellis Island and would write occasionally for the *Daily Worker* and for *The Communist*. One Saturday, a day when there are few editorial-board members at the *Daily Worker*, I was busily engaged in planning for the changes in the Sunday edition when Sam Don and Eugene Dennis appeared. Don, who co-operated in the editorial work on the *Daily Worker*, and Dennis had something big to show me. It was an article by Eisler, and it was to be run as though sent from Switzerland.

"The author is at Ellis Island or has just been released," Dennis told me, "we don't want any suspicion cast in his direction. He is here only on the sufferance of the government."

In November, 1942, the big assignment given the Communists here was to press for the Second Front at all costs. Even though American military supplies had helped to save the Soviet capital, Moscow was bitter because our men had not landed in Europe. The Politburo found it necessary to whiplash the comrades into renewed and heroic efforts in that direction—but it was Eisler who gave the comrades directives they could not misunderstand. In the November issue of *The Communist* he wrote an article demanding all-out American action for the Second Front and belaboring Americans for permitting "prejudice" to blind them to the virtues of Soviet Russia. Ironically, the man who had just slipped into the country under a blanket of misrepresentations and perjuries declared, as though he were the descendant of a founding father: "Toward the U.S.S.R. we failed to display that undaunted, forward-surging pioneer spirit with which our forefathers were so richly endowed."

His purpose was to give the comrades a handmade slogan with which to shout for the Second Front. Parrotlike, Communists repeat the words with which they are supplied on down the line until the expressions become heard in unions, lawyers' clubs and guilds, community organizations and neighborhood groups. By this constant repetition the Reds obtain acceptance for their ideas to an amazing degree. But Eisler wrote in that fashion, too, in order to conceal the alien background of the author.

Every active comrade recognized the article as a directive of the highest importance, and it was studied and explained and used to harangue other comrades into a frenzy of activity. In the stockyards area of Chicago, in meetings between shifts in Detroit, in a professional workers "cell" in New York, I heard the phrases of that article chanted—in so many places indeed that they spun around in my head. The Reds were busy making Americans ashamed of being so unworthy of the great Red Army led by that military genius, Stalin.

This was not the last of Eisler's big directives. When a year later, in November, 1943, the Communist International had allegedly been dissolved in order to lull America into slumber, he immediately explained the operation in *The Communist*. By stressing that the Communists were strengthening their "Marxist-Leninist principles, which know no boundaries," Berger gave the comrades to understand that the Communist International was not in reality dissolved no matter what might formally occur. The district organizers (state leaders) knew Berger was the Comintern representative and was continuing as such. This added to their understanding of his roundabout assurance that the C.I. was not dead.

When in early 1944 W. Z. Foster broke the traces of Communist discipline behind the little iron curtain on Thirteenth Street, it was Eisler who answered him for the comrades' benefit in the May, 1944, issue of *The Communist*. Foster had objected to the dissolution of the Communist party and the substitution of the Communist Political Association, but had been compelled to withdraw his objections for fear of being expelled from the party. Eisler, who had dictated the dissolution move to Browder, disposed of the matter thoroughly in an article ostensibly replying to Max Lerner of the pro-Communist newspaper *PM*, who had accused Browder of letting the liberals down.

These directives and many others by this able political tourist during his Hans Berger period were dispatched to the Ninth Floor from his office hideout at 162 Lexington Avenue.

After the international Communist apparatus had obtained his escape in 1949, something he had said at the 1936 Politburo meeting came back to me with full force. He had said then, as Edwards, and had repeated it in the '40's in a memorandum, as Berger: "We shall be able on the ruins of the Second Imperialist War to set up Communist cadres which will establish invincible international communication and information into the United States. That will be a distinct service to the Comintern and Comrade Stalin."

If we ponder that phrase, we can appreciate how injurious to America was the laxity which permitted him to roam around on bail after conviction and thus assured his escape. It was not coincidence that he left as he did, at the same time as the Hungarian J. V. Peters, master espionage director and Eisler's right hand man, and John Santo, the Rumanian Communist who was recalled by Moscow to his native country while deportation proceedings were pending against him. Reports of the Immigration Division of the Department of Justice show more than 3,000 known Red aliens are in this country illegally, and cannot be returned because the countries of their origin will not accept them. But the return of Eisler, Peters and Santo—who could have dragged out residence here through Supreme Court appeals and the Soviet satellites' refusal to take them in—was clearly facilitated by Moscow in order to train in Red-dominated lands those "cadres" for the extension of espionage in the United States of which Eisler spoke. This statement is based on more than Eisler's words; the plan was a continued point of discussion in the Minority Groups Commission, which met on the Ninth Floor, originally under the chairmanship of Mrs. Irene Browder, and later with Avram Landy presiding.

How well the Stalinist tourist, who resides here for years illegally and is then recalled, performs his services for the dictatorship is illustrated by the case of Boris Isakov. More and more we hear of him as directing English-language broadcasts from Moscow, assailing the United States and, in particular, on July 22, 1949, replying to the Papal excommunication of Catholics who become Communists. Who is this gentleman? He is none other than the immediate predecessor of Eisler as Comintern representative here, another of Gussev's pupils, who directed the party under the false name of Boris Williams. If he were caught in war, as Tokyo Rose has been, he couldn't even technically be tried for treason, since he was never an American citizen.

Among the other political tourists in the Communist conspiracy, echoing like a Greek chorus the words and work of Eisler, Peters and Gebert, were these men and women:

First, the big-boss inner-ring commission which co-operated with the Comintern representative in supervising the party—the illegal aliens Jack Stachel, Alexander Bittelman and the late Jacob Golos; the late Joseph Brodsky, the lawyer; the Russian-born Alexander Trachtenberg; and the illegal alien Robert William Weiner, alias Welwel Warzover, whose secret fund for conspiratorial purposes will shortly be heard of in a big way.

The men I have named were those who had "direct connections

with Moscow or Moscow sources," or as Trachtenberg dubbed them once, "the kitchen cabinet of conspiracy." They operated from the inner precincts of the Ninth Floor, pulling the strings that manipulated various men and women in public life, educators, editors and others favorable to pro-Communist causes. No matter what the party's public policy and regardless of who was general secretary, these men continued to function in their secret and powerful capacity as long as I was in a high Red post.

It is true that on the inner-party commission which worked with the Comintern representative there were two native-born Americans. The first of these was Earl Browder and the second was Eugene Dennis. But the chief reason for their inclusion, as I learned, was their conspiratorial work with the Communist International apparatus abroad, in China and India, for example. This had given them, as Bittelman once explained, the intimate association with the underground machine, and specifically with the Soviet secret police, that was indispensable in the Commission's work.

This thoroughly alien commission is of the highest importance in trying to understand the party apparatus—the illegal or hidden wheels within wheels which characterize its administration from abroad. One of the most-heeded voices on it was Bittelman, who under the name of "Ralph Barnes" or simply "Mr. Barnes" directed the thinking and often the action of the Communists in this country. He was the agent entrusted by Moscow with instructing the party leaders in the precise terms to be employed in the use of Aesopian language.

Many times I heard him lecturing the Politburo on exactly what words and phrases the party declarations should contain in order to be Leninist and at the same time legal. It is a measure of the difficulties that America has had in defending itself that he has been permitted to function in this role for so many years.

In late 1936, when I had become a full-fledged member of the *Daily Worker's* editorial board, I learned how efficiently this intelligent man molds the Aesopian language which the Communists use to conceal their purposes from the non-Communist public.

Bittelman was then operating from the Hotel Albert, where the entire editorial board conferred with him almost every day. So carefully were his whereabouts and movements guarded, and so carefully did he seek to conceal our conferences, that each meeting with him had to be arranged over an outside telephone, usually the drug store telephone around the corner from Thirteenth Street. Every day at noon, Harry Gannes, then foreign editor of the *Daily Worker,* a veteran member of the board, would rise from his desk and leave the building. In a few minutes he would return, to state generally that he had reached "Comrade Barnes" and that he would see us at such and such a time.

At the hour set, each member of the *Daily Worker* editorial board would stroll over to the Hotel Albert. Singly each would enter the lobby and then go up to Bittelman's room for a hurried hour on the paper's editorial policy. Bittelman-Barnes was the law and the line; particularly did he take pains to stress the exact manner in which a fundamental position should be presented. For the Communists, this is all-important, since they are constantly writing editorials with a view to presenting them as legal in courts.

The magic by which this man possessed such mastery of the line and the ability to present it properly was in reality no mystery. He was the chief of the small corps of Politburo members who were in touch with the Comintern representatives and the Soviet consulates. Others were Jack Stachel, Alexander Trachtenberg, and Robert William Weiner. To these should be added the general secretary of the party—Browder in my time, Dennis today. But not all members of the Politburo were so privileged. Elizabeth Gurley Flynn was never permitted to be one of this small corps, and even Foster, during the period when he was out of step with Browder, was denied the right. And though Robert Minor had been the party representative to the Comintern in Moscow for several years and was serving in that capacity when Browder was made general secretary of the party in 1930, he was seldom the direct contact man.

Unobserved, the chosen comrades entrusted with the reception of Moscow's directives got them by hand from a courier, some apparently obscure person who in turn had received them either from the Comintern representative or directly from the Soviet consulate or embassy. During the latter part of my work in the party this was Felix Kuzman, a former member of the Abraham Lincoln Brigade, who conveyed the brief directives from Gerhart Eisler to the Ninth Floor.

Another courier of this type who ran between the Soviet consulate and Bittelman was the former White Russian officer Sergei Kournakoff, who during the war wrote military articles in the *Daily Worker*. For a long time, because of his secret courier work, he wrote under the pseudonym of "Veteran Commander." Toward the latter part of the war, having given up this service for a time, he was permitted to use his own name at certain public meetings. Attached to the Communist Russian-language paper *Russky Golos*, he claimed to be a brother-in-law of the airplane designer Alexander de Seversky. Being of a genial disposition, he even used to entertain some of us with accounts of his quarrels with Seversky. Seversky, he said, criticized him for having changed his affiliations —from White Russian to Red—after coming to this country as a refugee from the Bolsheviks.

To continue tracing the chain to its original source, the Comintern representative—Eisler or another—got his information by courier from the Soviet consulate or embassy. At least, that was the procedure in my day. Someone in the offices there, in turn, received the orders in the diplomatic mail pouch or in code by cable. Supervising this operation was the Soviet secret-police apparatus, which has a finger in every Soviet pie.

It can readily be seen that this system of transmitting directives orally is calculated to defeat the most extensive counterespionage system. Agents of the FBI, as able and alert as that agency has proved to be, will have a most difficult time keeping so close to a courier that they can overhear a verbal message.

In my relations with the men who knew the political line because they were in touch from day to day with the Comintern representative or the consulate, I came to be a frequent inhabitant of the telephone booths near the Communist party building. One day I would walk around the corner to a small drug store in University Place, where there were only two booths. The next day I would stroll over to Union Square, to the busy Schulte cigar store. Then, down University Place, to the tavern opposite the Hotel Albert, to talk to this comrade and that, and get information or instructions. The outside booth was as much a part of the Communist communication system for me as the private line up to the Ninth Floor from my desk.

It was Stachel's peculiarity that he preferred often to phone me at the *Daily Worker*, always in cryptic terms as though he were someone else. He did not have a phone at his house because he wanted to be completely guarded from any surprise visitors or calls. The name "John," which Golos had also employed extensively, was Stachel's pseudonym when phoning into the *Daily Worker*.

To these "shorthand instructions" on the current party line, I had added—as all other active Reds do—the Communist "code," as I termed it, prepared in its Aesopian or slave language. This "code," as some other comrades came to call it following my example, is designed to educate and steel the active Red constantly and to embellish and explain fully the line which he has received in "shorthand," either through the underground channels or through the head of the party at National Committee meetings.

The code is nothing other than the several books, publications and documents which come from Moscow in excellent English translation each week or each half month for the guidance of the Communists here and elsewhere.

There are two parts to this code of instructions—each of them highly important. The first division consists of the works of Marx,

Engels, Lenin and Stalin, "the great Marxist classics," and those auxiliary works which serve as footnotes or additions to these classics. Their purpose is to inflame the party member with zeal, to provide him with the ideas that will confirm his devotion to the cause, and to steel him for the objective of overthrowing the government of his country.

The second division comprises the theoretical and practical organs provided as sources of direction and information. They explain and develop the immediate line which the party is following. Outstanding among these is the *New Times*, arriving here in English as an alleged supplement of the Moscow newspaper *Trud*: it is the successor in part of *The Communist International* magazine, which of course had to end when the Communist International supposedly ceased to exist. With that now goes the Cominform's publication, recently issued from Bucharest, and which under the guise of giving the official reports of the satellite states conveys a wider understanding of current tactics. Next there is *The Bolshevik*, the theoretical organ of the Communist party of the Soviet Union, "the model party" for all other Communist groups, and therefore read with the utmost respect and attention. Then there is *Political Affairs*, the theoretical organ of the Communist party of the United States, formerly called *The Communist.*

As a Red reportorial organ, although also containing directives, there is available *World News and Views*. This is a successor to the former famous *International Press Correspondence*.

Every leading Communist keeps himself abreast of all these publications, studying them carefully, line by line, to catch the nuance and emphasis of each quotation or expression. From that he learns with rare exactitude just what Moscow wants of his party and of him.

Americans, who have been much given to unraveling codes in detective stories since the days of Sherlock Holmes, have proved too impatient or too indifferent to pay much heed to this "code," though it immediately affects their lives. The comrades take great satisfaction from this; it is one of the reasons they contemptuously refer to all non-Communist Americans as "backward elements" and "immature."

The Aesopian language of the Communists is indeed the cleverest device ever hit upon to conceal subversive intentions and instructions. And the acknowledged master of it is the thin, graying Alexander Bittelman—the A. B. whose articles in *The Communist* are must reading for every member of the party.

Moreover, this man, who tells the American Communists what to think and say through his articles in their press, who shuns photographers, even of the Communist persuasion, who never appears on public platforms, never gives press interviews, and is even today almost unknown to the newspapermen of this country, carries on, in addition to his work as chief theoretician of the party, large-scale subterranean activities. I recall quite vividly a day when I came by pure chance to follow him up Tenth Street and observe his movements. He stopped at the corner of Tenth and Broadway to light a cigarette. Then he dropped his matches, and as he stooped to pick them up, made a half turn and glanced quickly back down Tenth Street. There was method in his awkwardness. Even his apparently nervous fumbling with his pack of cigarettes, which he seemed to have difficulty getting back into his pocket, gave him another half minute to check on whether he was being followed. He was on his way to confer with the Soviet secret police. This I know because he had just told me about it when I had had to disclose to him my own secret meetings with the NKVD, which of course took precedence over all my other duties. Some years later, in the fall of 1944, this fact was again confirmed, for I happened to be present when a messenger from the Soviet consulate in New York brought him instructions concerning his visits to Miami to arrange for the movement of Communist couriers back and forth across the border between Mexico and the United States. Again, I was present when certain pro-Communist members of Congress re-

ceived instructions from him in one of his hideaways in New York's
world of apartments.

The dual life of this intellectual leader of the Communists is,
like the lives of Gebert and other political tourists, symbolic of the
Communist party in America.

Another of the most trusted alien members of the party, and one
of the Eisler-Peters cross-country chain of mail drops and couriers,
was Beatrice Siskind, alias Shields, also known as C. E. Johnson.
At one time sentenced for deportation, she entered the country
illegally from Poland and operated largely from Chicago, which
was where I came to know her. Dark, grimacing noticeably when
under mental pressure, high-pitched in voice when giving orders,
she was not popular among industrial workers, who claimed she
was "autocratic." But this, I learned, was not so much her fault
as the fault of the nerve-racking work to which she was assigned.
For she was in charge of obtaining vital information in the big
industrial centers of northern Illinois and the Detroit area. That
she did well, which is why she was kept at it despite the complaints.

When I tried to find a home for my family in Chicago in the
late '30's, Beatrice Siskind shocked us by her ultrafanatical suspicion that every place we looked at might be subject to "FBI
stool-pigeoning." She wanted us to sign our lease and obtain our
telephone under a false name, which we refused to do. Her warn-
ings about the ease of approach by visitors, the possibility of dicta-
phones being planted, the questionable character of our neighbors,
were so intense that we looked upon them as a bit insane. We
found in time that her fears were the natural result of her long
years of furtive existence as an alien agent in America, and had a
real foundation in her experiences.

George Siskind is her brother. A former director of the Lenin
School in Moscow, he was dispatched here to supervise educational
work along Marxist-Leninist lines, and became one of the key
people in the training of conspiratorial cadres. In the recent Communist trial in New York, he was charged with advocating the

violent overthrow of the government while secretly teaching Stalin's writings. Siskind functioned best in the party's hidden circles, where his precise manner of presenting Marxist-Leninist views on violence and his fanatical devotion to Stalin made him popular and effective. During my first years in the party, he directed the secret schools that the party maintained for the special training of selected members. In later years, after I became managing editor of the *Daily Worker*, he was named news editor of the paper by the Politburo. This gave him an opportunity to carry out his real assignment, the examination of the political trends and Communist integrity of the comrades on the staff. In this capacity he acted as a Control Commission man. Since I was required to check with him, going over the records on the comrades every week, he and I were thrown much together during the late '40's. Many a night, on the latest shift of the paper, we discussed his conspiratorial labors in Moscow and America; they revealed him as a proficient operator.

Martin Young, alias Leon Platt, whose real name was Leon Plotkin, was another of the valuable Reds in the conspiratorial apparatus. Claudia Jones and Ferdinand Smith, Negroes from Jamaica, have been held for deportation, the one a particularly successful operator among the Negro people and in underground activity; the other for a considerable time national secretary of the National Maritime Union, although an illegal alien. Smith has now left America. George Pirinsky, alias Nicoloff, whose real name is George Zykoff or Zaikoff, has been a Moscow agent for about twenty-five years; he is now executive secretary of the subversive American Slav Congress, and was recently arrested for the second time for deportation. A close associate of Gebert in Detroit, he will be heard from again.

Then there is a man like Morris Childs, real name Chilevsky, who, though naturalized, was one of the most aggressive and active of the Comintern men, having long-time connections with Moscow. Not the least of his services was aiding the Soviet secret police at the Lenin School in the Soviet capital. His many trips to the South for his health had also a definite connection with his work with alien agents resident or operating in Mexico.

The list is a long one, of which these will suffice. The whole party was shot through with alien bosses, although it had solemnly stated in its revised constitution that only citizens could be members. That was, of course, one of the falsehoods to which the party constantly resorted, to hide the role of the Kremlin agents.

Of the additional scores of Stalin's political tourists who enter the United States for subversive purposes, many will parade through these pages. Coming into our midst illegally, as a rule, they put a permanent stamp of alienism on the Communist party and furnish another conclusive proof of its fifth-column character. They will be a living bridge in the days to come, as they have been in the past, with the growing Red espionage cadres trained in Europe and Asia.

(IV)

Climbing Joseph's Ladder

UNDERLINING the direction of the Communist party in America by political tourists is the fact that its *Manual of Organization* was written by the head Soviet espionage agent in its leadership, the notorious J. V. Peters.

If we consult his *Manual,* which Jack Stachel in a special introduction commends as highly accurate, we will learn that in 1936 the Communist party was organized in the following step-to-step manner:

Unit Bureau
Unit Membership Meeting
Section Bureau
Section Committee
Section Convention
District Bureau
District Committee
District Convention
Political Bureau of the Central Committee
Central Committee
National Convention
Political Secretariat of the Communist International
Presidium of the Communist International
Executive Committee of the Communist International—the
    ECCI
World Congress of the Communist International

This structure, as Peters tells us, is supposedly built up "in the order of responsibility." It does let us see at once the dependence of the unit on the section, of the section on the district, and of the district on the Politburo. Additionally, it brings out clearly the subservience of the Communist party in every country to the Communist International under Stalin.

Anyone familiar with Communist life recognizes at once, however, that the effort to indicate some democratic procedure is absurd. The bureaus of each division of the party—whether unit, section, district, or national—are not the servants of these organs. They are the masters in each case. In my ten years experience in the party, I never saw anyone elected to office who was not a member of an official slate selected by the leadership. This applied to national convention, state, district, section, and branch elections. Often the candidates were listed under false names, so that frequently the delegates did not even know for whom they were voting. Their choices were candidates without faces!

Once at an election of members of the Control Commission, Mike Quill looked disgustedly at the list of candidates that had been handed him and, turning to me, asked abruptly, "Who are all these people, anyway? I've never heard of half of them." I was a good Communist then, but there was more than a little cynicism in my reply. "I don't know," I said, "but we'll vote for them anyway."

In order to prevent any open discussion of candidates, the chairman of the nominating committee always resorted to an old Red device. He would announce in an abrupt and arbitrary manner that all the nominees were "trusted comrades, who had been tested in struggle, who were close to the leadership, and faithful to the line." To challenge them, he would add significantly, would be equivalent to an "anti-Communist act."

Just as there is no freedom of choice in any elections, so there is no parliamentary discussion anywhere. Even in the Politburo there is no such thing as decision by majority vote.

Some of the terms used in Comrade Peters' *Manual* have been changed since 1936, but their substance has remained always the same. Being a conspiracy, subject to the Kremlin's directives, the Communist party's setup has experienced many lightning transformations in the names and size of its divisions. The man looking in from the outside is inclined to be completely bewildered by these frequent shifts, but the trained comrade, educated to sharp turns in policy, knows that the organization continues always to be built on the "leadership principle," with directives coming down step by step from above.

To underscore this "orders from above" process, Comrade Alexander Trachtenberg, commissar for culture, made one of his frequently repeated jests. Dubbing the Red hierarchical system "Joseph's ladder" in allusion to the leader, Stalin, Trachtenberg would say with a chuckle: "On Jacob's ladder, the angels came down and went up. On Joseph's ladder, they go up when they accept the order coming down."

To climb the Red ladder was a much more difficult acrobatic stunt than Trachtenberg's words implied. The trained comrade not only had to know how to obey orders from abroad, but he had to master, among many other things, the shift in terminology for the party divisions, which changed as the party line changed.

The lowest unit of the party, which the rank and file member joins, has been termed in rapid succession a cell, shop or street nucleus, unit, branch, club, and now, in 1950, a branch again. The Politburo, ostensibly the most important body, has been officially entitled Political Bureau, Political Committee, and National Board. It has undergone drastic transformations in size during the course of a comparatively few years. When deemed advisable, it has shrunk to as few as six members. Normally, the aim is to have twelve—the present number—in imitation of the Politburo in Moscow.

The party's lowest unit has likewise been transformed repeatedly in size. In its "cell" stage, during the totally underground period of the party's history, it was a small group of no more than five people, only one of whom had any connection with the superior officer above them. The members met secretly in apartments or private homes. At the other extreme, in the "club" stage, which occurred during World War II, it often had as many as one hundred members and met frequently in public buildings. Outwardly the clubs were supposed to resemble Republican and Democratic local organizations. To get ready for this "club period," certain large sections of the party began to house themselves in more imposing buildings. As early as 1937, Section 24 in mid-Manhattan opened a four-story headquarters on East 29th Street.

Such a contrast was this headquarters to the disorderly, dirty quarters of the "revolutionary" period of the early '30's that the party played it up nationally. It was described as being clean, large, dignified, with a pretty receptionist. Particular pride was taken in the library, which the Reds were told contained books "ranging from *Love is Free* by Edworth to *Das Kapital* by Karl Marx."

During most of the time that I was a member, the local unit was irregular in size, its numbers depending on the particular industry or community being penetrated.

To get some idea of how the local units operate, let us take a look at one or two meetings of which I particularly remember. The first was in Peoria, Illinois, in 1938. That was during the Peoples' Front period when the Communists were succeeding through their Trojan horse tactics in penetrating political groups, civic associations, and trade unions all over the country. They were also recruiting members on a wider scale than they ever had in the past.

One evening I was asked by the district office in Chicago to go down to Peoria to talk to the party branch there. Beatrice Siskind was working as district organizing secretary in that area, and had run into difficulties with some of the local comrades, who resented what they called her bureaucratic manner. I was sent in to smooth the matter out, largely through staging an educational discussion.

We met in the home of one of the members, who like most of the others was a railroad worker. There were twenty-eight present, the entire unit membership. Beatrice Siskind, always conscious of what she called "the Red scare," had ordered that the meeting be surrounded with secrecy. In order to account for such a large number of callers, the comrade at whose house the session was held had told his neighbors that he was having a little party.

To give the session a good start, the educational feature came first. Since the party was then engaged in raising funds for the Chicago *Daily Record,* of which I was editor, in choosing delegates to the Pittsburgh Congress of the Red-controlled American League Against War and Fascism, and in a drive to increase penetration of the trade unions, the discussion was directed toward those ends. I first began, as the leading comrade who comes in from outside always does, by referring to the latest utterances of Stalin and of Browder, showing how exactly they met the needs of the hour, and stressing the tasks called for by their declarations. Since the members, who with one or two exceptions had not been too long in the party, had no critical opinion on such matters, they were putty in the hands of a skilled comrade.

Then Beatrice Siskind steered them into giving all their attention to what they should do, rather than to any analysis of what had been said. They decided, under her prompting, first, to collect money for the Midwest Red press; and second, to get a delegate to the Pittsburgh Congress from the local railroad lodge. It was decided just which comrade would take the initiative in persuading the secretary of the lodge, who was not a Communist, to make the motion to this effect. It was also agreed who should second the motion, and who among the non-Communist lodge members should be prompted to enter the discussion. Every little detail of the argument to be made was worked out that evening.

These plans led to a consideration of how the comrades could get out more into the community and, posing first as non-Communists, make friends among the industrial and professional workers. One tall, thin chap, known as Comrade Hill, was the sole teacher in the group. He had been recruited by friends at the University of Chicago, where there were a number of active Communists. These friends, as he explained to me, kept him on his toes politically, and through their letters and visits had made him realize that the party was deeply concerned with people in professional positions. They constantly sent him clippings and other information about the "big intellectual minds" who were supporting party fronts and causes. He looked forward to associating with "these big people" at the Pittsburgh Congress, which it was agreed he would attend as "an unofficial representative of the teachers in Peoria and Tazewell Counties."

Comrade Hill was in charge of party literature, which was the next item on the unit's business. The comrades were induced to buy all sorts of Red literature, which was there in abundance. This included *The Communist*, and a copy of *The Communist International* magazine. They were also urged to purchase the organ of the American League, a Red magazine on China, and various pamphlets published by the party.

Comrade Hill, supplemented by Comrade Siskind, made the sale of literature the occasion for another propaganda lesson. He stressed the Moscow purge trials, and charged that "every open and concealed enemy of American democracy" was "trying to use" the trials to slander the Soviet Union and the Communist party. He urged the members to read the literature, in order to be able to defend Comrade Stalin, who was therein shown to be "the greatest leader of democracy that mankind has ever produced."

In this way, most of the points I had made in my talk were drilled into the comrades again from another angle; for I had also emphasized the trials and declared Stalin to be "the greatest helper and guide of the common people of every land." If and when the comrades read the literature they purchased, especially the two official Communist magazines, they would find the same expressions used all over again. Absorbing these phrases by rote, they would then start circulating them in the community.

The section organizer, Comrade Melli, a stocky, dark-haired miner, took up the question of dues collection, saying that he would be at every unit meeting for the next several months. He told the comrades he had just come back from a secret party training school in the East, and that in his ten weeks there he had learned a great deal about a Communist's responsibilities to the revolutionary movement. He had clearly acquired considerable enthusiasm, which he poured into his explanation that collective work and Bolshevik self-criticism were the foundation stones of Communist activity. He was obviously repeating a speech that he had heard Pop Mindel, head of the National Red Training School, make to the students. Self-criticism would reveal at once, he said, that a much better showing had to be made on dues paying and recruiting.

Self-criticism is the method by which Communists are supposed to examine and declare frankly their own weaknesses and omissions in carrying out their responsibilities. It is most useful when a change in the line occurs. Then, even though the leading comrades, at least, all know that the change has been dictated by Moscow, everyone heaps abuse on himself for his mistakes and remissness in carrying out the previous line. Whether in accepting the Hitler-Stalin pact or doing a quick aboutface on the "peace for generations" propaganda, in accordance with the Duclos letter of 1945, they always blame themselves. It is an amazing psychological exhibition. But there is method in this madness, as Comrade Golos once shrewdly pointed out to me; for by having the individual Red blame himself for the change in line, the party itself is protected from criticism.

Comrade Melli's enthusiasm rose even higher as he told the group that he had learned at the National Training School that "the party is always right." At every historical turn, he said, the course of the party is correct, and he launched into a glowing description of the party's perfect unity, its freedom from factional quarrels, its mastery of the science of society through its great teacher Stalin.

The dues payments were made promptly that night. Comrade Dock, a heavy-set, deliberate engineman, had no trouble in getting the money then. Incidentally, he had been recruited by Art Handel, a railroad clerk who carried on concealed Communist activities for a long time on the Illinois railroad systems before coming out as an open, professional Red.

Although the hour was getting late, various comrades delivered reports on their success in penetrating mass organizations. This permitted Comrade Siskind, in commenting on what they said, to harangue them further on the "chief political points," which had already been covered several times. Again, the group was impressed with the urgency of carrying "the truth" about the Moscow trials to their organizations; again they heard about "aid for Spain and China," about the American League and the American Youth Congress. Again they heard that "all the weak-minded dupes of developing fascism in the United States have taken up the Trotskyite cries of slander against Joseph Stalin." Again Stalin was hailed as the genius who makes the Soviet Union a bulwark of peace.

When the comrades finally left for home, they had been converted into efficient parrots, able to surprise other people with what they "knew" of world affairs but in reality knowing very little. This is an example of what took place at the meetings of this group week after week. The only variation was the change of speakers who came from Chicago to "lead" their discussion.

What happened in Peoria is a pattern of what happened and continues to happen in every Red unit throughout the country. We can turn to a branch meeting not far from Union Square in Manhattan, in 1944. This branch was composed of veteran comrades rather than of the new recruits who were in the majority in the Peoria unit, but Sadie Van Veen, wife of Israel Amter, for years leader of the party in New York, supervised the branch's operations just as closely as Comrade Siskind had out in Illinois. Although not an officer of the branch, Comrade Van Veen represented the State Committee, and every time she arose to make an observation, everyone listened with the utmost attention. Even the officers of the branch corrected themselves when she said that they had made a mistake. Every suggestion that came from her was adopted, since it represented the will of the center.

On another occasion, I was assigned to an "industrial unit" of painters who were penetrating Local 905 of the American Federation of Labor Painters Union. There Louis Weinstock, leading Red in that field, and onetime secretary of District 9 of the Painters Union, dominated the comrades and directed all their motions. Out in Cleveland, where for many years John Williamson (one of the eleven Red defendants) ruled the party organization, I attended the meeting of a party branch connected with the Fisher Body Company plant. Here I found Gus Hall, also one of the eleven defendants in the 1949 trial, holding forth. He was leading the self-criticism, telling the party shop branch of its shortcomings. One of the major things he stressed was the necessity of relating "all political discussion" to the auto workers' conditions; that led him, as usual, to another long enunciation of the line.

When the meeting adjourned, the branch organizer went into a huddle with Comrade Hall over whether or not the branch would grant permission to one of the members to go on vacation. This particular comrade was in charge of literature, and there was some thought that his absence might hurt distribution; however, it was finally agreed to give him his leave. This practice of requiring the members to get permission before going away is one of the means by which the party keeps them under control. Not only must each comrade get leave to visit another city or to take a holiday, but he must also state where he is going and often with whom he is going. If he neglects this little formality, his case is handled in a disciplinary way. And that means possible expulsion from the party, sometimes with permission to apply for readmission after a certain period has elapsed.

In January of each year, the branches are given an added duty, the registration of the membership. The old party cards are then collected and new ones given out. A checkup of dues is made at the same time. Registration is something more than a routine affair; since this is the Communist party, it has its wider political aspects. It is made an occasion for reclaiming those who have slipped by the wayside; it also places upon the shoulders of the most active branch members the duties of visiting the other comrades in their homes and discussing their attitude toward the party. It thus has what is called a "control" feature, too—that is, a means of learning something more about the degree of loyalty of the individual party members.

"Control" data can be used in a number of ways. It may furnish a clue to a comrade who is turning sour politically, and supply a means of straightening him out. It may, in particular, lead to a comrade's promotion on selection as a student for a secret training school. If the control material jibes with the way in which a comrade conducts himself in the branch, he is sure to receive encouragement to rise higher in the official party family. Although the branch leader absorbs much of the meeting time in explaining the line and molding the comrades, some discussion is permitted the rank and file. The chief reason for this, particularly for having them report on their assignments, is to give the leader a chance to observe them and to note what Marxist readings they refer to, and thus to form some judgment of them as possible party functionaries.

Bearing in mind the complete bureaucratic domination of the branches, it is easy to see how the delegates to the section, district, and national committees are hand-picked right up the line. In the same way, they are picked for special training in the party's schools.

The communists maintain two types of schools. There are, first, the "open schools," formerly called workers' schools, which seek as students not only rank-and-file Communists but also sympathizers.

During World War II, the Reds, realizing the possibility of drawing in a much larger group, renamed the workers' schools after various American patriots. The workers' school in Chicago became the Abraham Lincoln School; that in New York was transformed into the Jefferson School of Social Science. In Boston it was the Sam Adams School, in Westchester County the Tom Paine School. All these institutions taught a variety of subjects, but were based strictly on Marxism-Leninism. The rigid party control is indicated by the fact that the Jefferson School switched its entire attitude on Browder when ordered to do so by the Politburo. All members of the faculty who opposed the party line were eliminated.

While these schools were designed to attract thousands of students, the other type, the secret party schools, headed by the National Training School, were created to develop a small and select corps of Red leaders and train them in "revolutionary theory and tactics." The National Training School was usually held at Camp Beacon, the party's summer camp above Kingston, New York, which originally was known as Camp Nitgedaiget. After the regular summer season was over, select comrades from all over the country were brought there for an intense six-to-ten-weeks training course in Marxism-Leninism. Among the outstanding instructors were Jacob (Pop) Mindel, a long-time associate of Jacob Golos and other leading Soviet agents, and also heavily entangled in espionage work. Mindel's job was to make certain that the students understood the force-and-violence doctrines of the party. It was also his duty to observe the students closely, to discover possible future operators for underground work. A quiet, sad-looking man, mustached and far from young, he was one of the important recruiting agents for the Soviet espionage rings.

Another prominent instructor was Jack Perrola, a small, hunchbacked man and a precise, fanatical Red, who was often called "the conscience of the party in the secret schools." It was his function to follow up Mindel's work, and to make certain of the Communist integrity of the student before he left the secret school.

George Siskind, of course, also taught from time to time at the National Training School, since he was considered to be a leading expert on the details of the doctrines of force and violence. His connection with the staff of the Lenin School in Moscow stood him in good stead in this respect. *61896*

The site of the National Training School was also used for courses of special instructions for comrades from the various concentration industries. Secret national schools for steelworkers, miners, and waterfront workers were conducted there. In 1937, the Washington *Post* startled the party by exposing the "Red Annapolis," the name given the party's secret marine training school, which operated under the slogan, "A Communist unit in every American ship." The *Post* charged that the school taught the use of force and violence to get control of the waterfront. After this exposé the name of Camp Nitgedaiget was changed to Camp Beacon, and some of the secret national schools were shifted over to Camp Unity, also in the Hudson River area. Once or twice, when the party embarked on an openly anti-American course, as during the Hitler-Stalin alliance, some of the schools were hidden away in the vastness of New York's maze of buildings.

In each district and section of the party, secret schools are conducted on a similar basis. Occasionally, the secret Illinois school was held at the Communist camp near Kenosha, Wisconsin. More frequently, for security reasons, it was conducted right in the heart of Chicago. For a time, vacant offices, obtained through the cooperation of comrades who were doctors or in other professional positions, were used as classrooms. To these secret state schools, there came as students men and women who were outstanding in their sections. The present leader of the Communist party of Illinois, Claude Lightfoot, was a student in one of the schools out there when I taught in it.

Elaborate measures were taken to prevent any surveillance of the National Training School while it was in session. Students were never permitted to leave the premises for the six to ten weeks of

the course. They were forbidden to write to any of their friends or
to receive letters, or to tell anyone where they were. In case clothes,
medical supplies or other accessories were needed by the individual
student, they had to be obtained through the officials of the school.
A special guard brought these supplies from the city.

Other precautions were also taken. No comrade was permitted to
use his own name while at school. Husbands and wives were not
permitted to be in residence at the same time. In one case, I arranged
for a special exception to be made in favor of a certain man and his
wife, and they were permitted to attend the school together. But
it was ruled that they should not have any association with each
other and should not recognize each other when they happened
to meet in camp.

It is upon the men and women trained in these schools that the
party depends to carry on its infiltration of trade unions and other
organizations and to wage war against the CIO and the AF of L.
Through these schools hundreds of loyal Communists are molded
for violent agitation of "the masses."

The more thoroughly one studies the actual functioning of the
Communist party, the more painfully apparent does it become that
its constitution exists only for decorative and protective purposes. In
the matter of organization, as in the matter of principles, it has to
be read from an Aesopian point of view. It has a strong resemblance
in this respect to the constitution of Soviet Russia. Free speech is
guaranteed in the Soviet document, yet there are millions in concentration camps for differing from the official view on politics or
science. Self-determination and the right to withdraw from the
Soviet Union are formally accorded the member republics. Yet
three of these republics were liquidated completely after World
War II; Moscow itself made the announcement.

Under the constitution of the Communist party of the United
States, the National Convention is the highest body. Actually, and
this is borne out by the discussions in the National Committee, the
National Convention dare not do anything against the will of the

Politburo. It is a puppet body to the utmost degree. It makes no decisions at all.

The National Committee is in the same predicament. Moreover, men who are not technically on the National Committee at all may rule it. J. V. Peters had no formal place on the Committee for years; but only a few minutes at one of the sessions would show him to be in authority over the members. Bittelman has been technically off the Politburo for a long period; what he says is nevertheless the law. Trachtenberg was listed simply as an alternate when I left in 1945; that was a deliberate effort to play him down publicly so that he could work more inconspicuously with Moscow. It arose out of the attempt of the Committee on Un-American Activities to spot Trachtenberg as a conspiratorial link (through his International Publishers) between Moscow and the party. The Congressional Committee was on the right track, but the party outwitted it and outfought it. I received instructions from Stachel that Trachtenberg was not to be mentioned as a member of the National Committee in the *Daily Worker* pages until the Ninth Floor gave permission. For a few months he disappeared completely from all public notice. Meanwhile, the party was organizing a campaign to discredit the Congressional Committee, and getting wide co-operation in that effort. Out of it all, Trachtenberg was protected. Soon the American people were reading other headlines, as Stachel predicted would be the case, and the whole business was forgotten. The link with Moscow remained.

The big gala event politically for the Communist bureaucrats was the enlarged plenum of the National Committee, which was held irregularly at the call of the Political Bureau. The conference was secret, as were the regular meetings of the National Committee. Generally no notice at all of where the session was taking place was given even in the *Daily Worker*. The Red secret agents, who came in sizable numbers to this enlarged plenum—for here the legal and illegal wings of the party blended in perfect harmony—had to be safeguarded against photographers or any other public observation.

Some three hundred to four hundred local leaders, in addition to the National Committee and the top leadership, attended the sessions, which generally lasted three days. The favorite meeting place was the Fraternal Clubhouse, a public hall, at 110 West 48th Street, Manhattan.

Each man and woman attending the plenums received a card of admission which had to be checked at the entrance. Everyone was instructed to enter the hall immediately and never to linger on the street in front of the building. On leaving, the comrades were supposed to go in groups of no more than four persons. A committee of chosen comrades, always under the supervision of J. V. Peters, examined each entrance card and identified each comrade as the person whose name appeared on it.

A memorable plenum of this character was held in Chicago over the Labor Day week end of September, 1939—the only session, enlarged or otherwise, of the National Committee ever held outside New York City during the ten years of my connection with the party. It had been called in Chicago on this occasion in order to allow more of the comrades from the isolationist Middle West to be on hand since the original purpose of the meeting was to organize the infiltration of organizations in the Corn Belt in order to offset the isolationist sentiment there. Stalin had recently discovered that Hitler was a threat to the Soviet dictatorship, so the party's assignment from Moscow was to whip up American friendship for Soviet Russia and American hatred for Hitler.

The Ninth Floor had labored for some weeks on the speeches to be made and the resolutions to be adopted at Chicago. Outlines of what Browder would say and of the proposed resolutions were carefully mailed in advance to all the leading comrades, so that they would be able to drive the line home in their own reports. Suddenly a political atom bomb hit the Little Kremlin. Stalin signed the pact of friendship with Adolf Hitler just a few days before the Chicago sessions opened.

It was a tense three hundred people who met, without the blare of publicity, in a large hall in Chicago that September Saturday morning. They were to hear Browder as usual tell them what the line was. He had spoken to more than 15,000 people at Soldiers Field the night before, persons of many political beliefs having been induced to go there through the usual Red high-pressure methods. Both at the stadium and in his report to the plenum, Browder defended the Soviet-Nazi pact and urged the United States to "cooperate with the energetic peace efforts of the Soviet Union." Both public address and secret report showed signs of hasty patching up, which was reflected in the declarations of the other speakers. Their path was not made smoother by the Nazi invasion of Poland, which occurred while their discussions were going on. Starting with Foster and with Childs, the Chicago leader, a number of the comrades did begin to label the war as "imperialist," but most of them, noting that Browder had not yet laid down a complete pro-Hitler line, contented themselves with quoting Stalin's famous words, that the Soviet Union would not pull anybody's chestnuts out of the fire. That quotation was safe.

While everybody put up a stereotyped front, and the usual unanimity prevailed, the uncertainty in Browder's utterances caused whisperings among knots of comrades at the end of each session. They all felt that sufficient instructions had not yet been received from the Soviet capital, and that the line would undergo further development within a few days. Some of them came out to my house on Saturday night, to engage in nervous speculation about what might be afoot. The Marxist-Leninist analysis had indeed failed them. They were far from being the exact scientists they always proudly declared themselves to be.

On Sunday, Foster and Bittelman cut short their reports to urge that the sessions be ended ahead of time and that everyone get home to begin the campaign in favor of the Soviet-Hitler friendship pact. At their instigation, several slogans were adopted. I recall particularly: "For jobs, security, democracy, and peace." It was explained hurriedly by Bittelman that this battlecry could be used to arouse the workers to halt by strikes, or other demonstrations, any move by America to interfere with the "friendship pact." Stating that information had not been received on what the Soviet Union would do about Poland, Bittelman told the comrades that they could rely on Soviet steps "for Polish liberation." A slogan was added, then, calling for America to help Poland defend its national independence.

Hurrying back to New York, the Red leaders learned that they had to go much farther on behalf of Hitler. All the National Committee members were immediately called into New York, ostensibly in connection with the Madison Square Garden celebration of the twentieth anniversary of the party. We soon learned from Peters and Bittelman that Poland had to be thrown overboard. Out of this announcement came the statement of the National Committee, dated September 19, summarized by the slogan: "Keep America out of the imperialist war." Poland was heaped with abuse for "bringing on its own destruction."

The following May, at its national convention, the party denounced Roosevelt in unbridled terms and pledged its allegiance to Stalin without reservation. It was then embarked upon the path of sabotaging all aid to Britain.

Another enlarged plenum of the National Committee which remains in my memory is that of December, 1941. Hitler had attacked Soviet Russia and the Reds were crying for America to enter the war. The meeting at the Fraternal Clubhouse was the largest that had been held since the Chicago gathering. Browder was in prison for passport perjuries, but the party was beginning to feel that pro-Russian publicity was permitting it to "come out of the underground" as Foster stated in his preliminary report. He now had to serve as the leader, in Browder's absence.

At the Sunday session, as comrade after comrade was rising to report on the efforts in his state to promote American aid to Soviet Russia, word came of the Japanese attack on Pearl Harbor. There was instant rejoicing, for it was recognized immediately that the

United States would now save the Soviet dictatorship from destruction. Foster was in high glee and in his concluding remarks called for "Victory in the battle for production." His words and the resolution unanimously adopted now stressed "America's national existence."

That plenum was also dissolved ahead of schedule. The delegates, as they left the hall to raise the slogan of "National unity," carefully tore up the typed reports they had given on the opening day. Those reports had warned that the Roosevelt government might still listen to Hitler's peace propaganda and had criticized Washington for not opening a second front in Europe.

Most of the enlarged plenums at the Fraternal Clubhouse had a much quieter course. Over the following years, comrades Morris Rapport and Henry Huff, leaders in the state of Washington, reported in detail on the penetration of political offices out there. We even were regaled eventually with the announcement of the creation of a secret Communist faction among the legislators, which met under the dome of the capitol at Olympia. From Dr. Albert Blumberg, the Red leader in the Washington, D. C. area, we heard of contacts made with senators and congressmen through the alert "Washington cell" of high-placed comrades posing as non-Communists. From Robert Digby, who under his name of Charles Coe had wide associations in the Department of Agriculture and among farm leaders, we heard of the successful penetration of that department during the secretaryship of Mr. Wallace.

At these enlarged plenums I renewed comradely acquaintance with John Santo, in whose hands had been placed the responsibility for disorganizing New York's economic life, should Stalin at any time require it. Having become a public figure as the national organizer of the Transport Workers Union, Santo had been requested by the Politburo after the Hitler-Stalin Pact to absent himself from Thirteenth Street, so that his Communist affiliation would not become known. But he did steal into the enlarged plenums. There also I was introduced to Nathan Gregory Silvermaster, "a most trusted comrade," who was later publicly accused of being an undercover Red agent.

The reports given at National Committee meetings make it clear that the Reds spend a good deal of time combating "enemies of the party" and "enemies of the working class"—who always happen to be those persons or agencies that at any given moment are most definitely opposing Soviet schemes. Prominent among them are the "renegades," those who have broken with the party and been expelled by it. Most elaborately the party seeks to show that they are all prompted by corrupt and degrading motives in their antiparty stand.

This is a comparatively easy task, since the trials by which erring members are found guilty are one-sided performances. On their small stage, they have a strong resemblance to the travesties of justice called trials in Red-dominated countries. The Reds here have no power to compel confessions and so they get none. But every comrade who is haled before a disciplinary committee is guilty in its eyes before his appearance. The "proof" against him has been gathered secretly, and in an overwhelming number of cases has originated with the committee carrying on the alleged trial.

It must be understood that the entire fate of a comrade within the party rests to an abnormal degree in the hands of the Control Commission and its subsidiary apparatus in the districts. When Clarence Hathaway, who had been high in the councils of the party, was expelled, he was merely called in by a subcommittee of the Politburo and the verdict handed to him. By this short shrift, the man who had been Communist leader in the New York district, editor in chief of the *Daily Worker*, and a member for years of the Politburo was disposed of. In his case, he took the punishment, kept quiet, and was allowed to function almost anonymously without party reprisals.

Another item which came up regularly at National Committee meetings was the matter of dues. When I first joined, party members paid 10 cents dues weekly if earning weekly wages of $15 or less. This was also the rate for housewives. Members earning over $15 and up to $25 paid dues of 25 cents a week. The rates continued to rise as the weekly income increased, until members receiving over $40 and up to $50 paid dues of $1 a week. Those getting more than $50 a week had a special tax of 50 cents for each $5 above the $50 earnings.

In the years that followed, the rate fluctuated; sometimes it was 1 per cent of the member's total wage and sometimes it was a flat rate. These constant changes made it as difficult to follow the financing of the party as it was to keep track of the names and locations of its various divisions.

When Miss Elizabeth Bentley in testimony at Washington in 1948 was vague about what dues had been collected for party purposes at a certain time, some people were inclined to raise their eyebrows at her lack of information. Thereby they revealed their own unfamiliarity with Communist practices.

The finances of the party were a complete mystery to most of the National Committee members. Reports on finances were sometimes given and sometimes not; but it made little difference. As they were presented, very few people could make them out anyway. It was quite clear that a much larger payroll was being met than the party dues and collections could account for. With the complication of district and section financing, for which separate books were kept, the whole thing became completely confounded.

The party always discreetly kept its financial records private until the Hitler-Stalin Pact period. Their publication then meant little since they did not include the big secret fund under Robert William Weiner's control. However, that there were huge sums of money in the conspiratorial fund handled by Weiner and the secret committee co-operating with him I know to be a fact. At times Weiner had deposits amounting to hundreds of thousands of dollars in various banks. On occasion William Browder also deposited amounts up to a million dollars, sometimes in his own name. The source of funds was frequently a mystery, further increased by the practice of conveying thousands of dollars in cash back and forth between Weiner and the various unions and other organizations under Red control. These transactions never appeared on the books of any organization since they were so arranged that the money appeared to be in the cash fund of the union or other body making the loan to Weiner.

A basic source of these mysterious funds is from abroad, flowing into Weiner's hands from Moscow. The late Joseph Brodsky was one of the connecting links in this transmission. But the Red international apparatus insists that every fifth column must stand on its own feet whenever possible. What Soviet financial aid does is to make the Communist group a going concern, always sure of "capitalization." Whenever a fifth column in any country is in dire need, it receives the assistance it requires. On that foundation, it is supposed to hustle for itself and, by influence with Hollywood stars of a Red tinge, tired businessmen who want a thrill, and wealthy young people who have inherited huge sums, to raise as much money as it can.

In the big *Daily Worker* drives for the subsidy of $200,000 needed each year, there were large sums of money given to sections and reported as their donation whose original source was vague. In 1944, business manager William Browder reported to me that we had $50,000 in the *Daily Worker* drive which we did not know how to handle. Weiner had delayed giving it over to us for fear of possible inquiry, which would be embarrassing. For weeks the money was on hand, but the fund-drive reports could not show it publicly. It finally got on the *Daily Worker* books by allocating it to various local groups.

Week after week Bill Browder as business manager and I as president of the corporation had to work out various ways of getting money for the paper. It was a trying experience, when we knew that $50,000 which could relieve us of most of our effort and worry was lying in the till.

The secret fund was used for a number of purposes. It financed the beginnings of Communist-created front organizations, setting them on their feet and giving them an initial financial advantage over any genuinely American competitor. It was also used to supplement the regular salaries of leading comrades with cash gifts for personal emergencies. Vacation trips, special visits to health resorts, extraordinary medical care, and similar items were paid for in cash by Weiner from this fund. Some comrades bought houses with this assistance; automobiles were also purchased the same way. But a more important use of this huge cash account was to finance the secret and illegal trips of the leading Reds to other countries. It was with the aid of this fund that Eisler, Browder, Dennis, Stachel, and all the others moved into Asia and Europe and back with forged passports. Since the expenses of these trips were laid out in cash and never accounted for, they did not appear on the books of the party. In this particular illegal financial work, Weiner often used the name of "Blake."

Active in the administration of the secret fund with the alien Weiner was a native American whose wealthy family was connected with Wall Street brokerage interests. He was Lement U. Harris, who has long lived in an exclusive section of Westchester County near Chappaqua. From him I learned that this fund helped initiate a number of enterprises, including Barney Josephson's Café Society Uptown. The purpose was to make that night club a rendezvous for artists and entertainers and people of wealth, with whom Communists could there establish acquaintance.

It might be illuminating to recount here a rather amusing incident that occurred out in Chicago, which had to do with this secret fund. The party's central apparatus was making the *Midwest Daily Record* sweat by its delay in sending out the subsidy which was to be furnished to start the paper. This is an old Communist trick which the Comintern itself practiced on its national parties. It is supposed to induce a certain type of humility in the dependent comrades—also it may help to bring bills down.

As a consequence of the delay, the printing concern that handled the paper was not being paid. But the owner of the print shop had dealt with the Communists before, having published several of their foreign-language papers, and knew their tricks. When I as editor and Jan Wittenber as business manager were obviously unable to pay his bill, he suggested that we wire to "William Blake" at the Communist national headquarters. This was the name under which Weiner had met him before and had made the initial financial arrangements. It was also Weiner's regular secret code name.

When I informed the Ninth Floor that the Blake wire might be sent, I was immediately told that Weiner would take the next train to Chicago. Not only did he get there the next day, but he had with him money to meet the bill in full. After Weiner had gone back to New York, the head of the printing concern took me aside and said with a chuckle: "That name Blake works wonders, doesn't it?" Then he confided: "I knew he was Weiner all the time."

The name Blake had been connected with so many conspiratorial transactions that the publicity of a telegram to someone of that name at Thirteenth Street would have necessitated all kinds of rearrangements throughout the country.

In his role of financial czar of the party, Weiner also supervised the "gifts" to the party coffers made by men and women with big incomes. Party members who earn large salaries or who receive large dividends from investments are "requested" to contribute proportionately large sums, generally based on a percentage of their incomes. Special committees sometimes make assessments on these comrades for sums above and beyond their constitutional dues, but the final word on how much was to be levied always rested with Weiner. I used to sit in on these committee meetings occasionally, and from the discussions know, for instance, of the $100,000 a year income of a Red lawyer much in the news. It was an amount he earned largely because of his connection with the party, which contrived to obtain for him clients in a number of unions.

On the basis of what has been said, it should be clear that the

formal structure of the Communist party of the United States conveys no idea of its real setup or functioning. The arrangements set
forth in the party's constitution are modified and changed by the
illegal and unofficial bodies that exist outside and above the constitution.

The baffling shifts in the names and size of each party division
are an efficient aid to conspiracy, and add to the handicaps of governmental security bodies whose job it is to uncover the workings
of the conspiracy.

One factor remains constant. Step by step, rung by rung, directives are transmitted down the Red ladder.

(V)

The Rank-and-Filers

UP TO this point, the people I have been concerned with have been for the most part either hidden or open members of the party's leadership. But since I left the party, I have often been asked about the lives of the Communist rank-and-filers. What is their daily routine, what part does the party play in their lives, what are their lives like—those people who never get into the leadership or even onto an executive committee except at a very low level?

The daily life of any one of them can be summed up in the word RUSH. It is a whirlwind of hurry from party conference to party conference, from the ringing of one neighbor's doorbell to the ringing of another's, from the peddling of papers and the handing out of leaflets to attendance night after night at classes and committees—always to the accompaniment of slogans and arguments taken from the *Daily Worker,* which must be read faithfully every day, and from the "theoretical" publications which few of the rank and file really grasp in full. These little people in the party accept the discipline of the party, do what they are told, think what they are told; and if these things seem contrary to reason, patriotic duty or common sense, they do them because the party says that is the correct thing to do "at this time."

Take, for example, a woman my wife and I came to know quite well—Comrade Ada Kutzov. Comrade Ada had a problem: she could not make up her mind whom she loved better, her first or second husband. She would visit at our house at all hours of the day, as she passed by coming and going on her party work. Sitting in the kitchen as my wife, Margaret, prepared the meals or the baby's formula, Comrade Ada's talk would frequently get around to her dilemma.

One day, for instance, when my wife was baking, Comrade Ada said rather wistfully that she could neither bake nor cook well. Her husband, David, the second one, frowned upon all domestic arts. He felt that she should not be imprisoned in the kitchen when she could be out doing effective party work. She was only a rank-and-file Communist, doing such simple things as typing, distributing leaflets, collecting signatures on election petitions, attending classes at the workers' schools, and making one of the audience at Red rallies and street-corner meetings. Although she had been in the party fully fifteen years, she had never held office in her branch, even the humblest. And yet David considered her petty party duties of such importance as to preclude any kind of family life in which she might play the part of housewife and mother.

On the other hand, Benny, her first husband, liked the little luxuries of life. Good food at good restaurants, entertaining at home, imported delicacies, were essentials in his way of living. But he was not too good a Communist, although a member of the party. Sometimes when he came, armed with a bottle of wine and a box of chocolates, to visit the Kutzovs, David would criticize him severely for political laxness.

Even though Ada knew that her life would be more comfortable with her first choice, both her Communist training and the advice of the Red section leaders in mid-Manhattan held her to David. The section organizer, Brown, looked upon him as a most valuable comrade, and told her so. Consequently, she did whatever David wanted her to do, chose her reading at his dictation, and even agreed when he criticized her at a branch meeting for not being apt enough at mastering the Marxist classics. What gave his views even more weight with her was the fact that for years she had been reading those same views in the women's columns of the *Daily Worker.* She was a product of the Young Communist League period when Communist women wore leather jackets and berets, and felt that good grooming was a bourgeois custom. This "revolutionary" attitude reflected the discipline from Moscow, which bade the comrades everywhere prepare for the immediate overthrow of their governments.

In 1937, while we were living on East 19th Street in Manhattan, we got to know the Kutzovs rather well. They sensed after a time that I was engaged in secret work for the party in addition to my public activities at the *Daily Worker,* but of course, as good Communists, they never referred to it. However, when we were preparing to move to Chicago, Comrade Ada unexpectedly asked me if she might be permitted to do "any of the extra work" in which I was engaged. Since I was actively co-operating with the Soviet secret police, I was obliged to answer her in the usual bureaucratic manner. I told her the party had no secret work, and therefore I did not know to what she referred.

She surprised me then by telling me of her own connection with the underground apparatus in the past, which included serving as a mail drop for secret communications from abroad to Politburo members here, and acting as a courier for Peters, who headed the Communist espionage activities. It was an education to me, for it showed me how valuable obscure people of her type could be to the party.

In the street branch which she served so faithfully, no one knew of her courier work, or of her other labors for the secret apparatus. Many of them would think her "too stupid" for such responsibilities, she volunteered with a smile. I was to learn through experience that comrades of her caliber, engaged in secret work, sat in branch meetings regularly all over the country without the majority of their fellow members having any idea that they were carrying out important party commissions. Upon inquiry at the

Ninth Floor, I was told by J. V. Peters himself that Ada was a comrade of the utmost reliability.

There is a human sequel to her story. In 1942, after we had returned to New York, Comrade Ada visited us at our Astoria apartment. She confided to us that she was about to have a child, and called our attention to her new clothes, particularly her hat. She was anxious that we note its contrast to the kerchief which she had always wound about her head in the old days. The party had changed, and she had changed with the party. It still was her law, and the distribution of leaflets and attendance at public party rallies in order to swell the throng were still her prime obligations. Her child was the result of Moscow's decision to "go to the masses." Since the comrades were supposed to look and act like other Americans, they were to have families as other people did, too.

With the rank-and-file Communist, if he or she can stand the strain, the obligation to the party and the party's rules become supreme. This point is well illustrated by a letter from a woman Communist to the *Daily Worker,* dated December 10, 1934. For many years afterward, the party leaders referred to it with approval. The woman wrote that her husband, who himself was a Communist and "read the workers' press every day," thought that she should devote herself to her home and two children. In some detail she recounted how one day she slipped out of the house when he was not looking, in order to attend a meeting. The next time he went to a meeting, she went too, leaving her children alone in the house. By such tactics she compelled her husband to yield to the desire of their branch that she do extensive party work. She told happily of learning to speak at street-corner meetings, of her frequent canvassing for the party cause, and of her attendance at demonstrations. Her children she took with her. This single-minded loyalty, with its all-absorbing demands, gives the humble member of the party a fanaticism most Americans cannot understand.

The demands upon the individual Red are so great that many

people cannot stand up under them. Every branch discusses frequently the loss of members who have yielded to "bourgeois customs." To this loss has to be added the defections, that take place when a sudden change in the line occurs. However, this turnover, which is a subject of discussion at every National Convention, is expected by the party leaders. They know that they can be assured of a good strong nucleus of disciplined Communists among those who remain. They also are aware that they capture the momentary co-operation of fanatics whose particular point of view happens to coincide with the current party line. During the Hitler-Stalin Pact, for instance, many pacifists and friends of Hitler became attached to the party and co-operated wholeheartedly as long as the line favored a Nazi victory.

The staunch rank-and-filer who remains loyal through all changes has one characteristic that stands out. He is always in motion. The party leadership keeps him continually busy with a thousand and one commissions, properly termed "tasks." That is a word constantly in use in the lexicon of Communists, from the Politburo leaders down to the members of the smallest branch. This perpetual motion serves as a substitute for thought. It keeps the rank-and-file Red from getting any view of life save that which the party leaders decree for him.

There come to mind two women Communists, remote from each other in education and family background, whose lives in their different ways were typical. There was Eva, living in New York on the outskirts of factory areas. A worried, frightened, nervous young woman, she was uncertain about everything but her loyalty to the party. She was married and had one child. Her husband, whom she had met on a picket line, did not make much money; he worked nights, she was alone a great deal, and the party absorbed all her neurotic energy.

Early in the morning Eva called at a local candy store where she picked up several copies of the *Daily Worker,* which she delivered to "sympathizer contacts" in the neighborhood, some of whom subscribed to the paper for a week, a month, six months, or a year. By delivering their copies personally, Eva kept in constant touch with them, her purpose being to influence their attitude on current events. Often she would take with her an addressed post card, on which was typed a message to the President or to the local congressman which the party wanted mailed. The sympathizer would be asked to sign the message, and Eva, after leaving her little girl at the public school, would mail the card herself, to be sure that it was sent.

Twice a week a section organizer called at her home, and the two would spend the morning going over work Eva was supposed to do. This might include collecting money for a half a dozen different causes sponsored by the Reds, arranging leaflet distribution at certain factories, persuading branch members to flood the neighborhood with the latest appeals on China and Poland, and seeing that the neighborhood comrades bought tickets and attended the meetings of the organizations they were pledged to infiltrate.

The biggest sorrow in her life was her feeling that the party did not value her services sufficiently. She was constantly in conflict with a woman organizer who assigned her the most menial tasks and even ordered her to leave her small daughter alone in the apartment at night while she went out on party work. But after a scene and sometimes tears, Eva accepted every assignment given her.

For years she attended every session and every event conducted by the local Parent-Teacher Association. Under orders from her section she introduced resolutions at every meeting, spoke on every subject, and was always first on her feet under "good and welfare." At first she was in a hopeless minority and was looked upon with suspicion by the other PTA members, but after a year she could not be ignored. Finally, when others grew tired of the job, she was elected secretary. She was then in a position to write letters to Albany and Washington in the name of the organization, even before such action had been endorsed. Through Eva's persistence, the PTA now became largely an echo of her Communist party section organizer. Eva kept up on sheer nervous energy; many of the resolutions she got passed her section leader had handed to her in writing, and she would have been unable to defend them successfully had they been intelligently challenged. But she swept all opposition aside by her aggressiveness and by having a program when many others were undecided what to do. Even before the entry of America into World War II, she had persuaded the other PTA members to begin knitting IWO wool for the Red Army soldiers. A woman so unskilled in spelling and the ability to express herself in writing that she had to obtain help from another comrade to write up the PTA minutes, Eva was made into another person by being the automatic instrument of party orders.

With only two other Reds in the PTA cell with her, Eva came in this way to dominate and speak for an organization of one hundred members.

One of Eva's assignments, from which she shrank, was handing out party leaflets at the gates of war factories during the Hitler-Stalin Pact. Since the leaflets were inflammatory in character, attacking the United States Government in violent language, the party had ordered the bulk of this distribution to be carried out by women members, fearing that the war workers would beat up any men who thus tried to sabotage war production. Although stricken with fright at the sight of a policeman, because she feared that her arrest might lead to the discharge of her anti-Communist father from his post office job, Eva led a group of women before a certain factory for a number of months. Though in time the leaflets changed from "The Yanks Are Not Coming" to "We Demand an Immediate Second Front," Eva kept constantly at the job of getting them handed out. Faithfully she reported back to section headquarters on the estimated effect of each distribution.

These local community activities were only the by-products of Eva's party commitments. As a member of the section executive committee, she was obliged to attend a great number of meetings and events and to get other people out as well. As a rule her schedule ran thus: Monday night, party-branch executive committee; Tuesday night, branch meeting; Wednesday night, early, workers' school class; Thursday, meeting on party literature in mid-Manhattan; Friday, section committees; Saturday, parties or open-house affairs for some Communist front, the section itself, the *Daily Worker* fund drive, or for recruiting new members.

Many of these inner-party events were staged early in the evening so that the leading section members such as Eva could swell the attendance at larger affairs. In talking to her in the first part of May, 1944, I learned that she was planning within a ten-day period that month to attend the following functions in addition to her regular round of meetings:

May 13—*Daily Freiheit* celebration in honor of Sam Liptzin, the man known as "Uncle Sam" in Communist circles, who was to be exposed later as having furnished Gerhart Eisler with his false passport. This celebration was held in Webster Hall, on the occasion of the publication of Liptzin's sixteenth Communist book.

May 14—benefit for the Joint Anti-Fascist Refugee Committee, featuring Paul Draper, the dancer and son of the outspoken pro-Communist, Muriel Draper. Every section executive member had been ordered either to attend the benefit with two friends or to sell three tickets.

May 17—showing of film, *The Buccaneer*, with comments by Dr. Phillip Foner. This was one of a series presented each week by the *Daily Worker* and Eva attended them all, including my own commentary on June 7.

May 19—special lecture at the Jefferson School on the Far East.

May 21—folk festival given by the George Carver (Communist) School at the Golden Gate Ball Room.

May 23—public session of the 1944 National Convention of the Communist party, with Earl Browder explaining "The Communist Program: For Victory and Enduring Peace." This was a highlight in Eva's life at that time. As the ace recruiter in her section, she received special free tickets and was privileged to lead several hundred new members to the Madison Square meeting that night. Among them was her own mother, whom she had brought into the party over the sullen opposition of her father.

Even when sitting with her small daughter in the public playground, Eva took advantage of the occasion to forward her beloved party. Armed with literature, petitions, or post cards, she engaged in conversation with the parents of other children. It was impossible to escape her, and many a person bought a ten-cent pamphlet or signed a petition in order to get rid of her. To my knowledge she obtained hundreds of signatures favoring the Second Front and even supporting the Communist party on the New York ballot, simply through the desire of those signing to be rid of her.

It may be noted that while she stood out conspicuously in her neighborhood as a known and active Communist, there were at least a dozen local concealed Communists wielding even greater influence in community organizations and trade unions because they were not known as Reds. It was one of Eva's greatest pleasures to attend special conferences with these undercover Red notables, to work out with them ways in which her open activities could supplement their secret labors.

There were moments when Eva threatened to crack up under this accumulation of tasks and emotions. One such incident occurred when Hitler attacked his ally, the Soviet dictatorship. Eva had built up a large following of pacifists around the local party and was almost driven to the point of insanity by not knowing how to handle them when the big turn came and the necessity of assailing Hitler became the order of the day. She got so busy, however, passing out the new leaflets and praising the Red Army, that she forgot her difficulties before two weeks had elapsed.

Here we have a person who was almost illiterate, despite her education in the New York public schools, and so neurotic that she made her close associates uneasy. And yet, in her excessive devotion to Stalin and "the revolution," and by her persistence in carrying out the party's orders, she was able to gain the goals set for her. Many such rank-and-file Communists are shrugged off as "crackpots"; nevertheless, in their smaller fields they are achieving their objectives for the Soviet fifth column quite as effectively as the Communist leaders at all costs fulfill Stalin's orders in a larger way.

Vera, in contrast to Eva, was far from illiterate. She was highly intelligent, had won a Phi Beta Kappa key, and had enjoyed unusual advancement in her profession. She had a quiet, commanding manner. Through her studies under pro-Marxists in political economy and European philosophy at a western state university, she had come to accept materialism as the foundation of her point of view. She was convinced that her allegiance to the party was intellectual, for she had studied the principal writings of Marx, Lenin, and Stalin before she joined up with the Reds. But she had deceived herself right in the beginning about how much independent judgment she had used. In her meticulous way, she had asked a skilled Communist to give her an idea of the books and documents she should read. What he had done—and he and I had conferred on how best to accomplish this—was to select reading that would lead inevitably to a pro-Communist conclusion.

From the moment that Vera signed the party card, she also went into motion. In her profession she soon assumed leadership among those of her colleagues whose allegiance to the party was emotional rather than intellectual, and came to dominate even those who had been considered competent and loyal enough to serve as secret couriers for the party's underground. Having a highly influential position in her profession, she did not hesitate to use supervisory conferences to persuade those under her to work with the party. She made it her business to learn the personal habits, associations, and political tendencies among both her party and nonparty colleagues. Whenever her immediate party superiors wanted someone for a task, secret or open, she knew whom to recommend. Particularly was she vigilant to note the things that could be turned into grievances and made issues in her profession. Through such devices she expanded the membership of the party to a marked degree and directed the successful capture by the Reds of the union organized in her profession.

Typical of Vera's methods was her appearance late on a stormy night in 1940 at the apartment of one of her women comrades. She excused her midnight visit by saying that she had attended a big party rally and had then gone to an executive committee meeting in preparation for the coming Communist state convention.

"I hear you are resigning from your job," she went on. "Why are you doing this when the reason is pregnancy?" Then she insisted that the woman apply for maternity leave, even though she had no intention of returning to work. The woman protested on that ground and also pointed out that no union agreement had ever been reached on the point. Besides, she was not feeling well and her physician had ordered her to rest.

Vera, however, was adamant. This furnished a case on which the issue could be fought out. And before Vera left, the woman had agreed to write out a demand for maternity leave, to supply the Communists with their fighting point.

So confirmed a Stalinist did Vera become that, unlike the Communist lawyers and other professional workers who use the Communists to build themselves up, she made her professional advancement secondary to party advancement. In New York, she became so skilled an organizer that the party leaders ordered her to obtain a position in another state where there was little party organization. With her usual respect for discipline, she obeyed these instructions, moved to the other state, and there increased Red infiltration on a large scale.

Every change of the line, no matter how drastic, was readily accepted by Vera. Never did she question the decisions which she knew came from Moscow, nor did they disturb her. Immediately upon noting in the *Daily Worker* or from party decrees that new views and arguments were expected of the comrades, she obtained the latest Red literature on the subject, her sole purpose to justify the line, never to examine it. With a certitude bred from faith in Stalin's wisdom, she bolstered up the spirits of any wavering Reds among her colleagues. It was interesting that one who claimed to have been won to Communism through intellectual conviction could become so intellectually servile.

The ceaseless preoccupation with party work starts with the young. In the Young Communist League, and later in the American Youth for Democracy, the youthful rank-and-filers devoted every odd moment to the Red cause. There was Molly out in Chicago, who was a dynamo among the young Communists. As a rank-and-filer she changed her role from day to day, being a member of a students' mass organization on Monday, one of the "working-class youth" on Tuesday, a young writer on Wednesday. So skillful was she in moving from group to group and gaining recruits among them that the Communist leader in Chicago, Morris Childs, ordered her to become a professional youth. But she was over thirty years old when she led the American young people's delegation to a recent international congress staged by the Reds in Europe. The echoes of this delegation's report are still to be heard in many of our colleges, and its laudatory view of the Soviet influence on the young people in the satellite countries has been accepted by many persons who are completely unaware that it is the work of veteran Communists.

So greatly did the party overshadow Molly's life that she went to the district headquarters in Chicago for sanction for her marriage, even though her fiancé was a young trade unionist and a faithful Communist.

From out of the ranks of the Chicago YCL there came a young couple whom we shall call Helen and Irving. While they were still teen-agers, they fell under the influence of pro-Communist teachers and dedicated themselves to the revolution and the party. They served their apprenticeship during their school years, doing all the chores that are expected of the Red in the ranks. So favorably did they impress the leaders of the Chicago YCL that both of them, becoming closer and closer friends and finally husband and wife, were assigned to dangerous secret work. Helen, being quiet and inconspicuous, was assigned to penetrate the Trotskyite groups. Irving, who went to Spain as a member of the Abraham Lincoln Brigade, was used as a special agent, under Steve Nelson and the forbidding George Mink, to detect and eliminate "enemies of the party." It was his responsibility there, as he told me one evening upon his return, to cultivate the friendship of those suspected of lukewarm interest or lagging spirits. Upon his reports depended the fate meted out to them by the Soviet secret police.

His service abroad won commendation from the national leadership of the Young Communist League. A short time after his return from Spain he was dispatched to Canada to work with the national organizer of the Canadian party, Sam Carr, who is now in prison for espionage. Under Carr's direction, Irving moved back and forth across Canada, strictly under cover, obtaining information connected with new weapons and Canada's military preparedness. Even though he was a mere cog in a big machine, this Canadian assignment was a mark of deep confidence in him on the part of the Red espionage apparatus, for Canada was considered a key spot in Soviet military plans against the United States.

Fear that he would be exposed led the Canadian espionage leaders to order Irving's return to the United States in 1938. He learned then that Helen had been instructed to move to New York, in order to penetrate the Trotskyites on a national scale. I was then in Chicago, and it was I who had arranged this transfer, on the orders of the Soviet secret police representative with whom I was working and who was known to me only as "Roberts."

Just before I went out to Chicago, in 1937 to become editor of the *Midwest Daily Record*, I had been instructed by Roberts to find a comrade who was engaged in penetrating the Trotskyite organization there. Through the reluctant help of Jack Kling, district leader of the young Communists in Chicago, I met Helen.

Our first conference was at Kling's house out on the West Side of Chicago. With curtains drawn so that no one could see who was there, we arranged the ways and means by which I could get in touch with her. She expressed an eagerness to work on a wider scale for the party among the Trotskyites and, before she knew what the mission involved, gladly volunteered her services.

Kling was opposed to this move because he did not want to lose Helen's truly effective services in the regular party infiltration work in Chicago. Her soft voice and conservative dress, which suited her position as a social worker, enhanced her skill as an underground agent. My relations with the Soviet secret police were unknown to Kling and Helen at the time of our interview, but since I spoke in the name of the National Committee my instructions prevailed.

I arranged to meet her privately at different places in South Chicago, where much of her social work was done. During these meetings I gradually broached the possibility of her moving to New York and also tested her skill in her present assignment. When I had satisfied myself about her loyalty and capability, I sent word to Roberts in New York through Jacob Golos of World Tourists, whom I could call on long distance for supposedly business purposes.

In the spring of 1938, Roberts accordingly arrived in Chicago and registered at the Hotel Stevens under the name of Rabinowitz. We chose the Drake Hotel for his meeting with Helen, since she thought it was unlikely that any of her Trotskyite associates or social-worker friends would be dining there. At dinner, Roberts gave her $300 in cash to cover her first-class fare to New York and her initial expenses there. He then told her how she was to proceed. She would have an apartment in mid-Manhattan; and arrangements had been made for her apparent employment by a woman doctor who was a trusted party member. This would explain her regular income and also her irregular hours. She could then volunteer to do stenographic and other clerical work at the Trotskyite national headquarters on University Place and 13th Street.

Helen listened with rapt attention, taking mental notes of her instructions. She demonstrated her adaptability by falling in naturally with Roberts' suggestion that the conversation be turned to the theater whenever a waiter approached.

Roberts had thought of everything; he had even made plans for Irving. For him, upon his return from Canada, the Soviet secret police would provide an apartment in the Bronx, and at least once a week Helen could visit him there. However, it was to be an unbreakable rule that Irving was never, for any reason, to go to her apartment; nor were they ever to be seen together in public.

The arrangements went through at top speed; Helen departed for New York, and Irving soon was located in the Bronx. And Helen so ingratiated herself with the leading Trotskyites that she became a close friend of James Cannon, American Trotskyite chief, and his wife, Rose Karsner. She had the full run of the Trotskyite offices, became Cannon's secretary, and made available to the Soviet secret police all the correspondence with Trotsky in Mexico City and with other Trotskyites throughout the world.

It was in Irving's apartment in the Bronx that I bade farewell to Roberts in the summer of 1939, when he informed me that he was returning to the Soviet Union. Irving spoke in the highest terms of the Soviet secret-police agent, though Roberts had compelled him for more than a year to live this peculiar, hidden existence.

These two were rank-and-file members of the party, performing tasks of great personal danger, always under orders. They were never to receive any party recognition nor hold any party office. Indeed, the very nature of their work cut them off from attendance at party branch meetings. They also ran the grave risk of being disowned by the party if their dual role were discovered.

This brings me to the case of Ruby Weil. She was another person chosen by the secret police out of the party's rank and file, and was coerced into becoming a leading figure in a great tragedy.

Even before she was given this particular assignment, the man in charge of secret work in the New York district, Comrade Chester, had selected her as a young woman with the requisite conservative background to act as a courier and in other secret capacities. She came from a respected family in the Middle West, successful in business and well regarded in community life.

Comrade Chester, an alien from Poland whose real name was Zuster, had noted her air of casual sophistication and had realized that she would know how to handle any social situation. Accordingly, he had drafted her for a secret training school for those who were to be called on to perform underground services.

It was while she was in this school that I approached her on behalf of Roberts. She had been a family friend before either she or I had joined the Communist party. What clinched her for Roberts' assignment was that she had also been a friend of the Ageloff sisters, before she had been a Red.

There were three of the Ageloffs—Ruth, who became Trotsky's secretary down in Mexico City, Hilda, who was Ruby's particular friend, and Sylvia, a Brooklyn social worker who was a special courier of the Trotskyites into Canada, Europe, and Mexico. They were the daughters of a substantial building contractor.

When at Roberts' advice, I told her what was required of her —to cultivate the Ageloffs in order to obtain information on the Trotskyites—she made excuses for declining. However, she finally agreed to see Roberts, and at that meeting he represented her obligation to be so urgent that she promised to follow his directions. To her, I might say, he was known as "John Rich," a name he and I invented just before he met her.

This was in the summer of 1937, and a few months later I was on my way to Chicago. Before I left, however, a complaint had been registered with me and with Ruby's section of the party that she had been seen with Hilda Ageloff, a known Trotskyite, and had once invited Hilda to her home. I was called into the conference with Roberts on this, since Ruby was much perturbed. Roberts, on his part, was pleased. He pointed out that to be suspected by the

Communists would make her more acceptable to the Trotskyites. Through me, word was sent to the section leadership that Ruby was engaged in vital infiltration work, but to her rank-and-file friends in the party no explanation was made and she remained under a cloud.

After I got to Chicago, I was called back to New York time after time to prevent Ruby from throwing up her assignment. As Roberts unfolded to her a plan to send her to Europe with Sylvia Ageloff, who was attending the international Trotskyite conference in Paris, Ruby's fears increased. On one occasion I was called to New York in great haste, and at Roberts' instructions met Ruby late at night as she left her work at the *People's Press*. Riding to the Grand Central Station in a cab, we had a bite to eat at Liggett's drug store there, and then went into the waiting room where for an hour I urged her to take the Paris trip. Both she and I had been told repeatedly by Roberts that our task was to halt the infiltration of Trotskyites into Soviet Russia and thus prevent Stalin's assassination. Ruby's attendance at the international congress would give her an opportunity to get at the roots of such plots. Neither of us suspected for a moment that we were engaged in steps that would lead to the killing of Trotsky in Mexico City.

Ruby was disturbed by the fact that mysterious plans of an elaborate nature had been made for her in the French capital. At the last minute, Roberts had said that he would not be there in person to direct her, and had sent her to a woman named Gertrude down in Greenwich Village. It was Gertrude who would be in Paris and tell her what to do.

Ostensibly, Ruby was going to Europe to visit one of her sisters in England, so it seemed natural enough that she should accompany her friend Sylvia—though as far as that aspect of it was concerned, she had already ingratiated herself with the Trotskyites by attending their affairs with the Ageloff sisters. While Ruby was stopping off in England, Gertrude reached Paris and was ready to receive Ruby on her arrival and introduce her to one "Frank Jacson," known also as Jacques Monard. Ruby in turn was instructed to introduce him as a Belgian count to Sylvia Ageloff. After this introduction, Jacson swept Sylvia off her feet with his attentions, pretending to fall in love with her at first sight and to be converted by her to Trotskyism. After a whirlwind courtship, Jacson induced Sylvia to get him into Mexico by the means used by Trotskyites. There she introduced him to the Trotsky household, where he became a trusted friend of the guards around the former Soviet leader and finally was able to kill Trotsky with an alpenstock. This took place in the summer of 1940.

After introducing Jacson to Sylvia in Paris, Ruby's work with the secret police ended abruptly. They did not remove the cloud from her name in the party. She felt alone and bewildered, since her party friends were suspicious of her, and she wanted to get as far away from the Trotskyites as possible. When the news broke of Trotsky's assassination, she was particularly upset. Rushing up to the *Daily Worker* office, she asked for instructions. Roberts had left New York the summer before, and I had to see Golos about such affairs. When I presented Ruby's case to him, he ordered that only the most secret communication could be held with her, and that only to keep her from getting too excited. He refused her a party card and said that hereafter she was to remain away from all party offices and demonstrations.

Repeatedly, up to the time of Golos' death in late 1943, I tried to get her party card restored and her party status re-established. Golos was always adamant. Once he did take the matter up with the Soviet consulate in New York, but told me that they would not hear of any association being established that might link her to the party, even in the remotest fashion. This is a classic case of the expendability of rank-and-file Communists when their sacrifice is necessary to attain party objectives.

"Discipline" requires the Communist to merge his personality in the movement, to do what he is ordered to do by the comrade next above him, to hide himself or appear in the headlines as may be thought necessary, to appear for years as an enemy of the party when engaged in espionage or other like work. I remember my own definition of "discipline" as given to the members of the *Daily Worker* staff. It said in part: "The staunch Bolshevik is even supposed to make what is really a supreme sacrifice, to immolate his reputation and what the bourgeois world calls his 'integrity' (as Lenin has indicated) at the feet of the party, on behalf of the cause." And the cause, we know, is Stalin.

I have stressed the work of rank-and-file women because they have been used extensively by the party in this country. In the early '30's they were required during demonstrations to stick pins in the horses of the mounted police, then known by the Red-chosen title of "Cossacks." They were placed at strategic positions in audiences on various occasions, such as the American Federation of Labor strike meetings, which the Reds were trying to break up, and instructed to scream or faint and thus precipitate an uproar. Their facility at inciting riots led several women comrades to leadership, and they became party functionaries or paid officials in the IWO. The education of women members in such tactics was carefully and minutely planned. I can remember in 1936 hearing George Siskind and Pop Mindel tell women party members that the riot tactics of the earlier period were not to be relied upon so extensively for the time being. When, about six years later, young Communist women were recruited into the "Sweethearts of Servicemen," to work among the enlisted men, special training squads were set up.

The men rank-and-file comrades are also given many responsibilities. They likewise are kept constantly in motion, and are frequently required to play several different roles during the brief course of one week. The case of Comrade Jacobs is typical of hundreds. In his own neighborhood, he was an active supporter of the American Labor party and openly known as such. He canvassed up and down the block in which he lived in New York, spoke at the local neighborhood rallies, and was regarded as a source of information on the ALP. But he had a regular assignment in another part of the city to distribute literature for the Communist party about once a week. On special occasions he also had to get petitions signed and other work done in the name of the CP. In his union he was known neither as ALP nor CP, but posed as a pure and simple trade unionist—except that coincidentally he always quietly plugged the Communist line. He had a great ambition to become a party functionary and devote full time to open party undertakings. He did not like having to change colors so many times during a week, and the idea of moving other people around in the puppet-like fashion in which he was moved appealed to him. Accordingly he pored over Marxist works at night, considering them a key to leadership; enrolled in the inevitable classes in the Jefferson School of Social Science; and asked for assignments of a special character which would put him near the person of a leading comrade. As a result of his solicitations he was given extra duties in "concentration" work, specifically on the waterfront, which was one of the chief concentration units in New York. He thus became a member of two local divisions of the party—his neighborhood branch and the waterfront unit. In the latter he perfected himself in editorial work, for there were always handbills to be distributed on the docks, calls to action to be written and mailed to party members, and leaflets explaining some particular item in the party's current line. With him on the editorial committee of the unit was a maritime worker, to give their writing the proper salty tang, and a woman comrade who was a secretary in a Wall Street law office. Comrade Jacobs' permanent residence in New York made it possible for him to do this more or less continuous editorial work, whereas the Red seamen who came in and out of port were given the tasks that could be passed from person to person, like the distribution of the *Daily Worker* through the waterfront area.

In spite of volunteering for all these extra duties, Comrade Jacobs was told firmly by his section organizer that he could not become a party functionary. He must stay on his job in his union and in his neighborhood, where he was more valuable. Once, when he was particularly insistent, the section organizer told him in my presence that the party preferred to take its regular workers from the tested ranks of the young people who had gone through either the YCL or the AYD. They had been "formed" by the party, and were therefore better disciplined in emergencies. With a wry smile he also added that they were more likely to remain loyal, since they had no other occupational training and were, in consequence, more dependent on the party. That observation, incidentally, was not original with him; I have heard it from the lips of Alexander Trachtenberg and other leading Communists in discussions in the Politburo.

During the war, Comrade Jacobs got an opportunity to go to Europe in connection with some service agency. This gave him the chance for a short but effective period to serve as a courier between the European and American Communist parties, at a moment when communication between them could not be of the best.

Comrade Jacobs was not alone in services of this character.

There was Comrade Ross, an eager and youthful seaman, who never held any official position in the party, even the humblest. He performed yeoman service, nevertheless, bringing with him on every voyage valuable secret communications from comrades in other countries. Always he went directly from his ship to Thirteenth Street, generally to the office of the foreign editor of the *Daily Worker*, who was a link with the international conspiratorial apparatus. Again, I can recall two brothers of a large family of Communists. Adam and Ben were members of the Abraham Lincoln Brigade, served as guards at party demonstrations, and had been specially trained to battle the police. They were kept so busy at this kind of work—which included acting as bodyguards for outstanding party officials—that they were not able even to become officers of their branch. They were expected always to hold themselves in readiness for the particular type of activity prescribed for them. One of their most valuable assets in their assignment was their ability to keep their mouths shut. Another was the total Communist character of their large family, which made it possible for them to come and go on delicate missions without questions being raised.

There is indeed one rule which the trained rank-and-file Communist must learn, as I once heard J. V. Peters tell a group of comrades. That is to keep a lock on one's lips, never to ask questions of one's party superior, and to say "Yes" to orders no matter how unrelated to any plan they may seem.

"There is an American game, isn't there, called Follow the Leader?" asked Peters. "Well, this is Follow the Leader, too. But it is not a game. It is in dead earnest. Each comrade anywhere in the party apparatus is wholly responsible to the comrade immediately superior to him. That is the first commandment of Communist discipline."

Peters was talking in this case to comrades who had just celebrated two years of party membership. The process of teaching them to keep their lips locked, however, begins at the first branch meeting. From the smallest branch organizer to the most powerful member of the Politburo, the leaders cultivate a bureaucratic manner which in itself prohibits questions. If any young or new comrade is rash enough to become too inquisitive, he is soon squelched with one of the special phrases used on such occasions. A favorite expression is, "Comrade, you are endangering party security."

From the moment of his entry into the branch, the rank-and-file member is made to feel his inferiority; he becomes conscious that he is to go through a series of "ordeals by fire" to test his party integrity, and that he is on a most severe probation which may last for months, years, or indefinitely.

To offset the bureaucratic atmosphere from branch to Politburo, the Red leaders every so often (usually before a National Convention when the members are to be given a new line) come out with an order for "more democratic discussion and elections in the branches." Nothing comes of this in reality. Certain democratic forms are more carefully observed for the moment; the nominating committee, for instance, may have on it one or two more new members than usual. But the one-slate system continues, and it happens to be the slate which the section organizer wants adopted in the branch.

One of the principal commissions of every rank-and-file Communist is to rid his neighborhood or union or civic organization of "antiparty elements." Under the direction of the section organization of the party, he will be required as a rule to spread a whispering campaign against any man or woman who leaves the party or who has Trotskyite or similar unfriendly leanings. In most instances the actual circulation of the rumors is entrusted to people who are not known to be Communists, which makes what they do and say much more effective. I have seen a former official of the IWO driven out of a pleasant apartment-house neighborhood by this method. The rumor in his case, absolutely false in every respect, was that he had been careless in the use of funds. The Reds could not go further in that particular neighborhood. But in the case of George Hewitt, a Negro ex-Communist living in a pro-Communist neighborhood, stronger tactics were applied. Obscene words were written on the door of his apartment; threatening notes were sent to him; his wife and children were harassed with vituperation. The Communists even whipped up anti-Negro sentiment in the neighborhood in order to drive him from the locality. In another instance, a Jewish dentist and his wife who were ex-Communists were isolated completely in a Jewish community by the Red-concocted rumor that they were "anti-Semitic."

The Communist in the ranks learns of the party's various activities only by degrees, and some of them he may never know about at all. The section and district leaders, on the basis of the individual member's circumstances and capacity for discipline, determine how far he shall be initiated into the mysteries of the professional revolutionist's craft.

Many rank-and-filers, for example, are never made familiar with any phase of the party's conspiratorial work. They are kept busy running up and down stairs in Vito Marcantonio election campaigns, or they are the faithful Reds who remain to the last minute in the union meeting in order to exhaust the anti-Communists and outvote them in the final hour. They are often told by their immediate Communist superiors that they are playing a "conspirative role" in that they are enrolled in the party under a false name and are not openly known as loyal to Moscow. But that is merely to weld them in the discipline eventually required of all; it does not often lead to any further secret or subversive activity.

On religious attitudes, a somewhat similar practice prevails. A new member is not required to make the profession of atheism that a leader must file with the Control Commission. In general, the party's aim is to lead the new member gradually into an antireligious attitude, according to Lenin's famous prescription. This atheistic education begins with the initial instruction given over a period of weeks in the new members' classes. The new Red is not openly criticized if he has some remnants of religious belief, but he is made to feel that such belief is a sign of political backwardness. It is also explained, when Stalin's discussion of historical materialism is being studied, that religion is the tool of the ruling classes.

So, too, with the celebrated pledge to Stalin. While every party leader is obliged to take this pledge and to renew it, to the Communist tenderfoot the pledge is presented in a different form. When I joined the party in 1935, a new member was required to take a solemn oath, on pain of punishment, "to rally the masses to defend the Soviet Union, the land of victorious Socialism." In addition, the new member swore that he would be a vigilant and firm defender of the Leninist line of the party, "the only line that insures the triumph of Soviet power in the United States."

Later on, for protection, the Communists stopped printing this pledge in their party documents. It was still required in most branches, however, the matter being left to the discretion of the section committee. In every instance, the Politburo ordered that the substance of this obligation be explained to new members in a solemn fashion, particularly that part which dealt with loyalty to the Soviet Union.

The rank-and-file Communist is drilled ceaselessly with the idea that the party must penetrate every phase of his life. Not only that, but his own interest must be made secondary to the interest of the party. If a friend breaks away, the party man must be the first to denounce him; if a spouse becomes disloyal to the Communists, the party member must end the relationship. The friendships and social life of the comrades, particularly as their years of membership lengthen, must be subordinated to party purposes. The Communist is not required to associate only with Communists; but he is expected to associate with non-Communists solely for the purpose of influencing them politically. Above all, he is forbidden to have anything to do in a friendly way with the party's enemies. That is strictly taboo, and constant watch is kept by comrade on comrade to see that the taboo is not violated.

A high party leader whom I knew well was sent to several foreign countries, one after the other, on a mission so lengthy and so secret that even his wife didn't know where he was. After he had been away for more than a year, she began to live with another Communist. Her excuse to herself was that the party leaders would give her no information about where her husband was or when he would return.

One day, after a long time, her husband did come back. His reappearance happened to follow immediately the proclamation of a sharp change in the party's line. The Red leaders, who knew that she was living with another man, ordered her to go down to the boat and welcome her returning husband. On the way down, she wondered how he would react to her conduct during his absence.

At the first possible moment she told him that she had become interested in another comrade. Immediately he shouted out: "What is his stand on the new line?" Even she, a trained Communist, was taken aback for a moment by this dominance of "party morality" in her husband's mind.

Not every rank-and-file Communist, nor every Red leader, for that matter, is affected in the same way by the party's control of their personal lives. But they all are influenced deeply in one way or other, and generally in many ways. There is nothing more pathetic than the women comrades who listened to the counsel of the party leaders during the wild and woolly period of "revolutionary" expression. As good Communists, they either severely restricted the number of their children or in many cases had no children at all, in accordance with the party's advice that birth control should be practiced and children for the time being eliminated "so that we can have more time for reading, study, and the enjoyment of life." Existing children were to be placed in nurseries, so that the home could be devoted solely to the Communist cause. That counsel appeared, among other places, in the *Daily Worker* of September 6, 1934.

I know several women comrades who followed this advice to the point of having no children during their productive years, and who bitterly regretted their act when the party changed its views as Moscow changed. They felt themselves defrauded, since now Communist women are permitted to have offspring. A man comrade of some importance, Avram Landy, told me in a moment of confidence that he had been criticized and even held back in his party advancement for years because he had dared to have several children and set up a home for them.

Few incidents symbolize this literal acceptance of Red rule as well as does the story of a furniture worker whom I knew in Brooklyn. He could scarcely read in any language, much less English, but he led me and everyone else who visited him to a bookshelf set up in the most conspicuous place in his house. In it were the red-bound volumes of all the *Collected Works of Lenin*. Next to them were two volumes of Stalin's *Leninism* and his *History of the Communist Party of the Soviet Union*.

"This is where I learn," said the furniture worker proudly, obviously indifferent to the fact that the books were untouched and unread. "Every night I take my family here and tell them this is the law for us."

When I asked him what he had learned from these books in his house, he replied that he knew that he must follow the party wherever it might lead. He looked forward with great expectation to the time when his ten-year-old son would be able to digest these volumes.

"The party is always right," this comrade said, with great earnestness. "I would kill or be killed for it. I want my son to have the same purpose. The party must be his life." And he meant every word of it.

(VI)

The Stalin Cult

O NE presence dominates the House on Thirteenth Street and that is the personality of Joseph Vissarionovich Stalin.

No one dares conclude an inner-party discussion—on the Eighth or the Ninth Floor—without a devout reference to the "greatest genius in the world," the man hailed as above all men. What Stalin says is the guide quoted and what he does is the blueprint cited by the Reds for the coming establishment of Soviet rule in America. Each step of the way to the seizure of power and the bloody crushing of the state machinery is charted for the comrades by Stalin's word and inspired by his example.

In Soviet Russia, it is known, songs have been written to the generalissimo of the workers' fatherland as "our glory, our conscience, our word." He has been proclaimed "great in eternity," the center of the universe. That an identical fervor grips his American disciples is something that is not well recognized, since the number of those who have had direct ties with the House on Thirteenth Street is comparatively small.

"Comrades: the name Stalin strikes the same chords of love in all the nations and peoples of the Socialist Fatherland, for it spells life and joy to them. The hearts of the working people throughout the world are filled with love for Comrade Stalin." Thus did William Z. Foster, Communist national chairman, lift up the spirits of the leading Reds when they were engaged in hard and uphill labors. They were then gathered in New York to plan further aid to the Hitler-Stalin alliance, and Foster's was the task of spurring them on to the incitement of larger strikes which would more extensively shut down American defense industry.

He had been paraphrasing the tribute paid by Lavrenti Beria, the efficient head of the Soviet secret police, to the "greatest man of our day." He went on, now echoing the words of A. I. Mikoyan, outstanding member of the Russian Politburo. "In the party," said Foster, "and among the people, unprecedented confidence in Stalin prevails, an unshakable belief in the infallibility of the general line of our party and in the success at every turn of the party's policy; for every one knows that since Stalin is at the helm, there is no cause for disquietude, victory is certain whatever happens."

The earnest faces of the comrades, sitting at that time in a small hall not far from the Thirteenth Street building, reflected their recognition of the "truth" in what Foster was saying. It was an almost palpable thing—this genuine belief in Stalin as one who could make no mistake, as one of the four outstanding infallible geniuses in the life of mankind and indeed the greatest of the four.

The quotations which Foster freely used were the tributes written by the Russian Politburo in honor of Stalin's sixtieth birthday on December 23, 1939, published in this country in book form by the party's corporation, the Workers Library Publishers. That book, *Stalin*, was required study for every leading comrade. Orders had been dispatched from Thirteenth Street that it should be the basis for all instructions to the sections and branches. The entire membership was whipped up to new fervor for Stalin's person, the giant who had mastered the mystery of mankind's destiny.

That sixtieth birthday was a gala event in all the party meetings and discussions from coast to coast. The celebration went on throughout the year 1940, the expressions of subservience to the dictator of the Russias rising in crescendo as the year progressed. The birthday of "the leader of oppressed humanity the world over" had come at just the right moment to have the effect of tonic on the comrades, for in 1940 the party was underground, so far as most of its members were concerned. The comrades felt the pressure of the nation's antagonism. Their leaders were openly assailing the "Roosevelt fascist war program" in the pages of the *Daily Worker*, because it was designed to aid battered Great Britain. Their branches had been broken down into groups of five, in preparation for sharp revolutionary action should the call come to "turn the imperialist war into civil war." Operating in disguise, American Communists were shutting down a considerable portion of American defense production through the Allis-Chalmers, North American Aircraft and other strikes.

Treading their way carefully under cover of night to apartment-house gatherings, the comrades received in whispered conferences instructions on how to undermine America's defenses. I attended no small number of these "get-togethers of neighbors" by which the party functioned in that troubled time. The group of five would huddle together in one room, keeping their voices down in order that no stray word should float into the corridor. They would salute each other by their "party names," even though they might have known each other for years, in order to keep in practice. These were generally first names only. Sometimes a party member would receive an assignment from the section representative which made him wince with fear. But as a rule, he or she gallantly accepted.

I remember an excitable woman Communist at one of these gatherings out in Long Island City who was ordered to distribute leaflets calling for a strike before a large defense factory. There was danger in such an assignment—from the workers specifically, since they did not want to be tarred as Reds. Like Eva, when she was assigned a similar task, Comrade Leah Paloni blanched when this order was given her and took the leaflets with trembling hands. But she went the next day to the factory gates, as she had been instructed, and many days thereafter.

What inspired her that night, as I saw with my own eyes, was the magic name of Stalin. The theme of the "educational" part of the evening's agenda had been the famed words of Georgi Dimitrov, the Bulgarian Communist, when he said that the working class in the capitalist countries "are learning and will learn from Stalin the Bolshevik art of fighting and vanquishing the class enemy."

The wrinkles of concern on Comrade Paloni's forehead were smoothed away, and the frown of fear on her face disappeared as Dimitrov's lesson was brought home to the little group: "Stalin is as international as the working class. Stalin is as international as Bolshevism . . . Comrade Stalin's theoretical and practical labors are concerned with the interests of the workers of all countries, of all nations and races."

Stalin was her leader, her guide—and for him she would betray her own nation. The conflict in her soul was cleared up, and she resolved to carry forward (so she said) "with the steel of Bolshevization, as Stalin has instructed."

What this semihysterical comrade had resolved, I heard more stolid Reds vow also in Stalin's name. With his Scotch burr, William McKie made a similar solemn pledge of "Bolshevization," in the Ford automobile district in Detroit. In the coal region near Pittsburgh, Tony Minerich was making the same fervent pledge and persuading certain Slav miners to act accordingly. In the New York garment area there were many such promises made. All over America, wherever Reds could meet in secret, this whispered oath-taking occurred—and its repercussions in the shutting down of industrial production gave silent evidence of Stalin's power in America.

Tens of thousands of Americans were induced to help Hitler in that year 1940 by downing tools and slowing aid to Britain. The incitement came from Reds disguised as non-Communists, who had been moved by Dimitrov's words repeated at these secret meetings: "We must learn from Stalin revolutionary audacity and revolutionary realism; we must learn from Stalin to be fearless in battle and ruthless toward the class enemy."

A number of professional intellectuals were mustered into committees to hurl abuse at Mr. Roosevelt, or to plead for the release from prison of Communist chief Earl Browder, or to work quietly for clemency to the party's convicted financial boss, Robert William Weiner. That each of these acts was subversion, organized by Stalin's fifth column against American security, never occurred to them. For these intellectuals had been thoroughly taken in by the comrades, who received their stimulus from that master of flexibility, "the genius who is carrying on the cause of Marx, Engels and Lenin."

From the Communist's political cradle to his political grave, the steeled perfection of Stalin imbues his life with a purpose and a plan. When I joined the Communist party in the fall of 1935, I was obliged by Jack Stachel, the American Politburo's clever and shifty liaison with Moscow's representatives, to express agreement with the pledge of loyalty to Stalin which had just been adopted at the Moscow meeting of the Seventh World Congress of the Communist International.

We were sitting in one of those cubicle-like offices which cover the Ninth Floor when Stachel, welcoming me into the party, pointed to "one weakness" which I had shown. It was "lack of full appreciation for the leadership of Stalin over the whole progressive section of mankind."

"Had you been to the Seventh World Congress," Stachel went on to say, with the sly smile he often assumed when correcting others, "you would have been reminded forever of how Lenin's successor dominated our entire thought and action. He was the beginning and the end of our discussions and resolutions."

He told me how even the children of Moscow had sent a representative, the Pioneer Pavlenok, to announce that they were "happy Stalinist children." And with a singular gift for prophecy this young Stalinite had declared amid shouts and applause: "The hour is coming when the streets of Berlin will be illuminated with the light of the Soviets. We shall be there singing the Stalin song. Great Stalin, your true hand guides us to ethereal heights."

Whereupon Stachel had handed me the pledge passed in the

form of a resolution of fealty by the Communist representatives of all the countries at the Congress. The American delegation, Stachel said, had joined in the enthusiastic unanimity with which the resolution was adopted.

"To Comrade Stalin, Leader, Teacher, and Friend of the Proletariat and Oppressed of the Whole World," its title read.

That pledge has been inspiring the Communist movement here for fifteen years. It has been the subject of devout discussion in many inner-party conferences. But it only came to the large-scale attention of the American people in my testimony at the trial of the eleven Communist leaders, that is, in April, 1949. This is a startling illustration of how little Americans actually know of the enemy within the gates.

Every loyal American should be thoroughly familiar with that resolution if he is to measure the nature of the Communists accurately. Every word of it stamps the Communist party as exclusively a fifth column of a foreign dictatorship.

Addressing Stalin extensively as "the beloved leader of the whole international proletariat," it proclaims that he is "at the helm of the struggle for the liberation of the whole of toiling humanity."

Then asserting that the Communists everywhere are under and follow his leadership, the pledge concludes:

"The Seventh World Congress of the Communist International, in the name of 65 Communist Parties, assures you, Comrade Stalin, that the Communists will always and everywhere be faithful to the end to *the great and invincible banner of Marx, Engels, Lenin and Stalin. Under this banner Communism will triumph throughout the world.*"

This pledge, with its constant repetition of adherence to Stalin and his teachings, specifically expresses loyalty to him as leader of the peoples of the world. It is a pledge to him as world conqueror.

This document is of the same pattern as most Communist declarations. The same slogan is repeated in numerous ways, with a monotony that would be boring to the normal person. By this means, however, the idea is implanted permanently in the mind of the Communist; at the same time, its real significance is frequently overlooked by non-Communists too impatient to examine it.

What attitude and acts does this allegiance to Stalin as the light of the world call for in actual life? One day in the late '30's, at a *Daily Worker* staff meeting, William Z. Foster asked and answered that question in frank terms. In a high, querulous voice which he frequently adopted when he wanted to make the comrades sit up and take notice, Foster said bluntly: "The toiling masses owe no loyalty or allegiance to the present political apparatus as set up under the United States Constitution. Their leader is not the President of the United States, since he is the representative of the ruling class, the capitalists."

To whom, then, do the American masses owe loyalty? Said Foster: "The leader of the American toilers and all those allied with them is the great scientist of Marxism-Leninism, Joseph Stalin. It is in his name that we shall turn the imperialist war into civil war, bringing about the destruction of our own bourgeois government as per the Leninist Formula."

That was in the inner sanctum of Thirteenth Street. But Foster said the same thing in public and in print, even in the year 1937, when the Communist party was wooing leading American politicians and liberals with the will-o'-the-wisp, of the People's Front. In his book of that year, *From Bryan to Stalin*, Foster wrote pointedly: "In nearly all countries there are now strong Communist Parties, under the leadership of the Communist International and ready to apply Lenin's decisive revolutionary war against capitalism. And behind it all stands the great fortress of Socialism, the Soviet Union with its powerful revolutionary Red Army."

At that time the Communists, through the pages of the *Daily Worker*, were offering excited support to President Roosevelt's plan to change "the Tory-tethered tribunal," the Supreme Court. They were making emotional pleas on behalf of the President and running his picture frequently on the front page, a signal to all the faithful in the country that the Reds were sidling in that direction.

But Foster's book reminded the same comrades that this aid to F.D.R. was merely for the purpose of gaining a wide voice among the masses, in order to persuade them that Stalin was their real ruler and guide. Sharp instructions were sent out by the Ninth Floor to all Communist district leaders to "safeguard the Stalinite integrity" of the comrades in the People's Front. There was to be no such nonsense as harboring pleasant illusions that Mr. Roosevelt could guide them anywhere. His name was simply to be the Open sesame! to contacts with high places in the governmental apparatus—for the greater glory of Stalin. The more warmly that Mr. Roosevelt was publicly embraced, the order said, the more emphatically were the local leaders to stress Stalin in the inner-party circles as "our real leader, our guide to the world proletarian dictatorship."

Little onionskin papers, the kind that conveyed all conspiratorial orders, flew about the country to this effect. They were dispatched to obscure mail drops in each city—in Chicago to a boardinghouse run by a woman Communist—and thence transmitted to the district leaders. It was a game at which the Reds excel: speaking in public one way and in their conspiratorial meetings and magazines another. The result was tragic for America, and remains so to this day.

Right at the beginning of the People's Front maneuvers in 1936 —which were to dress the Reds in "patriotic" garb—this allegiance to Stalin had been made paramount for them in an outstanding speech by Earl Browder. On January 20, 1936, I attended my first Red meeting at Madison Square Garden as a member of the party. Thousands of comrades overflowed the huge auditorium, to cheer as Browder acclaimed Stalin's "incomparable wisdom, clarity and boldness," and hailed him as "our present leader, who has taken his place unchallengeably beside Marx, Engels and Lenin . . ."

The words of the Reds' national leader, uttered on such a solemn occasion, are not merely to be applauded; they are to be studied diligently and carried into life, as the comrades so often say. I was one of those specially commissioned to take the Browder message out to the branches, to units of the International Workers Order, to fractions in the trade unions. We directed the fire of our anger at the "Liberty-League-Hearst-Republican combination," which was the Reds' indirect way of backing Roosevelt's election campaign, but above all, we warned, our chief devotion was to Stalin—"our great and wise Stalin," as Browder had put it—and to the socialist fatherland, the Soviet Union. The comrades were made to understand that.

The 1935 pledge of fealty to Stalin was now making itself felt in the sober realities of American life. Through every subsequent twist and turn in party history, it has continued to animate the Reds. During the Hitler-Stalin alliance period of 1939-1941, when the Kremlin cast the party in the unpopular role of an aid to the Nazis, the necessity of maintaining allegiance to Stalin turned attention to a book which put a special stamp on the comrades everywhere. The *History of the Communist Party of the Soviet Union (Bolsheviks)*, written under Stalin's eye and now acclaimed by Soviet writers as entirely his creation, was published in America by the party's own house, International Publishers. It has become the chart by which the comrades think and act to the detriment of the American Republic.

Nonbelievers in communism will have difficulty in correctly estimating the power of this volume. If there were to be an accurate survey of the works which have most intensely influenced recent history in the United States, Stalin's *History* would stand high on the list. Its pages imbued the party bureaucrats with a sense of the righteousness of their cause and a certainty of ultimate victory that gave an aura of sanctity to all their Moscow-born commands. Its arguments fired the Reds working in disguise with a conviction that led them to lie and to ingratiate themselves in the highest social and political circles.

Let us consider some cases, illustrating how a book by Russia's dictator has damaged America on certain critical occasions. In late January, 1940, I received instructions to confer with A. W. Mills in his underground hideout in Columbus, Ohio. I was in the Ohio capital covering the convention of the United Mine Workers for the *Daily Worker*, being then one of the few members of the party's National Committee who was not undercover. Scarcely had I got settled in my room at the Neil House, across from the state capitol building, when I received a telephone call from "Comrade Nettie," the wife of a local newspaper man.

She was the person I had been told would bring me in touch with Mills, so I accepted her invitation to meet her in the hotel lobby. From there she drove me far into the outskirts of Columbus, and in the rear of a small and obscure restaurant I met the undercover comrade.

An alien long in this country illegally, Mills' true name is Milgrim. Quite short in stature, with large and conspicuous ears and heavy features, Mills seemed anything but the dynamic source of violence in mass actions that he had proved to be. He was an expert at organizing clashes with police or other authorities which would lead to bloodshed. To him goes the credit for the tragic outcome of the Bonus March on Washington during the Hoover administration. Because of his record, the government ordered his deportation in 1936. Soviet Russia, however, refused to receive him. All the United States felt it could do then was throw up its hands and permit him to remain. Now, in 1940, he was secretly going from city to city, tapping on the doors of reliable comrades late at night and stimulating them to incite walkouts in defense industries.

"Here are two sealed envelopes," he said, passing them to me. "One is my report for the National Committee on shutdowns in defense matériel; that is for Comrade Foster. The other has to do with expenses for conspiratorial purposes; that is for Comrade Weiner. Do not let either of these envelopes for one moment away from your person; no matter what the circumstances, keep them on you."

And then, with a light in his eyes, he pulled from a workman's lunchbox a copy of Stalin's *History* and began to comment on several passages. He was particularly wrapped up in two of them— one on page 346 dealing with the promise that out of the Socialist State would emerge the Communist Society. Stalin repeats the familiar prediction that then the Communist principle will be established as the guiding one: "from each according to his abilities, to each according to his needs." The other passage was the conclusion, where Stalin says emphatically that now we have entered the Leninist period when the violent overthrow of governments like that of the United States is imminent. Or, as he puts it, "when forces are being directly mustered for the overthrow of imperialism and the seizure of power by the proletariat."

The hardened Mills, whom I had known heretofore merely as a cool and calculating bureaucrat, appeared suddenly as a devotee of the master of Bolshevism. Stalin the infallible had spoken, and that gave him hope in his hideaway places; that red-bound book was the holy book which drove him to acts that gravely injured the country in which he lived.

All that this zealot wanted to discuss—"in the half hour we dare be together"—was the significance of these phrases, when considered with Stalin's famous article of 1937 on "Mastering Bolshevism." And against these he wished to measure Stalin's later statements (early in 1939) in which he postponed indefinitely "the withering away of the State." That seemed to delay for a long time the coming of the final Communist Society—and Mills was "hungry to discuss with a leading comrade," as he said almost pitifully, all that Stalin had in mind in these various declarations.

Not that Mills had any doubt of the basic objective of Stalin's legions. He had dedicated his life to the destruction of the American government and of all others standing in the way of Moscow's march to world empire. But the continued consideration of "theory" is always on the order of the day for the Red activists.

"We have to stand firm on Bolshevik principles, advancing the revolution as rapidly as objective conditions permit," said Mills himself, "and at the same time, as Comrade Stalin says so well, be flexible enough to keep in touch with the masses."

At that moment, weighing this double duty, Mills was convinced that he would shortly be called on to advance open civil war in the United States. As a true Bolshevik, he rejoiced at the possibility of chaos and conflict. And out of his rejoicing, factories were shutting down in the Middle West from the impetus furnished by his machinations.

Meanwhile, the Politburo members went quietly around the country in Stalin's name, urging the Reds to be prepared for civil war against this nation. Outstanding in these labors was Eugene Dennis, the rising star of the bureaucracy, who had made his name prominent in the party by an article in the May, 1940, issue of *The Communist*, designed to steel the comrades for the desperate deeds it was expected they would have to do on behalf of the Hitler-Stalin alliance. It was Dennis, with a copy of this article under his arm, who went out to Milwaukee and gave the orders for the Allis-Chalmers strike. A good section of our war production was thus paralyzed in early 1941, and Hitler given no small assistance.

If that had turned out to be the end of the matter, Americans perhaps could afford to let it rest. But the 5 to 4 decision of the United States Supreme Court on June 27, 1949, in the Harold Christoffel case, has encouraged the comrades to new seditious work in the basic industries. The man who engineered the Allis-Chalmers strike, who in 1948 was convicted of perjury for swearing before the House Labor Committee that he was not a Communist, was released on a minute technicality. His retrial and reconviction in February, 1950, put the matter again before the high court.

The whole affair brings back a statement made to me by Dennis during that Hitler-Stalin alliance period: "The legal technicalities built up by bourgeois democracy can be used against it. Comrade Stalin, who knew how to work both legally and illegally, has given us an example that can spur us to defeat bourgeois democratic justice."

The comrades, as evidenced by issues of the *Daily Worker* for June, 1949, were jubilant at their success in the Supreme Court. In the whole matter of seditious organization in the heavy industries, as we shall learn in detail as this narrative progresses, Stalin has thus far badly beaten America. Red work continues virtually unimpaired and uninterrupted in spite of trials and convictions.

Stalin worship reached its official climax in the Eleventh National Convention of the Communist party held in upper Manhattan in the later part of May, 1940. Amid banners denouncing "Roosevelt's War Policies" and proclaiming "The Yanks Are Not Coming" and "Keep America out of War," the convention unanimously denounced President Roosevelt as "a willing servant" of American imperialism and for "leading the nation along the same path as Hitler had led Germany." Then, in an outburst of enthusiasm, the delegates with equal unanimity "associated" themselves "proudly" with one man, the genius who had brought peace to one sixth of the globe, the greatest man living today, the great Stalin.

There remains with me still the memory of that scene. Americans, with red badges, rose in a body on the call for the vote, crying: "Long life to the great Stalin! Long live our leader! Long life to the protector of the socialist fatherland! Down with Roosevelt's war program!"

That resolution of open "association" with the ruler of a foreign state was completely overlooked by the "capitalist press," though the omission can readily be explained by the peculiar definition of "democratic procedure" that the party adopts. All reporters were barred from the convention sessions. They got merely what the Red bosses handed out. But as obscured as the resolution was in the general press, on the comrades it was the most binding of any there adopted.

Elaborate preparations had been made that it might be "a living thing." The Workers Library Publishers had been ready in advance with the adulatory volume, *Stalin,* and the party writers had been called together by Alexander Trachtenberg to plan a campaign to make the book widely known among the delegates.

I remember that conference with some amusement. Tall, white-haired Vern Smith told us of a New Zealand delegate to the Seventh Communist World Congress in 1935 who had compared Stalin to a kauri tree. That arboreal splendor happened to be the highest tree by far in that South Pacific land. And the "kauri tree" allusion struck Trachtenberg as so exotic and "typical of what should be said about Stalin" that Smith was commissioned on the spot to write the publicity piece for the *Daily Worker.* It duly appeared two days before the convention opened.

The delegates went out of the Royal Windsor Palace, where they had met, to spread Browder's promise that "the existence of the Soviet Union" and "the realization of the teachings of Marx, Engels, Lenin and Stalin" would bring about "a repetition on a larger scale of the great outcome of the first imperialist war that gave birth to the Soviet power and socialism on one sixth of the earth's surface."

The promise of Stalin's triumph over new countries and eventually over our own is contained in Browder's book, *The Second Imperialist War.* Its distribution was made a leading task for the delegates to the 1940 convention, and with their usual alacrity they peddled it by the thousands within a few months.

During the year that followed that convention—until Hitler foolishly decided to assault his Russian ally—I saw the comrades do almost impossible things against the United States. They rallied the International Workers Order, the Red insurance front, and through its ranks spread the message against adequate defense into faraway places that had scarcely seen a Communist as such. They spread isolationist and pacifist sentiments, although both are in contradiction to Marxist principles. With my own participation, they persuaded 300 prominent writers and artists to assail Mr. Roosevelt and his "imperialist war program." I heard them in small mining villages repeating the words of Foster and Browder against the "imperialist war" and the "warmongers of Wall Street." I heard them in drawing rooms on Park Avenue speaking of the cost to American business that would result from Roosevelt's "wild adventures." And always the dynamic force that moved them to speak and act was the devotion to Stalin represented by the words of Foster and Browder at the convention.

In 1944, after the anti-Axis war was on in full force, pressure from Moscow upon the comrades became heavy to safeguard the glory of Stalin in the postwar world. None was to be like him; the Soviet Union and his military genius were to be proclaimed as having won the war. The comrades were to do all in their power, through their influence and contacts, to assure America's agreement to the Red Army's occupation of key areas. Thus America was to be deprived of a strategic position in Europe—or in Asia—so far as possible. That directive was transmitted to the Ninth Floor through Moscow's mouthpiece, Gerhart Eisler.

There was some question whether these hopes should be reflected in the columns of the *Daily Worker*, in order to tip off the comrades everywhere to begin a big campaign on the Red Army's superiority to the American troops. After some consultation with Eisler, Jack Stachel (the Politburo's liaison officer with the *Daily Worker* as well as with Moscow undercover agents) held this to be unwise. Such a course, Stachel asserted, would arouse indignation here against the Communists and imperil the shipment of American lend-lease matériel which Russia needed so badly.

Some comrades, however, let enthusiasm get the better of their discretion and almost let out the anti-American animus in the Red plans prematurely. Late one morning in mid-December I arrived at the *Daily Worker* office to find a lump of comrades gathered in the managing editor's room, excitedly examining the yellow ticker slips that were bringing in the war news. Among them was Joe

Starobin, foreign editor of the *Daily Worker* and knee-deep in knowledge of the conspiratorial apparatus and its aims. Others included some of the men from the fifth floor, the office of the New York State Communist organization, Gilbert Green among them. The ticker told of the big Nazi offensive in Luxemburg that was driving back the Yankee troops.

The comrades were jubilant, and immediately discussed comments in the *Daily Worker* which would compare the "heroic advances of the Red Army with the inefficiency of the American military operations." They referred back to Red criticisms of America's alleged slowness in launching the Second Front, and declared that this Battle of the Bulge—for that is what it was—proved that America was still not fighting whole-heartedly.

Green and Starobin were particularly elated, and particularly set upon the *Daily Worker's* hailing the Red Army as the sole guarantee of victory in Europe.

Starobin's face, generally troubled in aspect, was lighted up with genuine pleasure. "We can now hammer hell out of Washington's collaboration with the Polish government-in-exile and its failure to aid Red China," he said.

I raised a strong objection that this would place upon the Reds the onus of breaking the "coalition" which publicly the *Daily Worker* acclaimed so often. That objection would have been brushed aside had I not telephoned Stachel about what was afoot and asked him to come down before the editorial board convened.

Stachel, who was always alert to the delicate shades of Moscow's exact views, immediately vetoed any proposals for publicly exulting at American defeats. He put this decision solely on the ground of expediency.

"Such an expression would be premature and injurious to the Soviet Union at this hour," he stated, in his rasping voice. "It would have an element of insanity in it."

But he had a suggestion about how to take advantage of the American setback in another way. "What we should do," he continued, "as Comrade Berger [Eisler] has suggested, is to use this difficulty in which the Americans find themselves to show that political backwardness causes it. We can make it the starting point for an attack on the Polish government-in-exile and for a plea for a Red-supported China."

Since Stachel's word (particularly when backed up by Eisler) was law for the party, that decision stood. And it was reinforced by the fact that the gaining of a Red Poland and a Red China was the big and specific task assigned to the American comrades at that time.

Out of Stachel's decision, then, came the piece by Starobin in the *Daily Worker* of December 20, 1944, which the comrades spread throughout the country—"Hitler's Drive—Challenge at Home and Abroad"—and which aimed its big blows at the Polish government-in-exile. We were losing in the Battle of the Bulge, it said in effect, because we continued to fritter our resources away with "reactionary political allies."

The comrades' spirit of satisfaction at the difficulties of the American armies continued through December and added to the holiday spirit on Thirteenth Street. Many comrades, Starobin with his soft-spoken voice among them, went around the halls saying: "The day will yet come when we can tell that the Soviet Union, through the military genius of Stalin, won the war!"

And they did get that chance, after two years. The Soviet military triumphs became the propaganda line by which the Soviet Union and its fifth columns everywhere proceeded to advance the so-called cold war. It is well put from the Red point of view by Max Weiss in the November, 1946, issue of *Political Affairs*, the new name of the official theoretical organ of the party: "Led by the Bolshevik Party headed by Stalin, the Soviet Union and its heroic Red Army—despite the most frightful sacrifices—was able to make the chief contribution to the defeat of the Axis powers."

Weiss then went on to say: "Today, the Soviet Union stands at the head of all forces which are struggling to guarantee that the

peoples of the world will accomplish the aims they fought to
achieve against the fascist powers."

The Reds thus transmuted the war slogan of the "Four Freedoms" into a postwar cry for all-out aid to Soviet aggression.

With the unfolding of that aggression in the years immediately
succeeding World War II, Stalin worship rose to new heights and
by 1949 every article in every official organ of the party, here and
abroad, contained hails and hosannas to Stalin. The reports of the
leaders of all the satellite states acclaimed him as world leader, and
the party leaders in America promoted his name on every big question, as though it were magic. In *Political Affairs*, the organ for the
most advanced comrades, Stalin's name is repeated in litany form.
Is it the theoretical work of the party? In numerous articles, Foster
and others call upon the brilliant works of the leader. Is it about
science? The scientists are told abruptly they must follow where
Stalin leads. Is it an explanation of certain "nationalist" errors in
leading Polish comrades? Tribute must be paid above all to "the
great and brilliant leader." Is it agriculture? Stalin's "graphic description" must be drawn upon. Is it a discussion of the necessity
for Communists to know Lenin's methods? They must go to Stalin,
the man who "saved the world from a fascist fate." Is it to show
the comrades that the present cold war is in reality a prelude to a
hot war? Then Stalin's letter to the Russian Professor Razin to
that effect has to be published. Whatever the subject, Stalin is the
master mind of last appeal.

In the literature distributed to the American comrades, the salu-
tations to Stalin are innumerable. He is called everything from
"our beloved" to "great driver of the locomotive of history." And
behind these terms is the iron fist of Communist discipline. Men
committing treason against their native lands whisper the name of
Stalin and gain courage. Well-manicured gentlemen steal secret
military documents from our State Department for Stalin's glory
and are happy. For him, certain scientists prepare to betray their
country, as did Dr. R. Boyer in Canada and Dr. Alan May in

Britain. Other scientists like Dr. Klaus Fuchs steal the secrets of the atom and hydrogen bombs. Still others work night and day for the power to paralyze American defense when Stalin so orders. Others kill ruthlessly in gangster style in order that this man of "immortal deeds" may go forward to world rulership.

Stalin worship is a reality. The average American, who goes to bed at night totally unaware of the future it lays down for him, should be made to understand that fact. Stalin worship is the mighty dynamic force which is killing off Chinese peasants, murdering men of religion, making great sections of the world huge concentration camps. His is the magic name that is beating down the United States—"the focal point and mainstay of world reaction"—as the Cominform's organ boasted at the beginning of 1949.

America must realize that this "supreme master of bold revolutionary decisions" is the man whom the Soviet fifth column's members, operating from Thirteenth Street, plan to make ruler of a Soviet America. They assert that the cry, "For Stalin!" is the watchword of liberation.

That was what I taught, as did the other Red leaders, to the *Daily Worker* staff and to the branches, using the official biography handed us by the party and published at Moscow's orders in 1941.

Every Red inner-party meeting, large or small, introduces in some vivid way the theme of devotion to Stalin. Every theoretical article written for Communist direction is scanned carefully in advance to determine whether it contains allusions to Stalin or to his teachings in proper measure. I have seen V. J. Jerome, who has served for years as editor of the inner-party publications, poring over manuscripts with this emphasis in mind. The purpose is to confirm the active Communist in that primary loyalty which will make him in a crisis abandon home or country for the Soviet dictatorship, disrupt his union, turn upon his family or his closest friends, and risk his own life if necessary. If conflict arises between Stalin's aims and a stanch Communist's native land, the choice will be made—no matter how painful or difficult—on the side of this dominant loyalty.

Without understanding the cult of Stalin worship—and that is what it has come to be—it is impossible to understand the Communist conspiracy. It is impossible to understand the life of the party member, especially the member who has been thoroughly trained, unless one appreciates what the constant repetition of Stalin's name, attributes, and works has done to him. America must realize that these hosannas to Stalin are not fantastic ravings, but part of a cold, deliberate program designed to undermine any remnants of patriotism among Communists in capitalist countries and to obliterate democratic sentiments everywhere. If the average resident of Middletown, U.S.A., is inclined to shrug off such statements as bombastic, he would have a different view if he knew what rigid discipline can accomplish.

From the Baltic countries to China, Stalin worship records its victories in the conquests by the armed bands under Stalin's banner. In the United States, it has also achieved its successes.

(VII)

S-Day

O^N "S-DAY," when Stalin gives the order for the Red Army and Air Force offensive against the United States, he will count on many aids within this country. The Communist apparatus has long been set up—to help make targets of our industrial cities, to prevent our scientific equipment from being effective, and to paralyze our economic life. The main preoccupation of the Ninth Floor is seeking every avenue to enlarge the possibilities of this apparatus.

The basic program for undermining America in case of war was laid down at the Comintern's Seventh World Congress in Moscow. The resolution was adopted on August 20, 1935, and reads: "If the commencement of a counter-revolutionary war forces the Soviet Union to set the Workers and Peasants Red Army in motion for the defense of Socialism, the Communists will call upon all toilers to work, with all means at their disposal and at any price, for the victory of the Red Army over the armies of the imperialists."

Since the United States is the greatest of all "imperialists" (being today stigmatized by William Z. Foster, chairman of the Communist party as more dangerous to the world than was Hitler's Third Reich), the preparations for undermining America have been particularly feverish. The continuation of this anti-American network, in spite of all the talk of scotching it, caused Foster to boast in the August, 1948, issue of *Political Affairs* that the United States would be defeated in a war with Soviet Russia. "For the forces of

democracy and socialism are much too strong to be defeated mili-
tarily by American imperialism," writes Foster exultantly.

S-Day—Stalin's Day, Soviet Day, the day for Seizure of Power
—is the term by which the leading comrades dramatize the "inevitable" crushing of the American government by Soviet arms. It
is a term heard only in the secret councils of the party's higher
leadership, and then on infrequent but vital occasions. It was most
vigorously used in the late summer of 1940 by William Z. Foster
when the United States was preparing for "M-Day" and when the
Communists everywhere were aiding Hitler. White-faced and
tense, speaking in a high-pitched and complaining tone, Foster declared that these M-Day plans of the United States "must be
smashed by mobilizing the workers, farmers, Negroes and youth
around the leadership of the Soviet Union, their true fatherland."
If that were done, he went on, "the Roosevelt war and hunger
policy, dictated by American imperialism, can be crushed, and the
force forged stronger to threaten the very existence of the capitalist
system." Then growing more indignant, Foster stated that the trade
unions had to be taken away from their "reactionary leaders" (he
specifically mentioned Sidney Hillman) to show that "if the Roosevelt imperialists propose an M-Day, we can plan our S-Day, when
the Soviet Power will make itself felt, through the proletarian internationalism of the American workers."

In order to keep the comrades everywhere alive to their obligation to prepare for the day of Stalin's triumph, they are constantly
inoculated with official Red declarations. Again and again in *Daily
Worker* staff meetings, I read and expounded the famous report of
Georgi Dimitrov at the Seventh World Congress in which he states
categorically that the Communist aim is to overthrow all non-Soviet
governments and to set up the dictatorship of the proletariat in
every land. Those who were in court during the trial of the eleven
Communist leaders may recall that the defense started to introduce
this Dimitrov report, because it refers to the Communists' opposition to "fascism," and was considerably taken aback when the

prosecution read paragraph after paragraph from the same report advocating the violent overthrow of all governments.

One of our favorite quotations during our "educational discussions" on the paper, when the whole staff met for the purpose of being inspired, was the concluding words of William Pieck as chairman of the Seventh Communist Congress: "Our road is revolution of the peoples against the oppressors and exploiters. Our will is the will of Marx, Engels, Lenin and Stalin. Our goal is Socialism for the whole of humanity. Our main slogan is the establishment of Soviet Power."

At this term, "Soviet Power," every speaker who ever addressed the staff would pause to refresh the memories of the comrades on the famous blueprint for world conquest and the overturn of the U.S. government set down by the Sixth World Communist Congress in 1928. So inevitably did this happen that every person present unconsciously reached for the printed report containing that outline for S-Day whenever the speaker came to this point.

Called *The Program of the Communist International*, it was printed and widely distributed in several forms by Workers Library Publishers, the official Communist publishers in this country. In no uncertain terms, it called for: (1) the establishment by force and violence of a world Soviet dictatorship; (2) the stimulation of political strikes to dislocate the economy of the country under attack; (3) the turning of political strikes into armed insurrection; (4) basic and permanent loyalty to the Soviet Union.

The Seventh World Congress in 1935, the last so far to be held, made some additions to this program. A special resolution declared sharply that with the victory of socialism in Russia it had become the principal obligation of every worker and every "progressive" person to defend the Soviet fatherland against his own country.

Both in peace and war, it was their duty "to help with all their might and by all means to strengthen the U.S.S.R. and to fight against the enemies of the U.S.S.R." The colonial peoples were told they had a like obligation.

This resolution, voted for unanimously by the American Communists and the sixty-five other Communist delegations present in Moscow in 1935, was compulsory reading throughout the party. In countless inner-party conferences, the comrades drilled themselves in the necessity of aiding the Soviet Union in every emergency and specifically in case of war. I can remember Alexander Bittelman, painfully and precisely, asking the *Daily Worker* staff what the words of the Seventh Congress resolution meant, and giving the answer as "eternal active preparation, to aid the Soviet Union in every struggle, particularly including military conquest."

If you could have accompanied me into the branch meetings of the party while I was a member, you would have learned to respect the power of this program. It is perused and talked over seriously night after night. With even more intensity this study continues on the higher rungs of the party's hierarchical ladder, and on the Ninth Floor the document is quoted repeatedly and at great length.

The precepts of that document have been put into effect in the paralysis in the Pacific caused by the Hawaii strike, in the spreading of the seamen's strikes to England in mid-1949, in the Allis-Chalmers and North American Aircraft shutdowns in the Hitler-Stalin Pact period right here in the United States. Each of these, as the two last were specifically called in my presence, were "exercises" for revolutionary action against this country.

What does this program tell the Communists to do? In the beginning it lays down its aim, and only the most obtuse can fail to grasp what it signifies: "This program of the Communist International . . . *becomes the program of struggle for the world proletarian dictatorship, the program of struggle for world communism.*"

It will be observed, as every leading Communist (including myself) when explaining this sentence did observe, that it is the *world* proletarian dictatorship which is the goal—a dictatorship to be set up, as the Communists have declared in all their official proclamations, under the leadership and guidance of Stalin. That includes specifically and above all the United States, which the document calls derisively the "Dollar Republic." The contest must go on until all opponents of the Soviet State are destroyed, for "two antagonistic systems are now contending with each other," and they cannot be reconciled.

If war should come between them, the orders are explicit: "In the event of the imperialist states' declaring war upon and attacking the U.S.S.R., the international proletariat must retaliate by organizing bold and determined mass action and struggling for the overthrow of the imperialistic governments with the slogan of: Dictatorship of the Proletariat and Alliance with the U.S.S.R."

Another objective set forth in the program is revolt in the colonial countries—China, for instance. The Soviet dictatorships thus created are to be brought into the "growing Federation of Soviet Republics" headed by the U.S.S.R.

By way of preparation, the Reds are ordered specifically to cultivate legal and illegal forms of activity. This is the tactic recommended by Lenin—to work within the framework of the law as far as possible in order to develop better those violent and subversive forms of action clearly in violation of the law. This also includes interpreting the law in such a way as to throw a mantle of "civil rights" around subversion. The Reds are further ordered to keep always before them the slogans of the Communist International: "Convert imperialist war into civil war; defeat 'your own' imperialist government; defend the U.S.S.R. and the colonies by every possible means in event of imperialist war against them."

Upon all Reds everywhere is rigidly imposed what they refer to as "international proletarian discipline." On many occasions and in many different places—from the home of the Hollywood writer, Albert Maltz, to tiny apartments in the Bronx—I have lectured on the importance of "discipline," the iron necessity of thinking with Stalin, speaking as does Stalin, and acting with Stalin. The one army thus created, a huge army of sedition, is the guarantee of that Soviet world conquest to which the Communists now so confidently point.

When the hour of insurrection arrives—and Stalin is the guide and leader who will decide that hour—the Reds are to resort to mass agitation for defeatism and the government's overthrow, and to mass action, "a combination of strikes and demonstrations," becoming ever more violent and insurrectionary.

On that day—S-Day—as the Reds plan it, the American people will find it too late to defend themselves. Stalin has given the Communists a rule for conspiracy and they preach it zealously: "It takes a thousand men to build a bridge but one can blow it up." It was said originally in reference to the Trotskyite conspirators, but it is also the law of conspiracy for the Stalinists. One Red is supposed to be "as a thousand men or more," an expression that remains in my memory from its frequent repetition in Communist discussions.

Through the acts of Red agents at first disguised as non-Reds, coal would not move rapidly enough. Steel production would be shut down. Our aircraft would be turned out in insufficient quantities. Transportation and communication would be paralyzed. Concealed Communists would spread confusion in many of our organs of public opinion. Rancors and dissensions over racial and religious matters would be intensified, leading to wide divisions among the people. Too late the American people would learn that they had been victimized by their own complacency, their desire to be "liberal" to the Reds. They would be confronted with a colossal national Pearl Harbor.

The political strike, whipped into hurricane proportions in the armed insurrection of the workers, is the device by which the Communists plan to attain their goal.* The political strike, provoked and manipulated by disguised Red agents, begins often as a demand for rises in wages or changes in working conditions; it is

---

* The political strike is a paralysis of industry brought about primarily in order to win a political end rather than merely to gain better wages, hours or working conditions. The final goal of the political strike in Red hands is the overthrow of the government and the establishment of the Soviet dictatorship on its ruins.

then stimulated by Communist agitators and armed bands into a frenzy of destruction. Therein lies its peculiar advantage: it gives disguised Communists, using the original economic demands, a chance to move thousands of completely non-Communist workers and others into action against their country.

The essential idea, as we Reds learned over and over, is the seizure of power by a small but disciplined Red minority. The Red bands are to be thoroughly armed, and taking advantage of the strike crisis they have whipped up, will speak in the name of the workers. Wherever possible, they are to prepare the way through "coalition governments" in which they will have charge of the police and if possible the military. This will give them additional arms and destroy resistance to Communist violence.

The plan relies upon a state of collapse or confusion, induced from within and without, in the country to be conquered. This is the way in which a handful of Reds, aided by the Soviet Union's economic strangulation of the eastern European countries, have seized Poland, Hungary, Czechoslovakia, and Yugoslavia.

No better explanation has been made of the political strike and the machinery set up by the Communist fifth column to make it deadly than that given in 1939 by Morris Childs, district leader of the party in Chicago. The talk was presented to the secret class in leadership, known as the District Training School. Childs and I had ridden out there together, to a nondescript business block in the West Side of Chicago. Up one flight of stairs was the office of a doctor connected with the International Workers Order; proceeding through his suite, we were conducted to a room which was vacant save for some chairs around the walls. There sat the wife of an Italian-American coal miner, Mucci, from southern Illinois; Claude Lightfoot, an alert young Negro; and four other women and six other men in all.

In his talk Childs emphasized the part the political strike had played in the Bolshevik Revolution and showed how it had allowed Lenin's followers to seize power. Then he pointed to the San Francisco general strike of July, 1934, in which "the Communists [led from underground by Comrade Edwards, the representative of the Communist International] turned the demands of the marine workers into a demonstration of strength paralyzing all San Francisco."

"That was a political exercise in revolution," Childs went on to say, "which was the answer of the Communists to Roosevelt's refusal to recognize the Soviet Union's campaign for peace. It was a demonstration that munitions to China could be shut off, if sometime in the future there should be a continued flow of war goods against a Soviet China. At the same time the party sent John Howard Lawson, the playwright, to the Alabama coal-mining areas to speed up the political strike there, and sought a general strike when the workers walked out in Toledo and elsewhere. We were striving to give the American workers an education in the necessity of 'storming the citadels of capitalism' by force, as our great leader Stalin has directed us to do."

Talking out of the side of his mouth and chewing gum violently, as he generally did, Childs then outlined the "apparatus" that had been established to assure the success of political strikes. The key to this success was the system of concentration districts to which so much attention is given at every session of the party's National Committee. The men at the head of these districts are "veterans in revolutionary tactics," as Childs stated, "trained in the Lenin School at Moscow."

It was up to these trained revolutionists, Childs continued, to bring forward gradually in the political strike "radical transitional slogans"—such as nationalization of banks, workers' control of industry—which would be raised publicly by the Communists as such. Then, solemnly, he picked up the master textbook, *The Program of the Communist International,* and turned to the section on "Strategy and Tactics." Slowly he emphasized the importance of the "mass action" of which the political strike is a part.

Deliberately he read: "This mass action includes: A combination of strikes and demonstrations; a combination of strikes and

armed demonstrations; and finally, the general strike conjointly
with armed insurrection against the state power of the *bourgeoisie*.
The latter form of struggle, which is the supreme form, must be
conducted according to the rules of war."

The American Communists must be particularly thorough in
making preparations for revolutionary mass action, Childs stressed,
since Lenin and Stalin had particularly singled out the United
States as a country in which such tactics would have to be used.

"Since in our day socialism has been victorious in the Soviet
Union, under the leadership of Comrade Stalin," the speaker con-
tinued, "and since Stalin is the great scientist who has succeeded
Marx, Engels and Lenin, it is Stalin's call through the international
communist movement that will alert us for this gigantic task. It is
Stalin's revolutionary works we must study above all, Stalin's every
statement we must follow, and loyalty to Stalin as pledged at the
Seventh Congress must be the keystone to our conduct."

The concentration districts created by the Extraordinary Conference of 1933—the political offspring of Gussev and Eisler—
here loom up in their proper proportion. Into these areas which
contain the basic industries—steel, coal, automobiles, aircraft, maritime, machine manufacture and electrical equipment—the party
pours its chief resources in money, personnel and planning. In the
1948 party Convention, again, the vital urgency of enlarging Red
power and influence in the concentration districts was stressed.
The reason which was given then is the reason always receiving
consideration: the key character of the basic industries in war.

Indeed, the plot was given new life in the Convention's chief
report and resolution dealing with the "Concentration Policy."
In order to be able to prostrate America, there must be *concentration within concentration*, it was decreed. "Concretely," said
Henry Winston of the Politburo, making the report, "while we
must strengthen our base in all industrial states, we must above
all shift our main emphasis to such states as Illinois, Ohio and
Michigan and to Western Pennsylvania. While we must

strengthen the party in all basic industries, we must particularly select for major concentration such industries as steel, auto, mining, maritime, electrical and railroad. Within these industries, we must pursue a policy of concentration in key industrial towns and key plants and departments—with special concentration in the most underpaid sections of the workers, the unskilled and semiskilled. In some districts additional industries may be selected, for instance textile in the South and New England; in Ohio rubber, in addition to steel and mining, etc."

With the utmost detail, in one-two-three order, Winston—who was one of the eleven defendants in the 1949 trial—works out the methods by which each industry may be penetrated. He shows how the workers can be trained in "class consciousness," and how effective cadres can be built. The guiding slogan in this work is Comrade Stalin's famous phrase, "Cadres decide everything." (This expression in itself is a military term. The cadres of the Communists are the trained key Reds in each plant, union, or community vested with the responsibility of instructing others. They are the noncommissioned officers of the revolution.)

In his report, Winston complained that the Communists had not made so much progress in rooting themselves in the key industries as they wished. But that is an old Communist dodge to keep the comrades on their toes, to intensify the frenzy with which they plunge into their assignments. All the years that I was in the party, I heard at every National Committee session the claim that we Reds had not reached the mark set for us; and a big change of line, when it came, was always blamed upon the fact that the comrades had not worked hard enough for the previous line. Sometimes solemnly, sometimes hysterically, the comrades would repeat their self-accusations, over and over again, even though every one knew (in the National Committee, at least) that the change had been dictated by Moscow.

Political strikes, as a matter of record, have always been a potent Red weapon. At a meeting of the Politburo in the early summer of 1941, before the Germans marched into the Soviet Union, I listened to several members boastfully estimating the amount of damage Communist-led and Communist-stimulated strikes and slowdowns had done to America's preparedness program, and to the flow of supplies to England. This was "the Soviet Union's contribution to the pact with Germany."

That meeting on the Ninth Floor I shall not soon forget. For there I heard Foster threaten the American workers. If they "did not rise further in their responsibilities and fight against the coming war with all weapons," he said, they would suffer punishment. Punishment was to come obviously from the combined Soviet-Nazi forces. The threat was repeated in the resolution prepared for the 1948 National Convention of the party: "Let the American working class," says this blackmailing resolution, "guard against a course that would bring upon it the judgment pronounced upon the German working class for deserting its vanguard party—and for sharing the guilt of the Third Reich against humanity!"

In effect, the American workers were told that they would be exterminated or beaten into slavery by the victorious Red Army (who else could mete out this punishment?) unless they were willing to betray their native land. It is a threat that struck me in the early '40's, and should strike you now, because it gives a new indication of the fact that when the Reds talk of the best interests of the "proletariat," they do not mean the working people but the Soviet dictatorship.

The backbone of the party in concentration work and in preparing for political strikes is the party cadres to which Winston referred. These key men of the Soviet fifth column, working in the shadows, as Eisler and Peters worked, are the faithful and well-trained comrades who are sent into the basic industry areas; as Winston said, "our most capable comrades were assigned to these key districts, national coordinators were assigned to key industries." Specifically, they are charged with the task of making the concentration-district plan and the political strike successful when Moscow so decrees. It is also their duty to Russify active party people in these key centers, teaching them to think in Russian terms and drilling them in Russian experiences, so that their loyalty, as I heard Trachtenberg say, will be "more and more associated with the Soviet fatherland."

Among men who stand high in Red estimation for their subversive work in the key industries are the Russian-born William Schneiderman, who was saved from citizenship cancellation and deportation by the Supreme Court, and the alien John Williamson. They are regarded as masters in the art of establishing cadres trained for the political strike and its culmination on S-Day.

There are two others, however, who have not been so much in the public prints (not at all in fact), who have contributed even more to the setup. One is Martin Young, who directed on a national scale the formation of secret cells, i.e., organized groups of both open and concealed Communists, in the steel industry while ostensibly functioning as district organizer in Pittsburgh. The other leader in Red infiltration is John Steuben, who directed both steel and automobile infiltration while supposedly section organizer in Youngstown, Ohio.

Early in my Communist career I heard of Young as "a comrade of such extensive revolutionary education and experience" as to be a right hand to Eisler and Stachel in cadre-building. Since it was Stachel who told me this (it being essential that I know of Young's status in my work then as labor editor of the *Daily Worker*), I always held Young in great respect as a Red leader.

When I first met him, at a National Committee meeting in 1937, I was surprised to find him such a mild-mannered man. He was unnaturally slight in build at that time, as though he were ill, and he spoke in soft and almost whispered tones, inclining his head to one side as though he were always listening as well as talking. Yet the party had gone to great extremes to make sure that he would be able to function in the United States. Through elaborate preparations engineered by party headquarters, he had been illegally smuggled off a ship into this country and had been protected by a number of false statements about his residence and citizenship here. I had been told a thrilling story of his being ordered into this country from Europe by those who rule the underground for the Communist International, of his escape from the ship in New York harbor as planned, and of his being hidden in Manhattan tenements until a name and explanation for his presence could be invented.

During the Hitler-Stalin alliance, Young was one of the first of the leading Communists to go undercover, and from his concealed post became even more active than he had been before. Besides directing Red infiltration of the steel industry, he took on the added job of controlling the leaders of the Greater New York CIO Industrial Council. And when John Santo, political representative of the party in the Transport Workers Union, was drafted for the army, Young secretly took over his responsibilities.

Since social life from an undercover post can become somewhat irksome, I was instructed to visit Young and his wife from time to time as he changed residence (or at least changed apartments for meeting). My wife accompanied me, and on one of these occasions John Steuben and his wife were also there. They were living a strictly concealed existence since he too was directing concentration work.

Steuben was regarded as an expert at imbuing the comrades who were later to be trained for special concentration work with a consciousness of things Russian. Requested to enlighten others about his methods, he wrote a detailed article in the *Daily Worker* of January 11, 1936—at the very time when the Communists were beginning to talk as though they were for Roosevelt. Citing a successful campaign for *Daily Worker* subscriptions, a vital educational task in concentration areas, he wrote: "We brought to the comrades the experiences of the Russian Comrades, how they established the 'Iskra'; we combined this with Lenin's recommendation for a revolutionary newspaper in the U.S.A. We have also read to the comrades from the book of Comrade Piatnitsky, *Memoirs of a Bolshevik,* how they distributed the paper. It was on this basis, on these facts, that we were able to develop real enthusiasm."

This was no casual comment. It was an article recommended for study and appropriate imitation to all section organizers.

It was during one of the undercover visits with Young that I learned of the "creeping blitzkrieg" planned by Soviet Russia against the United States—and coincidentally I was told by Young himself of his contact as a courier with the Soviet consulate. This was not a social evening but a secret apartment-house meeting, called to acquaint the comrades functioning openly at Thirteenth Street with what was occurring in the underground work in the basic industries. When Young told me of the plan for taking over one country after another "in Hitler fashion but in slower motion, in order not to arouse America too soon," he revealed himself—both in that knowledge and in his co-operation with the consulate—as indeed an important agent of Moscow.

The comrades' reasoning on concentration is that if they control labor action in the basic industries (for they may never acquire control of the trade unions completely) they will be able to wreck American economy any time they choose to do so. It is in that spirit that the head of the Communist-led World Federation of Trade Unions recently boasted of Red control of the United Electrical, Radio and Machine Workers Union and some other labor organizations in the United States. If they cannot succeed in capturing the head offices in many trade unions (though they will try for that by every means at their command) they will be content with substantial hidden nuclei in every key industry and industrial locality. These will form the centers of disaffection and unrest in case of any internal or external crisis.

But the comrades also pay much attention to other groups in the key American industrial communities—Negroes, veterans, women, and youth groups. Such labors are commanded by the

Program of the Communist International, and it is followed scrupulously.

The principal stronghold of recent Communist influence in the youth movement has been the American Youth for Democracy, which, though the comrades try to deny it, is the successor of the Young Communist League. The latter organization was not successful in attracting wide groups of young people, largely because of its name. A projected change of name, but not of purpose, was advertised long in advance by the *Daily Worker* and other Red papers. In one article, Max Weiss, former chief of the organization, made a lengthy analysis of the league, emphasizing that the proposal "to change the program and name of the YCL and to broaden its leadership" must be accompanied by continued education in Marxism within the league. That meant that Communist control should continue, though now concealed. At the meeting which definitely changed the name, Israel Amter, New York Communist leader, solemnly warned Carl Ross, then an important league official, that the organization had been born under the banner of "Long live the world proletarian dictatorship," and that this must continue to be its guiding slogan.

Overnight the name of the Young Communist League was changed to the American Youth for Democracy, and Ross was metamorphosed from executive secretary of the YCL into national secretary of the AYD. This change was dictated in part by the Communists' experience with the American Youth Congress, which had proved to be a valuable agency for them during the Hitler-Stalin Pact. The AYC was a federation of youth organizations, whose capture by the Reds had been ordered by the Politburo, and achieved by the YCL. It was regarded as a medium through which the Young Communist League, which became a member of it, could reach out and influence wider sections of young Americans. The Communist control of the AYC, which became increasingly obvious as time went on, drove many young people away from it. The adoption of the name American Youth for Democracy by the

Young Communist League was designed to recapture some of the unwary among these young men and women, and again broaden Red influence among the youth of the nation.

The change occurred in 1943, when the Communists were under instructions to make America believe they were about to fold up. In the National Committee meeting to which the AYD's creation was reported by Ross and Weiss, the old 1927 orders of the Young Communist International to its youth were read and emphasized as still the guiding objective of the party's youth work. The resolution was entitled "War Danger and the Importance of the Factory Nuclei of the Young Communists," and is therefore most pertinent to the S-Day plans.

It said in part—and it was this portion which was emphasized in the National Committee—"The factories producing war materials are the vital nerve of imperialist war. Imperialist war can be hit at its weakest spot by a cessation and sabotage of the production of shells, cannon, submarines, and every description of war material. The strikes in the ammunition and poison gas factories and in ship-building yards are generally the reflection of the mood of the soldiers at the front. In this manner, imperialist war may be dealt a fatal blow by the mass strike, that is, civil war begins, waged by the proletariat against imperialist war.

"We must therefore attach special importance to the creation of nuclei in the undertaking of supplying of war materials. We must strive tenaciously to capture these strongholds for our fight against imperialist war."

Thus the Reds, with their usual proficiency, were able to draw in thousands of young people who were not Communists and to put them to work under the AYD for Stalin's purposes. Meanwhile, the solid core of genuine Communist youth (trained in the undercover schools of the party) was steeling itself for the real goal of all this activity—and through its contacts recruiting new agents from the AYD ranks.

Today, the Soviet fifth column has decided upon a new tack, in order to mobilize young people more effectively for militant work against "American imperialism." In its 1948 Convention, it resolved to launch a "new" organization as a supplement to the AYD, one that will be more definitely committed to Marxism-Leninism. This is in line with the decision made informally, while I was still in the party, that the necessity of aiding Soviet Russia in the battle against the United States required a more consciously "revolutionary" youth group. Such an organization would establish closer ties with the concentration districts for the sabotage of work in the war plants, as provided in the classical resolution of the Young Communist International.

In addition to the youth, Negroes, women and veterans were the subjects of the recruitment refrain than ran through all Communist reports in all committee meetings.

Owing to Stalin's emphasis of the "national question," and to his command to arouse the "colonial peoples" against the United States along with the "workers," the chief of these groups, as far as Communist propaganda goes, is the Negro community. The thunder of revolutionary guns was scarcely stilled in Russia before American Communists were busily trying to sow discord among Negroes. Taking advantage of the Negro's legitimate complaints, the comrades began to raise the issue of "self-determination in the Black Belt."

When I joined the party in 1935, the Reds were still clamoring for the creation of a Negro republic, to be separated from the United States, by force if necessary. Many leading Negroes rightly denounced the proposal as putting them in a false and dangerous position; it was a cruel trick to sacrifice the Negro people to the propaganda needs of the Soviet dictatorship. But in 1936, when the Communists decided it was expedient to support Mr. Roosevelt and make more friends, they withdrew their "self-determination" slogan. However it was, like all Red "revolutionary" programs, only shelved temporarily and not actually withdrawn. During the next dozen years the manner in which the Communists handled the Negro question showed, as clearly as anything else has done, their utter subservience to Moscow and their complete cynicism toward the colored man. Whenever the Soviet dictatorship's opposition to America was strong, as during the period of the Hitler-Stalin Pact, the Communists' cry for "Negro rights" reached a shrill height. In March of 1940 the party appealed to the Negro people to fight "against the imperialist war," and special men were dispatched into the big industrial areas—Detroit, in particular—to stir up racial differences. When Russia was attacked, the comrades immediately called upon the Negroes to make no demands!

Behind the scenes, the opposition to Negro rights was even more pronounced. I recall one meeting early in 1943 at which Alexander Bittelman sharply reprimanded the Communist Negro leader James Ford for suggesting that the issue of Negro discrimination be raised. Since Bittelman was recognized as the voice of Moscow, Ford humbly reversed himself and wrote an article, in accordance with his instructions, urging that Negroes resign their rights and proclaiming that "the defense of the Soviet Union" was above all other considerations.

It is a sign of the new times that the demand for the Negro republic was revived at the 1948 Communist Convention. There it was agreed, in effect, to return to this objective if and when the time seemed ripe. In a subsequent issue of *Political Affairs,* Claudia Jones, alien Negro Communist, presented a graphic description of the area to be covered by the projected republic. It included most of the southern states.

A new and intense campaign among the Negroes has now been inaugurated. By June, 1949, the party was convulsed with trials charging certain of its members with "white chauvinism"—an incorrect attitude toward the Negroes. This became a major concern, receiving the entire issue of *Political Affairs* for that month, though the offenses for which the comrades were tried, it was admitted, had existed for some time in the party. Trials of this sort are always the prelude to the renewal of an old line. In this case they forecast a return to the old tactic of stirring up widespread feeling about Negro discrimination. The legitimate hopes of the Negro people for a broadening of their opportunities are thus made the front for the Soviet program of dividing America. The reason for this sudden all-out campaign is stated by John Williamson for the Politburo: it is the comrades' reply to America's determination "to achieve domination of the world . . . and to unleash imperialist war against the Soviet Union, the People's Democracies and the freedom-striving colonial peoples."

The harsh lot of the Mexican-Americans also figures largely in the Communists' plans. The abuses to which they have been subjected were retailed at some length in resolutions at the Communist National Convention and in subsequent directives to the comrades. Secret schools for training Mexican-Americans to work for the Red cause among their own people have been set up. The agency of infiltration in their case is the Communist-controlled Food, Tobacco, Agricultural and Allied Workers of America, which was recently expelled from the CIO. Not only in Texas, but in California and a number of other states, this union has always sought out the Mexican-Americans, with the aim of making these migratory workers and their undoubted exploitation the occasion for additional disruptions in American life.

There is not room for one thin doubt that the comrades are preparing in a deadly, intent way to paralyze American production by every means and utilizing every possible group. These plans are not static; they lead to results. Too many incidents illustrate how the Soviet fifth column has been able to unsettle American industry. There was the conference on the third floor of Thirteenth Street (in what were then the classrooms of the Workers School) which took place in 1936, shortly after I entered the party. My sworn statement on this affair has been given in my testimony under subpoena on James Matles of the United Electrical, Radio and Machine Workers Union and his relations to the Communist party, before the subcommittee of the House Committee on Labor. The sole purpose of that third-floor conference was to determine how far the Reds could go in tying up the Port of New York, in case of "imperialist war." The leader of the discussion was John Santo, the powerful representative of Moscow among the transportation trade unions here, but the report was given by James Matles, who still has a dominant position in the Red-controlled UE. He stated that the aim of the Reds around New York was to get such a grip on subways and busses, the maritime unions, and the radio and telegraphers' organizations as to make it possible to bring New York to a complete standstill. By way of accomplishment, he reported, the party already was beginning to get a good foothold in the Transport Workers Union; an equally good start had been made in the National Maritime Union; and a third target was the American Communications Association. (Incidentally, Mervyn Rathborne of that organization was sitting in on the conference.) President Michael Quill of the TWU, when he announced his break with the Communist party in 1948, confirmed that secret meetings of this character, i.e., between Communist leaders and top union officials, had been held.

While Joseph Curran of the NMU and Rathborne, too, have since also broken with the party, it still retains a series of cells in the unions of the Port of New York. Its hope is now, through the Red-dominated Fur Workers Union and other such groups, to extend its control as it did originally when Santo directed the proceedings. The United Electrical, Radio and Machine Workers Union is also scheduled to play a large part in the spread of Red control, by supplying both funds and organizers for the infiltration of other unions.

Another incident in my memory is the meeting at the home of Mrs. Meta Berger, in Milwaukee, at which Eugene Dennis (denouncing Roosevelt as "another Hitler") ordered Harold Christoffel to strike the men at Allis-Chalmers. That particular "exercise in revolution" was directed against Great Britain, which was then making a last-ditch fight against destruction. It is a matter of record that the strike did take place, that Christoffel and his associates stuffed the ballots for the strike with two thousand false "Yes" votes, and that war matériel of the most valuable kind was tied up for months.

As a final example, there was the never-to-be-forgotten Politburo session in the Fall of 1945 (one of the last I attended) which heard Foster's impassioned plea, based on Moscow's orders, to get busy on big strike preparations once more. Plans were made then for American Red participation in shutting down all shipping in the free world. The plan, as outlined by Foster, included "activization" of AF of L members, and counted heavily on working through the World Federation of Trade Unions, which is Red-ruled. Significant of the callous manner in which the Reds use the workers were the bald instructions to the comrades (later repeated in print by Williamson) to hunt around for issues that would "radicalize" the AF of L members. It was a bold admission that they will manufacture these "issues" if necessary for their purposes.

Although these schemes have not gone through exactly as mapped out, they have had a big influence on recent shutdowns throughout the free world.

Americans have meanwhile sat quietly by, doing little about such plots and preparations on the part of the Reds. The master key to the Soviet conquest of the United States might well be our own complacency.

In his book, *Toward Soviet America,* Foster prophesied: "People who think the revolution is impossible in America are going to be deceived." And, let us remember, "the revolution" has always been the conquest of a country by small but well organized armed bands fanatically dedicated to Stalin, aided by Soviet secret agents and the paralysis of the country's economic life. The keys to conquest have been forged here, too; the question is Can America break them?

(VIII)

Red Web in Labor

WHEN the Second Congress of the Soviet-controlled World Federation of Trade Unions met in Milan during July, 1949, it was revealed that the organization planned to set up world departments for each of the different trade unions—that is, to solidify the unions in each industry or group of industries into one world-wide trade department under Soviet control. From the discussion it was plain that the purpose of the departmental arrangement was to make it possible, under pretense of "defending the trade union, economic and social rights of the workers" in various industries and countries, to tie up the production of the whole democratic world, and by calling strikes at critical moments to create chaos in the economies of all the democratic countries, if desirable, simultaneously. And the man publicly introduced as the official in charge of the trade departments of the WFTU was my former comrade in conspiracy, Boleslaw Gebert.

To put it bluntly, Gebert (who fled on the *Batory* with the connivance of the Red Polish government) is now responsible for directing a shutdown of factories or transportation in the Atlantic community whenever possible, feasible or desirable in Moscow's eyes.

An outgrowth of the WFTU's departmental activities, as directed by Gebert, was the creation of the Red-ruled world organization of maritime workers, under the presidency of Harry Bridges. This development followed shortly after the close of the Milan congress, and led to official threats by the CIO to expel Bridges from that federation.

When we link the new departmental setup with Moscow's open threat that the western European countries will never be permitted to trade on a healthy basis with eastern Europe, we understand much more clearly the peril involved. The entire plan is not only an iron-fist answer to the Marshall Plan, as it purports to be; it is obviously a rounded-out scheme to create artificial depression conditions in the United States and among its friends by cutting down their domestic production and their foreign trade.

How completely the Second Congress of the WFTU was under the Kremlin's thumb may be learned from the proceedings. The workers of the Soviet Union were hailed as "emancipated brothers," enjoying that "freedom" which the rest would like to possess. The leaders of the American workers in the American Federation of Labor and the Congress of Industrial Organizations—who have won conditions and real wages which the workers in Russia have never dreamed of as present-day possibilities—were denounced as "servitors" of "the American and British imperialists and their criminal plans."

Several weeks prior to the congress the Soviet organs throughout the world had laid down a bitter barrage against President Philip Murray of the CIO and President William Green of the AF of L as "agents of the American monopolies." The cause for this prolonged outburst was the withdrawal of the CIO, the British Trades Union Congress and a number of other national trade-union centers from the WFTU. Their withdrawal was a prelude to the formation of a new international federation of free unions, anti-Communist in character, with which both the AF of L and the CIO affiliated.

What the British and American labor movements would have had to swallow as members of the WFTU was brought out with typical Red arrogance at the Congress. In the address of the president, Giuseppe di Vittorio, the line was laid down thus: "*The imperialists of the United States and Great Britain broke the soli-*

darity among the Allied Powers. . . . They launched a disgraceful campaign of calumny against the Soviet Union and the other countries which have rid themselves once and for all of every species of exploitation." (The italics are mine.)

Di Vittorio's keynote was another piece of Soviet propaganda— the statement that the United States is wracked by unemployment, and "only in the Soviet Union and in the other countries that have put an end to the capitalist system crises, depressions and unemployment are unknown."

It is hardly necessary to point out that any country could proclaim it had no unemployment if it stowed away fifteen to twenty million workers in concentration camps. Hitler, too, could make such a boast.

For America and all Atlantic-community countries the Congress went even further and resolved—through the directives given the delegates by V. V. Kuznetsov of the Soviet trade-union delegation— to carry the "fight against the splitters" into their own organizations everywhere. That move was ordered by Comrade Kuznetsov and endorsed by the Congress in July, and in August the Communist and pro-Communist leadership of certain unions in the CIO proceeded to carry out these instructions.

These seasoned followers of the party line and tactics met in New York and resolved to place the burden of the split which they meant to make, if necessary, on President Philip Murray and the CIO. The advance arguments for the move were given by the *Daily Worker*:

"Just as some 10 unions who in 1935 formed the Committee for Industrial Organization to advance industrial unionism and organization of the unorganized *within the AFL* were expelled, so an approximately like number of unions with about a like number of members are facing expulsion now from the CIO." Then comes the knockout sentence: *"The CIO is fast taking on the image of the AFL of 1935."*

That then will be the tune: that the Congress of Industrial

Organizations, once a worth-while union grouping (when it took in the Reds in leading positions), has now begun to decay. As a "bureaucratically controlled" group (a favorite Red phrase for its enemies) it is expelling the "progressive-minded" unions under Red and pro-Red leadership. From that premise warfare will be opened against both AF of L and CIO, with the strikebreaking witnessed during the days of Red trade unions in the late twenties.

The Communists were able to plan such a strategy with some confidence because they have successfully penetrated a number of divisions of the labor movement. Everyone knows of such infiltration, but few people have any but the foggiest idea how it was accomplished.

The Red technique of gaining control of a labor union is the same, on a smaller scale and with slight modifications, as that used by the Soviet Union in taking over the governments of its neighbors in eastern Europe and the Far East.

When the Communists set out to infiltrate a local union they join in pairs, or in larger numbers if possible. All of them have been carefully trained in special schools for the work. In a variety of ways they try to make themselves indispensable. If a thankless office is unfilled, they volunteer for it; if a difficult or distasteful job is undone, they do it. Thus they build up reputations as hard workers for the union.

As time goes on, they try to get themselves into such strategic posts as executive secretary, educational director or legislative agent. Each one of these positions can be used to commit the union to certain stands without its full approval, to aid causes which forward Soviet Russia's immediate objectives and to influence the membership favorably toward Red purposes.

Once the Communists have established themselves as important members of a union, they begin to test their strength, trying to uncover potential party members or fellow travelers. They do this by the process of introducing at union meetings resolutions which express progressively the current Communist line. Careful notes are made of those voting with the comrades. Finally, a hotter resolution is brought forward, denouncing the United States for its "imperialistic foreign policy," and perhaps even endorsing the "peace policy" of Soviet Russia. Those who favor that resolution are secretly asked to join the Red "fraction."

If enough members join, the party then prepares to take over so far as dominating the union is concerned. A resolution plainly Red in aim is introduced, such as a proposal to donate money to the defense of Harold R. Christoffel or of the eleven Communist leaders; or perhaps a statement denouncing President Truman as "imperialistic" is brought to the floor. By bickering and arguing the Red fraction delays adjournment until most of the non-Red members have tired and gone home. Then, usually without even a quorum present, the resolution is passed and the party line or party resolution becomes the official pronouncement of the union. It will be cited by other Reds in other unions as evidence that their organizations should do the same thing.

Once small and active units of Communists have been planted throughout the union, at the proper time the demand is made for a united front of all groups within the organization. Often the proportion on an original executive board of the union may be as great as 4 to 1 against the Communists. But it is often in an amazingly short time that the Reds have changed this to a majority in their favor. The procedure in general is simple. Among the four non-Communist members on the board may be a concealed Communist who pretends to be something else.

This concealed Communist will approach the most ambitious or malleable of the board members with a program of action which he suggests this ambitious one forward in the organization. This will make a leader of him, the concealed Communist says. Jumping at the chance, our ambitious board member submits the program; to his tickled surprise he puts it over, since of course the open Communist votes with him as well as the concealed Communist. Thereupon, it is suggested that the new leader get rid of the most obstreperous of the "opposition members." Again the vote is 3 to 2. The new board member, it goes without saying, will be either another Communist or someone they can count on. Thus in time the "leader" finds himself at the mercy of the Communists. The united front has proved to be a device for Red control.

Sometimes the board members will wake up to what is happening before this dire fate is meted out to them. Then the Communists will seek to ruin if they cannot rule. They will create disorders, cry fraud, and endeavor to confuse the issue in the public mind.

(This is the procedure, incidentally, that the Communists use to get control of any kind of organization, not solely of labor unions.)

If a union member or official refuses to have anything to do with the Communist fraction, and divulges whatever Red offer has been made to him, the comrades immediately smear him without mercy. Scandalous rumors are circulated about his private life. If he is an official, demands are made that he be investigated. He is denounced as a Red-baiter, a labor spy and a gangster. Sometimes the Reds even accuse him of being a Communist or of asking to be one.

William Z. Foster once fired this last accusation at Walter Reuther. In June of 1941, when Reuther was fighting the Communists who were trying to prolong the strike at the plant of the North American Aviation Company in California, Foster asserted that Reuther had "even tried for membership in the Communist party, and was rejected on the grounds of his obvious opportunism." The charge was even published in an article in the *Daily Worker*. I know Reuther made no such attempt, because only a short time before I had been sent out to Detroit by the Politburo to try to persuade him to join the Red "top fraction" in the UAW. He flatly refused to do so. But what Foster was doing was provoking the recollection that Reuther had gone as a very young man to Soviet Russia, had worked in some of its auto factories, and originally had not been hostile to the Soviet regime.

When the Communists complain of "Red-baiting," which is one

ot their favorite ways of intimidating liberals, this sample of their own Red-baiting can be produced to show their utter insincerity. It is only one of a number that could be drawn upon. When a number of National Maritime Union officers broke away from Communist control, the *Daily Worker* revealed that they had been secret party members all along. It is true that some of them, like Tommy Ray, had often been mentioned as notorious Reds, but the majority of them had always denied having any Communist affiliation.

If a union official indicates a willingness to go along with the Reds, the Communists immediately make a great to-do about "co-operating with the leadership." This tactic is a duplicate of their "coalition government" proposals, and is used always with a view to slitting the political throats of their newly found friends.

It is a co-operation, then, which leads to destruction, even for men admittedly alert and able. James B. Carey, first president of the UE and now national secretary of the CIO, is Exhibit A in this respect.

Carey was head of a small local union organized in 1935 in Philadelphia under an AF of L charter. About a year later, in late 1936, he took his local into the CIO and with it as a base organized the UE. In 1937 one of the few labor units then dominated by the Communists—a group in the light-metals industry—left the AF of L and joined Carey's new international union. The Communist leader of this group was James Matles, a man of considerable ability, who recently indicated his disaffiliation from the party. It was then that Donald Henderson, president of the farm workers' union, stated that he had resigned. The CIO accused them, nevertheless, of pursuing Red policies. Another leader in the group was Julius Emspak, a veteran of William Z. Foster's old Trade Union Unity League and a Communist organizer.

Matles speedily ingratiated himself with Carey and his associates and by promising whole-hearted co-operation managed to be chosen as an organizer for the UE in the light-metals field. He soon became national organizer, whereupon the Communists rushed into the union to form locals. Emspak, as we saw earlier, in time became general secretary of the UE. There is evidence that Carey knew what was going on but thought he would be able to handle the comrades and defeat them in a showdown. But the Communists turned many of the members against him with a whispering campaign in which he was denounced as a "yellow Social Democrat" and a "class collaborationist," which everyone understood to be a bosses' man. They fought him because he was an obstacle to their campaign to halt war production in 1940 and 1941 when the Reds were helping Hitler.

In September, 1941, when the UE held its Camden convention, the Reds worked out a scheme to take advantage of one large local union's dissatisfaction with some of Carey's inner-union policies. Hitler had by then attacked Soviet Russia, so the Communists were prepared to continue Carey in office if he would agree to go along with them in the future. This he wrathfully declined to do. The Reds then picked as their man Albert E. Fitzgerald, chief representative of the dissatisfied local, although he was not a member of the party.

The comrades' report on Fitzgerald noted that he liked "long week ends"; they promised themselves that if he would play along with them they would make him president of the UE and give him as many long week ends as he liked. The union of his forces and those influenced by the Reds supplied enough votes to win, and Fitzgerald was elected. Since then, Fitzgerald has been in policy accord with Emspak and Matles. Now in 1950 he joined them in leaving the CIO.

Carey's defeat, the result of thinking that smart labor leaders can control the Communists by co-operating with them, put 500,000 American workers under the domination of the Soviet fifth column in this country.

A roll call of the UE's officers, if the full truth could be told about them, would uncover a long list of Red devotees. The educational department, for instance, is directed by Ruth Young, a trustee of the Communist party's Jefferson School of Social Science, who was chairman of one of the New York party's convention sessions and spoke from the same public platform as Foster. Nominally she is secretary of one of the UE's largest districts, but from that post oversees the union's educational work. The union's newspaper, the *U. E. News,* is edited by Tom Wright. When I was managing editor of the *Daily Worker,* Wright often consulted with our editorial board.

When those unions which had been denounced as Red controlled by the CIO decided in late 1949 to take advantage of the National Relations Board, the officers of each swore to the non-Communist affidavits. Both Matles and Emspak did this, although at the same time refusing once more to tell a Congressional committee under oath whether or not they were or had been members of the Communist party.

The tactic of pitting one non-Communist against another, as in the case of Carey and Fitzgerald, is a favorite Red method of splitting up an anti-Communist majority. The fostering of quarrels and the furthering of inner-union bickering has always been one of the Communists' effective weapons.

I recall vividly a time when Bill Gebert, who was then supervising the penetration of the auto workers union, went so far as to offer Red support for the international union presidency to two different leading auto workers who were not permanently allied with the Communists, and thus managed to keep them welded together against Walter Reuther, whom the Communists wanted politically liquidated at all costs. Fearing that President R. J. Thomas of the union and General Secretary George F. Addes would run against each other and split the anti-Reuther forces, Gebert first had a prominent Detroit Communist, Nat Ganley, visit Thomas. Promises of support were made to him provided he would work closely with Addes, who was the long-run choice of the Reds for the presidency. Then Ganley and others were dispatched to

Addes, to urge him to be patient and bide his time, and to back Thomas for the time being. At that time, Thomas had too large a "conservative" following to be squelched in his ambitions, since he could have defeated Addes, though undoubtedly at the expense of a Reuther victory.

I sat in on many secret conferences in hotel rooms when various automobile workers' conventions were in session, and heard many such proposals gone over with Red delegates and their friends.

To make certain that there is no deviation from the party line by Communists, and to see that the Reds take advantage of every break, a high-ranking representative of the Politburo attends every labor convention held in the United States. When I was in the party, the representative was usually Roy Hudson or Rose Wortis, though in my first years as a Communist Jack Stachel also fulfilled this function; he was, I recall, at the United Mine Workers convention of 1936. And Gebert of course attended the automobile and steel conventions.

They would usually take rooms in an obscure hotel and from that point direct the comrades' activities. I have accompanied Hudson, Wortis and Gebert on many such trips, and have seen them, with the aid of a small minority of comrades, throw a labor convention into a turmoil which required days to settle.

There was a striking series of such uproars in the conventions of the United Automobile Workers during the presidency of Homer Martin. They arose in part from the fact that the auto workers were newly organized, but they were also stimulated by the Communists. In like manner, by organized booing and cheering, a number of vital meetings of the National Maritime Union in New York were brought under Red control. Almost all these demonstrations were aimed at the president, Joseph Curran, despite his then long-standing alliance with the Communists. Whenever he showed any sign of independence, in the early days, he received this kind of treatment.

I have also seen the Politburo representatives at the labor conventions call in a labor leader who had displeased them and give him a severe dressing down. During the United Automobile Workers Convention in Buffalo in 1941, for example, Lou Michener, who had led the strike at the North American Aviation plant, was soundly berated by Hudson and Gebert for not having conducted the strike skillfully enough. Harold Christoffel, in a somewhat similar scene, was told that while the Allis-Chalmers shutdown had been more effective than the North American, he was to avoid certain mistakes in the future. The lesson was read to him by Hudson, as he walked up and down the hotel room, slicing the air with his arms.

In hotels near the Boston convention of the CIO in 1943, I was present when men like Arthur Osman, president of the large Local 65 of the Retail and Wholesale Workers Union, CIO; Ben Gold, president of the wealthy International Fur and Leather Goods Workers Union; and members of the CIO staff who were Reds met to receive instructions from Roy Hudson. They went so far as to work out phrases which they planned to slip into President Murray's speeches in order to be able to use them later for their own purposes. In the old days, before 1949, when the Reds had many concealed posts at the CIO national headquarters, this game was played over and over again.

During the years that I was in the party, I helped to develop the labor infiltration technique, and I saw it operate many times to bring a labor union under the domination of the Communists. I know of no union in which the Communists comprise more than a small minority, but it is a minority often able to control thousands. For example, about 90 per cent of the *officers* of the United Electrical, Radio and Machine Workers Union are either Communists or under Communist discipline, while the *membership* is fully 95 per cent non-Communist.

Joseph Curran, president of the National Maritime Union, reported in 1947 that out of a total membership of some 70,000, not more than 500 were Communists. Yet this comparatively small group of comrades filled 107 of the Maritime Union's 150 national offices! They had been occupying those jobs in like proportions for a number of years.

An even smaller number of Communists kept the huge United Automobile Workers Union in constant turmoil under Gebert's direction, and for all practical purposes dominated it, until they were finally defeated by Walter Reuther.

Such successes, and the official actions of the Communist-dominated unions, illustrate what the Reds mean when they say, "One party member should be able to move at least a thousand persons in support of the party line." In many instances, a comrade in a key post moves many more than that number into pro-Soviet acts.

In their infiltration, "boring from within," the Communists literally stop at nothing and keep everlastingly at it. "Trade union democracy" and "unity" are slogans under which they cloak their designs—while through small Red groups they meet secretly in their own caucuses to push things through the union meetings in anything but democratic or united fashion. Fraud, falsehood and double-dealing on an unlimited scale are in their arsenal.

Three big aids to union infiltration in this country are the subversive office worker, the labor lawyer who is under Communist control, and the International Workers Order. To take the last first, this "fraternal insurance agency," with headquarters at 80 Fifth Avenue, New York, is so important that it might be called the first front of the Communist conspiracy. It was organized by Communists and has been under the control of Communists from the beginning, having been formed from a Communist split-off of the Social Democratic insurance organization, the Workman's Circle. It has had as national officers such conspicuous Communists as Max Bedacht, former general secretary of the Communist party, and Robert William Weiner, the party's financial agent. Outwardly giving the appearance of an ordinary insurance agency, it is everywhere heavily staffed with Communists and helps the party in innumerable ways. Its local offices throughout the country are used for secret Communist conferences, and its representatives (most of whom are not known as Communists) push the party line with great industry. The IWO also provides money for the work of the party. These funds, obtained from insurance payments, are contributed in one large sum through the device of taking big advertisements in the *Daily Worker*. In 1949, for instance, it contributed $4,000 to the defense of the eleven Communist party leaders, announcing that the sum represented donations from members in New York.

Most of the labor lawyers who work with and for the Communists are members of the National Lawyers Guild. As early as 1939, Earl Browder characterized the Guild as a "transmission belt" of the Communist party. Because of its persistent refusal to denounce Communism, many members have resigned from it, including former Attorney General Robert H. Jackson, now a Supreme Court justice, former Assistant Secretary of State Adolf A. Berle, Jr., and former Governor Charles Poletti of New York, who all left the Guild in 1940 because they held it was Communist-controlled. And indeed everything that it came out for while I was a Red was in accord with the party objective of the moment.

The Communist secretary in a union office turns over carbon copies of her employer's important letters to her Red political leader, reports confidential conversations overheard in the union office, and notes the names of her employer's visitors. It is as though an X-ray picture were being taken for the benefit of the Ninth Floor, to which all this material finds its way. Much of it got to me, as managing editor of the *Daily Worker*, to aid me in knowing how certain people should be handled editorially or in our news columns.

There have been two main phases in the Communist campaign to capture American labor, and we are now witnessing, in the program laid down at the Milan conference of the WFTU, the beginning of a third. The first phase opened in the fall of 1921, when William Z. Foster returned from an extended visit to Moscow. Having gone to the Soviet capital a non-Communist, he secretly joined the Communist party at that time. Publicly he organized the Trade Union Educational League. This organization made little headway, but it prepared the way for the Trade Union Unity League, formed in Cleveland in 1929. The Unity League immediately became the Communists' principal labor front; it was supposed eventually to supplant the American Federation of Labor.

During the half-dozen years that followed, the Communists worked openly toward their objectives. Not only did they boast of receiving orders from Moscow but, convinced that the world proletarian revolution under Stalin and the Communist domination of the globe were just around the corner, they filled their newspapers and magazines, and the party's own manifestoes and resolutions, with undisguised calls for the violent seizure of power in the United States.

To find material for organizing the Red corps from among the workers for this seizure of power, the Communists created independent unions, officered entirely by Reds and affiliated with the Unity League, or the TUUL as they called it. Among these were the National Textile Workers Union, the National Miners Union and the Steel and Metal Workers Industrial Union.

All these so-called unions were organized upon directives from Moscow in line with Stalin's prediction of an imminent "revolutionary situation" and the Kremlin's tactics of fostering the Red International of Labor Unions under S. Lozovsky in Moscow. Almost all the Communist unions, however, existed only on paper, for American workers refused to join them. Nevertheless, the Communists managed to do a great deal of harm; they were largely responsible for the slow progress of non-Communist labor organizing. Everywhere that union movements were launched, the Reds came into the picture to unloose vituperation upon the labor leaders and often to break up the AF of L unionizing efforts.

During the early 1930's, before I became a Communist, I was a special organizer for AF of L unions, working among the hosiery and other textile workers. I saw the Communists virtually destroy the textile drive of the federation in Paterson, New Jersey, Allentown, Pennsylvania, and Kenosha, Wisconsin.

In 1931 at Allentown, Pennsylvania, for instance, at the most critical moment in the American Federation of Labor's textile strike, the Communists sent in several scores of goons from Philadelphia to break up a key strike meeting which had been called to halt the return to work. Placing themselves around the stage in military formation, in which they clearly had been drilled, they held Carl Holderman, now president of the CIO in New Jersey, and me prisoners on the stage for about two hours. We had gone into the city especially to help out at this particularly serious time. Through interruptions, catcalls and other disorders they prevented the meeting from proceeding. Only the presence of mind of the local chairman, a young Italian-American textile worker, who talked almost the entire two hours, saved the day from the Red hoodlums. Having accomplished their purpose in halting the meeting, they permitted the people from the stage to retire.

They did a neat service for the antiunion mill owners by way of strike-breaking that evening, for after the failure of that meeting, the return to work the next day was pronounced. In Paterson, New Jersey, where I was in direct charge of the strike, the Communists tried the same thing, but our meetings were well guarded by our own men and they failed there.

In Kenosha, Wisconsin, in 1929, during the Allen-A strike, of which I was in charge, they likewise performed yeomen service for the antiunion company. They published an attack upon the AF of L strike leadership, charging it with so many crimes that the corporation delightedly reprinted the Red handout and gave it wide distribution.

But that was a regular feature of the outbreaks against the

AF of L strikes and organizing drives during that period. Branding all legitimate unions as "Fascist" and their leaders as "gangsters" and worse, the Communists sought to smash them from without and weaken them by spreading dissension within.

At the Eighth Party Convention of the Communist party held in New York in 1934, the main slogans were: "Forward to winning the American workers for Soviet power," with its natural accompaniment for violent action, "Concentrate our forces in the basic industries," and a third, "Smash Roosevelt and AF of L strikebreaking." These slogans were not only adopted by the convention as the party's chief aims, but ran in huge headlines across the pages of the *Daily Worker's* convention issues.

When, after the so-called People's Front Congress, they pretended that all this had changed, they persuaded me they now had learned that the best interests of Soviet Russia and the Communist cause would be served by working harmoniously with labor. It was a sad mistake on my part, of course.

The period of the People's Front and the end of the campaign to organize out-and-out Communist unions was forecast in the open letter and the Extraordinary Party Conference of 1933, for the order to "go out to the masses" was bound eventually to compel such a change. It finally came in 1935, as I have earlier described, following the Seventh Congress of the Communist International in Moscow. From the American delegation, both Earl Browder and William Z. Foster were elected to the Presiding Committee, on which also sat Joseph Stalin.

Out of the decisions handed down there, the second phase of the Communist fight for the conquest of the unions—the inauguration of the infiltration and boring-from-within process on a large scale—was begun. Communists everywhere throughout the world were instructed to embark upon a program of pretending to cooperate with democratic organizations and governments. The Red unions were to be dissolved in all countries, and the comrades were to join established unions. Georgi Dimitrov, who was elected general secretary of the Communist International at that congress, appropriately called this a "Trojan horse" policy. Those who rushed forward to grasp the Reds' proffered hands forgot to read the Congress' resolutions and Dimitrov's speeches, which explicitly committed the Comintern to the same blueprint for violent seizure of power that had been adopted in 1928.

In the United States, Reds were ordered to support a then new labor movement, which was to become the CIO. In the period shortly after the Seventh Congress, John L. Lewis suddenly became a "great labor leader," although as late as June, 1935, Jack Stachel, writing in the *Daily Worker,* had denounced Lewis and George L. Berry, head of the printing pressmen's union, as the *"most outstanding and infamous strikebreakers in the country."* (Italics mine.)

Detailed instructions concerning the new technique of expansion were brought back from the Moscow congress by Browder. The task of carrying them out, insofar as they concerned labor unions, was entrusted to two newly organized bodies—the New York State Trade Union Commission of the Communist party, and the party's National Trade Union Commission. The former group, for several years at least, was of particular importance. Its nominal head was Rose Wortis, but it was actually directed by Browder, Stachel and Foster. These three made no secret of the fact that they were in continuous communication with Lozovsky in Moscow.

The New York Commission met one evening every week on the third floor of Thirteenth Street, in one of the larger unused classrooms of the Workers School. From January, 1936, on, I attended every Commission session as well as the meetings of the National Trade Union Commission, being a member of both bodies. Among the Communists who regularly reported to the New York Commission for instructions were many who in later years became outstanding figures in both the CIO and AF of L.

As early as 1935 I can recall seeing Matles, who as we know

became national organizer and Red political representative in the UE; Jay Rubin, afterward a power in the Hotel and Restaurant Workers International Union; John Santo, then and for many years thereafter national organizer of the Transport Workers Union; Louis Weinstock, who rose to be secretary of the strong District 9 of the Painters Union; Irving Potash, in later years a national officer of the Fur and Leather Workers Union, an ex-convict and one of the defendants in the trial of the eleven top leaders; I. Rosenberg, who became national organizer of the United Shoe Workers; and James Lustig, now an organizer of the UE General Motors division. (This "division" of the UE has just been rejected by the GM workers in favor of the new CIO union.)

Another regular attendant was Mervyn Rathborne who became head of the American Communications Association, and who later was to break with the party and be replaced as chief officer of the union by Joseph Selly. In 1949 Rathborne announced that he would be a witness for the government against Harry Bridges in his trial for perjury. There was also Donald Henderson, whose union tried to invade the Catholic cemetery workers in 1948 and tangled with Cardinal Spellman, the workers as a result going into an AF of L union. Henderson delivered one of the most pro-Red speeches made at the Paris Conference on Peace in July, 1949, pledging that American unionists would stand by Soviet Russia.

These men, all of them more or less obscure when I first met them, were among the several hundred chosen for special training in the new technique of infiltration practiced after 1935. The major place of instruction was the Lenin School in Moscow, which most of these men had attended. There everything had been taught from street fighting to penetration of labor and liberal organizations. A great deal of the training after 1936 was carried on at the two summer camps near the Hudson River not far from New York—Camp Nitgedaiget and Camp Unity.

That Moscow wanted the Communists to put on the "sweetness and light" act in the labor organizations only in order to secure a wider field of influence for themselves was soon underscored by Gerhart Eisler when he sharply declared on the Ninth Floor in 1936 that "the party was not to go overboard in support of John L. Lewis. While giving him aid in the formation of the CIO, the party is always to remember that it must be prepared for the role of vanguard; it must so strengthen itself in all People's Front endeavors as to be able to dispose of class collaborationists like Lewis when that becomes necessary." Eisler's oral command was backed up by a written order to the party to the same effect, and a special article in the Soviet press criticized the *Daily Worker* for being too eager to grasp Lewis' hand.

This was brought out again during the rubber strike at Akron, Ohio, in the same year. The Politburo was trying to discover the proper balance which Eisler had laid down as essential—to "get out to the masses" and yet advance the Communist control at every step. It required some maneuvering, and in the rubber strike I was dispatched to the scene to try to work the whole business out. Owing to my past activities in the labor movement, I did succeed in arranging a conference between the local Communist leaders, then John Williamson and James Keller, and the CIO representatives, the late Powers Hapgood and Leo Krzycki. (Rose Posetta was there also for the International Ladies Garment Workers Union.)

The whole conference was taken up by the Red representatives in laying down the law to the CIO leaders—they even attacked several of them for "betraying the workers." This did not sit well with some of these men, and when the Akron strike was finally settled on the terms worked out by the CIO it looked as though the Reds were thoroughly rebuffed. But it wasn't so simple as that. The whole Williamson-Keller message had been in substance: "Give us a place in the official family or we will find ways and means to criticize every strike settlement you make." These threats of disruption had their final effect, especially as they were repeated later. And when in time a weak spot developed within the leadership of the United Rubber Workers, the Reds obtained a firm foothold in the union. This situation, fortunately, has recently been changed considerably.

Their progress in union infiltration was made easier by the fact that Leo Krzycki, then a vice-president of the Amalgamated Clothing Workers, was already showing secret signs of that friendship with the Communists which has now made him one of Moscow's favorites in this country. All of us who came in touch with him had orders to play upon his vanity—and it worked.

Krzycki is an excellent example of an active and ambitious personality manipulated by the Communists. His career in this respect parallels that of others in larger and smaller spheres. When I first knew Leo Krzycki in 1928 he volunteered to help me in my direction of the Kenosha strike. One of the prominent organizers of the Amalgamated Clothing Workers of America, he was then not a Communist. He had been Socialist assistant sheriff of Milwaukee County and was a popular speaker at workers' strike meetings.

As the CIO campaign developed after 1936, the Amalgamated Clothing Workers lent Krzycki, who by then had become vice-president of the union, to the CIO to help in its organizing drive among the steelworkers. Boleslaw Gebert, being Polish as was Krzycki, made it a point to cultivate the ACW man, and pupils of his were close to Krzycki when he directed the steelworkers march which led to the "Memorial Day massacre" in Chicago. Gebert was also aided in his cultivation of Krzycki by his close relations with the Fraternal Organizations Committee, which was composed largely of representatives of the pro-Communist foreign-born groups, and which offered its aid to the CIO in the days when the new union was getting under way. These groups were the wedge Gebert used to penetrate further into the CIO unions in the basic industries. They also became the heart of the American Slav Congress, outstanding among the subversive groups on the Attorney General's list.

The first and only president of the American Slav Congress from its foundation in 1943 was Leo Krzycki. On the governing body of that Congress, he was largely surrounded by men known to me to be Communists.

The Gebert-Krzycki association became ever closer during the forties, and one day in 1945 I met Krzycki leaving Gebert's offices in the IWO national headquarters at 80 Fifth Avenue. "I have made a great decision," he told me. "The hour has come for men to take sides—and my side is with the Soviet Union and against all who oppose it."

Later that day Gebert also told me of Krzycki's great decision, saying dryly that he had convinced Leo that "it is better to be a world figure as president of the Slav Congress and with us than one of several vice-presidents of the ACW."

It was, consequently, no surprise to observe the two of them as brothers-in-arms in the same photograph in the souvenir journal, *Rally for Peace,* of the Third American Slav Congress in 1946. That was an assemblage which cheered a message from Joseph Stalin and booed the name of the American Secretary of State, James Byrnes. It listened to a call for *"the unity of the Slavs under the U.S.S.R."* and assailed the United States for its "saber rattling," Krzycki himself voicing the last phrase.

There is no doubt that Gebert was an excellent forecaster. As president of the American Slav Congress, Krzycki made a noted trip to Soviet Russia, was received by Joseph Stalin in a longer interview than he had granted Secretary of State Byrnes, and then went on to comradely receptions by all the Soviet satellite Quislings from Dimitrov down.

It is perfectly clear that Krzycki's name in the labor movement and his connections with the foreign-born groups will now be used by the Communists in building those cells in the steel and other big industries which are designed to cause trouble later in the CIO.

When I left the party in 1945 plans had already been made for the third phase of the labor campaign, to include elements of both the first and second. These plans were to be put into operation when the Communist high command considered the time propitious, and in an article in *Collier's* on October 23, 1948, I predicted that this hour was near at hand. It was a safe prediction, for in the January *Political Affairs* of that year William Z. Foster, in an article designed to trim down the late President Roosevelt's reputation among the Reds, had written: *"Today only a Marxist leadership can lead the workers effectively, even in the daily struggle of the trade unions for bread."* (Italics mine.) Since President Philip Murray of the CIO is certainly not a Marxist, he was declared by that sentence to be unfit to lead the workers today, and the advancing shadow of the "new Red federation of labor" was cast over the scene. Also, as I have written elsewhere, the leading comrades had ordered me just before I left the party to prepare an indictment of Murray for future use.

It is a notorious fact that at that time the Reds thought they had the CIO in such a position as to be able to ruin it if President Philip Murray finally balked at their demands for an anti-American policy. Their big slip-up in this case was that President Michael Quill of the Transport Workers Union, whom they had counted on to lead the fight against Murray, turned against them. So likewise did Joseph Curran, president of the National Maritime Union, who was slated to be a strong aid to Quill in the anti-Murray fight.

We have heard from Michael Quill himself what occurred. In 1949 he was summoned to the national offices of the IWO at 80 Fifth Avenue, New York. There, in the presence of John Williamson of the Politburo and several other leading Reds, William Z. Foster as leader of the party ordered Quill to attack Murray. The TWU head refused, and the Red plans misfired.

If all had gone according to schedule, the United Electrical, Radio and Machine Workers Union would have been the largest contingent to walk out of the CIO into the Red labor center, its officers crying all the while that it had been "expelled." It would have been associated with the International Fur and Leather Workers Union, led by Communist Ben Gold and Communist Irving Potash (the latter a member of the Politburo tried in Foley Square). A third would have been the United Office and Professional Workers Union and a fourth the Food, Tobacco, Agricultural and Allied Workers of America, which was a Communist-dominated group before it entered the CIO and whose president Donald Henderson was a member of the party's National Committee with me for some years. Instead, Philip Murray carried the fight to the Communists.

Among the Red-controlled unions which the CIO has at this writing booted out are the United Electrical, Radio and Machine Workers Union; the Mine, Mill and Smelter Workers Union; the United Public Workers, which invades federal, state, and local municipal jobs, and through which the Communist party gets a grip on the strategically placed secretarial workers; Henderson's Food, Tobacco, Agricultural and Allied Workers Union; the United Office and Professional Workers Union, formerly headed by Lewis Merrill, who was forced to resign by orders of the Communist party; and the Farm Equipment Workers, which has been notorious in following the Red party line.

Among the Communist-dominated unions still remaining in the CIO in early 1950 are the International Fur and Leather Workers Union and Harry Bridges' International Longshoremen's and Warehousemen's Union, which as we have noted has established fraternal relations through Bridges with the World Federation of Trade Unions. It is noteworthy, however, that the California organization of the CIO, which was under Bridges' influence, has been dissolved and a new state body set up.

If these expulsions are rigorously followed up, they will tend to cut the Reds off from the legitimate labor movement in America. Such steps are therefore to be welcomed. However, we cannot close our eyes to the fact that the Communists are now in a position to make use of these expulsions to advance their own program of economic disruption and espionage. They will have bodies which they will call unions completely under their control, and can readily use them for strikebreaking purposes and to quicken the infiltration of key spots in shops and factories.

In their new plan of campaign, which is a revival of the old "united front from below," the Communists count on the money hunger of certain business interests to aid them. In Politburo discussions before I left the party this was often brought out. To achieve their ends and defeat the CIO unions, the Reds were prepared as early as 1945 to offer company-union terms to the employers. Recently, as a result, several managements have worked in collusion with the Communists to defeat the newly formed CIO union in the electric industry.

The lines upon which the Communists plan to battle are clearly drawn—they echo the command of V. V. Kuznetsov and the Red-run WFTU to "fight the splitters." Instructions, putting the comrades on the alert and advising them how to proceed, were given in two illuminating articles in the August, 1949, *Political Affairs.*

The Communist "code" is here at work overtime, preparing the entire party—and its trade-union agents in particular—for the fray. One of the articles is the product of Alexander Bittelman; the other was written by Sid Stein, hitherto an obscure man in the party, who is now acting as assistant to John Williamson in directing Red work in the unions.

The battle cries raised by Comrade Bittelman are strongly reminiscent of the outcries against President Roosevelt up until 1936 and during the Nazi-Soviet alliance. They are worth mention, for every American will now have them served up to him in many forms, and will hear them sometimes from the most surprising sources, as a comrade or some one under a Communist's influence slips them into the columns of some daily newspaper or persuades some well-meaning minister to utter them in his pulpit.

The major immediate demand under which the Communist party and the Red federation of labor will now function is, ironically: "For the curbing of the power of the monopolies and for a people's government." The second part of this slogan, the call for a people's government—which specifically entails building up the "Progressive party" ostensibly headed by Henry Wallace—is put forward, it should be noted, by those who applaud a dictatorship which has not permitted even its *one party* to have a congress in ten years, as Marshal Tito pointed out on August 21, 1949. *The last congress of the "model party" for all Communists, the Communist party of the Soviet Union, was the Eighteenth, held in 1939.*

But the Communists count on such slogans being raised by those who do not acknowledge their Red affiliations or associations and among people who do not question what is being told them. Under such slogans the Reds can take advantage of any weakness in present labor-management relations or in the functioning of government to turn the issues involved into a major crisis, and conditions which the Reds urged people to accept when they aided Soviet Russia in the war will now be made the occasion for "mass agitation."

"Protect the living standards of the people; make the monopolies pay for the cost of the economic crisis," is to be a second battle cry for the comrades. As in the days of the Hitler-Stalin alliance, that will furnish a pretext for interfering in organizational work, staging demonstrations and inciting violence.

From that, necessarily, proceeds the condemnation of President Truman for his "betrayal" of the workers in not getting the Taft-Hartley Act defeated and for his alleged "aid to the monopolies." This again is an echo of the assault upon President Roosevelt in 1939 and 1940.

The marked danger in this Red slogan is that it can be smuggled into genuine controversies over wages and hours and cause chaos in settlements; it can also help to weaken President Truman's own fight for the repeal of the Taft-Hartley Act. A grave responsibility rests upon management and labor—and upon management in particular—to see that no deadlocks occur which make capital for the Reds.

The Red program also lays down the inevitable barrage against the labor leaders who stand in their way, an outcry already heard in many places and which will increase in intensity as the days go by. "The Murrays, Dubinskys, Careys, Greens and Reuthers" is the new formula for assailing those who do not see eye to eye with the Reds. It recalls the blasts against the "treacherous roles" of "the Hillmans, Murrays, Greens, Dubinskys and Van Bittners" for backing Roosevelt's "warmongering" views. These labor leaders, who had for some time enjoyed immunity from Red assaults, are now attacked because they have been *"successful in committing large sections of the trade union movement to the war program foreign policy of the Administration, exemplified by the Marshall Plan and North Atlantic Pact,"* and because they serve as "agents" for the United States in "promoting 'the cold war' " against Soviet Russia. In brief, they are indicted for their refusal to knuckle under to Soviet aggression and its agency, the WFTU (*Political Affairs,* August, 1949, page 39). (Italics mine.)

The principal charge of the self-styled "progressives" is that "the Murrays and the Reuthers are attempting to impose by dictatorial means an anti-working class, procapitalist, proimperialist policy upon the various international unions." Again, it has the same tone as the Communist accusations in 1940 that "the Hillmans, Dubinskys, Greens, Murrays and Van Bittners" were turning the workers over to the mercies of the "Roosevelt Administration's reactionary, warmongering, imperialist policy."

In the uproar which the Reds will stir up in the third phase of their labor campaign, we shall hear again their contention that they "have been in the front line of every struggle for better wages, shorter hours, improved working conditions and against the speed-up." That is an exact quotation from a noted document within Red party circles, "Twenty Years of Communist Trade Union Policy," by William Z. Foster, written for *The Communist* of September, 1939. It is, however, a statement which has been reiterated almost mechanically by the Communists through the years. Labor history shows that it is far from true.

When the occasion requires co-operation with the unions to advance Red aims, Communist agents in the labor groups will be among the most zealous of union men. But when antiunion activities serve the Kremlin better, strikebreaking, rough stuff and union-busting will be and have been resorted to by the comrades.

Among the agencies at the disposal of the Reds in their present endeavors to weaken the CIO and the AF of L, I have already mentioned the IWO and its ally, the American Slav Congress, with its members in many industrial centers. In addition, on this past October 1 there was launched in Chicago a National Labor Congress for Peace, "initiated by a number of mid-West trade unionists," as *Political Affairs* modestly puts it.

The purpose of this Congress, according to Sid Stein, is to offset the efforts of the CIO leaders to bring about "an increasing mass war hysteria among the working class." It is therefore another channel through which to reach unsuspecting workers, attracted by the magic word "peace," and organize them against the established union leadership. Stein's analysis of the purpose of the meeting, which he blessed in advance, is precisely that. For he writes: "This opportunity must be fully utilized by all militants and progressives within the AF of L, CIO and Railroad Brotherhoods. An outpouring of a great labor delegation backed by millions of workers can be the beginning for a powerful peace movement of the organized workers which can tremendously *advance also the economic interests of the workers.*" (Italics mine.)

Since that was written as part of a program to defeat Murray and the CIO leaders, it takes no deep knowledge of Aesopian language to know that the "peace" group will be used to create disturbance in labor circles.

Another transmission belt for internecine labor warfare prepared by the comrades is the New York Emergency Committee for the Freedom of the 12. Although this committee was ostensibly set up to raise a clamor on behalf of the Communist leaders tried at Foley Square, Stein puts it down as a challenge to the CIO leaders for their "wall of silence" on the trial. With the usual Communist audacity, he associates the rights of the unions with the government's charges against a conspiratorial setup which faithfully supports every policy of a foreign dictatorship.

In this the comrades are bringing out the old bogeyman—that "Red-baiting" leads to trade-union injury. That was what they said when the Roosevelt Administration sent Earl Browder to jail for passport fraud, and obtained the conviction of the Communist financial agent, Robert William Weiner. The attempts of the Communists to prove that Mr. Roosevelt was thereby antilabor were as insincere and ridiculous as their present strained efforts to show that Mr. Truman is prosecuting the Communist leaders because he is an enemy of labor.

The only grounds on which that attitude could be justified is the Communist premise that Stalin represents all that is good for the working people, being their "leader and guide." If that were true, then necessarily anything that treads on Stalin's toes would be a crime against the workers. But it is thoroughly untrue, as the case of the Berlin rail strikers who were greeted with Soviet strikebreaking demonstrated.

The *C. I. O. News,* the official organ of the Congress of Industrial Organizations, declared on June 13, 1949—at the time of the Berlin walkout—that a lot of union people "are wondering if the inexcusable Communist strikebreaking in Berlin doesn't show what the Reds really are when their false whiskers are off."

Then that paper went on significantly to state: *"After the war ended and the party line went back to its normal twisting, it became obvious that the Commies' main objective was to use the C. I. O. to advance the cause of Communism, not American trade unionism.*

"That's when the process of giving them the heave-ho began— and it's been going on ever since. And it's likely to reach larger proportions in the near future.

"One of the principal reasons for this is that more and more persons are learning that the Reds are not free agents but act as puppets attached to a string leading to Moscow." (Italics mine.)

The issue is there well joined.

(IX)

Capture of the Innocents

Nᴏᴛ the least of my official assignments on Thirteenth Street was setting the nets to capture intellectuals and professionals —writers, artists, actors, educators, churchmen, scientists, editors, politicians and the like. As the thirties advanced into the forties, this fishing for nonproletarian innocents increasingly occupied a number of leading Reds.

From the Eighth Floor (and frequently from the Ninth) I watched, fascinated, as men and women of world-wide reputation were duped into carrying out plans laid for them by Stalin's secret police and special emissaries. Wrap party-line bait in "liberal" phrases and certain celebrities would bite over and over again. There was also help for us in the fact that a great many well-meaning and intelligent men and women, genuine liberals who were independently sympathetic to some of the causes—worthy enough in themselves—that the Communists sponsored, were often too busy or too unsuspecting, or both, to investigate the nature and backing of the organizations to which they were persuaded to lend their names. And though in some cases they may have known Communists were also involved, they were too unfamiliar with Communist practices to realize that the comrades were not interested in the cause itself but only in the way it could be twisted and used to further Soviet objectives. Again, many people lent their names to these organizations at a time when our relations with Russia were much better than they are now.

I was constantly amazed at the facility with which the Red agents operating among the intellectuals escaped exposure, though detection was comparatively simple. Their records proclaimed loudly who they were and what they were up to. Yet whenever their true allegiance was suggested, some reputable newspaper was certain to express indignation at the charge. To many of them the public paid huge royalties, out of which they turned over large sums to the party for subversive work. They hoodwinked their colleagues in the cultural field as easily as they did the public.

A recent exhibit among those who successfully concealed their Communist membership for a long time is the Canadian scientist, Dr. Boyer, who is now serving a prison sentence for espionage. Another case is that of Dr. Norman Bethune, the Canadian surgeon. All his life he had asserted staunchly that he was not a Communist, but on his death, helping the Reds in China, his allegiance was announced. I was present at the meeting at which Earl Browder stated that Bethune's last request on leaving for China was that in case of his death his party membership should be made public. In America there have been men like Howard Fast, the writer, and Frederick Vanderbilt Field, who for a long time passed themselves off as non-Communists, only later to acknowledge their membership.

The Congresses of Peace, which claimed continuous newspaper space in 1949, are a tribute to the Kremlin's astuteness in manipulating professional groups throughout the world and aligning them on the side of the Soviet Union. "Peace," at all these Congresses, suffered an Aesopian transposition and became endorsement of the political war which the Soviet dictatorship is waging against weaker nations from the Baltic to Shanghai—a war aimed at the United States.

The first of these assemblages, held at Wroclaw, Poland (formerly Breslau, Germany), in August, 1948, was officially named "The Congress of Intellectuals in Defense of Peace." The second, at the Waldorf-Astoria in New York City in March, 1949, was hailed by the chairman of the succeeding World Congress at Paris as "the great peace congress of intellectuals held in New York some time ago."

At the first Peace Congress, which was staged in Red Poland in order to start things off under completely correct auspices—as the Soviet always like to do—the theme song which was to be heard at all of them was sung by Alexander A. Fadeev, general secretary of the Union of Soviet Writers. It was a tune heard before and ran as follows: "After the Second World War, the entire world was divided into two camps: the democratic, anti-fascist, anti-imperialist camp led by the Soviet Union, and the anti-democratic, reactionary, imperialist camp led by the ruling circles of the United States of America."

The line dividing these "two camps," the Soviet representative stated, "passes through the interior of each of the capitalist countries, through every city and village—through New York as well as London, through Paris as well as Rome, through Brussels as well as Rio de Janeiro. Each camp has its own program, its own aims and tasks."

It would not take much consideration of the facts of life to know that Mr. Fadeev was referring to the Soviet agencies in these various cities engaged in what is popularly called fifth-column work. The report in *Pravda* notes that his assertions were received with tremendous applause.

This Congress, like those that followed, spanning the globe from Red Poland to New York to Paris to Moscow to Mexico City, concentrated on denouncing the "war plans of American imperialism" and applauding Soviet Russia as a citadel of peace.

Some of the British and American delegates couldn't take the anti-American things that were said. The attacks on both the United States and Britain were so raw that a number of them protested strongly. It did them no good. The Congress formally condemned "American imperialism," charging it with "war" plans, while praising the Kremlin's "peace" policies. All but a few of the thirty-two American delegates joined in the typical Communist vilification of their own country.

Heading the list of those who sponsored and attended the Waldorf-Astoria sessions the following spring were Thomas Mann and

Albert Einstein, neither of whom are Communists. Mann is the noted novelist who has long been a warm defender of Moscow. His name can be found on many Communist fronts, including the successor to the Young Communist League, the American Youth for Democracy. The world-famous Einstein, though occasionally dissenting from Communist views, has likewise sponsored a number of Communist-concocted groups.

The relationships with Mann and Einstein were established by what the Communists called "remote control," while I was still part of the Red leadership. The chain of communication with Mann ran through associates of his daughter Erika; while with Einstein, means of reaching him were set up at Princeton. In both instances, these men were persuaded to their pro-Communist stands by playing upon their hatred of Nazism. This I know from what I heard said in Politburo meetings. No more striking illustration could be found of the way well-known men and women of unquestionable integrity are deceived and exploited by the Communists.

Among the sponsors there was also, of course, a solid core of veteran supporters of Communist views or Communist fronts. There we find Albert Maltz, whose party card numbered 47196 was identified before the House Committee on Un-American Activities, though Maltz refused to tell the Committee whether or not he was a Communist party member. Maltz, who has a pleasant personality and who gets around a lot, is one of those we relied upon to induce non-Communist intellectuals to join Communist-sponsored groups.

Another name is that of Rockwell Kent, the artist, whom I came to know well when I was a Communist. Mr. Kent, among his other services to the party, acted as chairman of the conference supporting the *Daily Worker*, in May, 1944. When Robert William Weiner could no longer serve as president of the International Workers Order, since one convicted of a crime is not acceptable as an official of an insurance agency in many states, Kent was chosen as his successor. In that post he now collaborates with the Red underground agent for the Communist International, A. W. Mills, who is secretary of the IWO.

Others of the pro-Communist core around which the various fronts are always formed include Dashiell Hammett, the mystery writer, who is an instructor at the Communist party's largest school, the Jefferson School of Social Science, and who openly supported the Communist party in the 1946 elections in New York; Howard Fast, the novelist, who writes for the *Daily Worker* and who has been mentioned as a Communist by that paper; Dalton Trumbo, whose party card number 47187 was produced by the Committee on Un-American Activities and who also refused to answer under oath whether or not he was a Communist; and Howard Selsam, a former professor who is now director of the Jefferson School of Social Science.

From the recitation of these names—to which can be added such others as Muriel Draper, an officer of the American Division of the Red International women's organization; Clifford Odets, the playwright; and Louis F. McCabe, lawyer for the eleven Communists in 1949—we can see how the circle begins to expand. One or two persons under control of the party can in the course of their work relationships or social contacts quite easily and naturally induce others to join the group. They, in turn, may reach out further and persuade acquaintances who are not Communists or even sympathetic to the party to follow along and to bring in still others.

It is not surprising, knowing this method of operation, to find that the staff of even such an anti-Communist newspaper as the *New York Times* was invaded in order to get sponsors for the Waldorf-Astoria affair. Jacob Deschin, photographic critic; Olin Downes, music critic; and John Martin, dance critic were all persuaded to lend their names to it.

To capture the innocents and the unwary for the Communist-controlled groups, every natural association is taken advantage of. Just before I left the party in 1945, a writer for a popular weekly publication visited me at the *Daily Worker* to bid me a temporary farewell. He was about to leave for what many people would consider an exciting experience in order to write a book secretly ordered by the Politburo. Because of the adventurous nature of his assignment he was lionized among intellectual circles as he made his rounds of farewells. With the instinct of a true Communist, he was, he told me, "signing up future sponsors for fronts" in the course of his good-bys. He had with him that day a little book in which he had written a number of names; and many of them did later appear with his own in the list supporting the Waldorf-Astoria Congress.

The ease with which people in public life could be persuaded to join up on grounds of friendship, or because they favored some specific issue, sometimes astounded even the Communists. Shrewd Trachtenberg, who was charged with supervising these operations, said once that he was constantly reminded that a man who is wise in his own specialized field may be quite a child politically.

How many who signed up for the Congress of Intellectuals here really knew how far they were committed to pro-Soviet purposes cannot be accurately discovered. That, nevertheless, is what they lent themselves to by this move.

At the World Congress at Paris the following month, the Soviet writer, Ilya Ehrenburg, seized the spotlight by associating the Ku Klux Klan with all American culture (as Hitler had) and by referring derisively to "the American upstarts" who claimed to be defending "Western civilization."

At the same Congress, Boleslaw Gebert (a delegate from Red Poland) denounced the "criminal designs" of the United States. In order to defeat the American "warmongers," he made a move to set up a Permanent International Committee for Peace, and national peace committees in all countries. Since this proposal emanated from the Kremlin, the delegates assented unanimously.

By making that motion, Gebert proclaimed himself to the faithful as one of the chief Comintern (or Cominform) representatives at the congress, carrying on in the tradition of his former teacher, Gussev, and his old colleague, Eisler. The "new turn" made in the

thirties to "win the masses" and hence the intellectuals, voiced by
Gussev and Eisler as a command for the American Reds, was having
results on a world scale.

The Soviet oligarchy expressed its approval of the World Congress by labeling it "a major international event" in *New Times* of
May 4, 1949. "The calls of the World Congress reverberated
throughout the world," declared this Soviet organ. "They reached
their destination. All the gold of Wall Street is powerless against
their influence on the masses. The doors of the Salle Pleyel (where
the Congress had been held) had scarcely closed when the formation of organizations in defense of peace began in various countries."

Never does a Soviet organ such as the *New Times* approve of an
organization in such glowing terms unless it is acting in complete
obedience to Soviet directions.

How the Communist international apparatus took advantage of
and exploited the non-Communist reputation of some of the partici-
pants is also revealed by this judgment on the Congress. "Is it not
clear to everyone," writes the *New Times* with an air of innocence,
"that former special assistant U.S. Attorney O. John Rogge, Nikolai,
Metropolitan of Krutitsky and Kolomna, the French Abbé Boulier
and all the men and women in general who gathered at the Salle
Pleyel did not come to Paris because they were followers of one or
another political party."

Since then Abbé Boulier has withdrawn from participation in the
Congress and its work. But innocents will continue to be corralled
into the fold of "peace" fronts serving Soviet ends. It is their public
non-Red reputation that is valuable, as this instance proves, to Soviet imperialistic designs. And Red agents who are intellectuals or
professionals of one sort or another will continue to worm their way
into the confidence of these innocents and influence them to take
stands and sign statements the full import of which they do not
realize.

The way is made so easy for the comrades. Often unexpected
channels of influence were opened up by honest liberals who did

not understand the requirements imposed by Communist discipline, and who sometimes turned to us for information or advice.

When I was out in Chicago, for instance, I wrote and published in the *Midwest Daily Record* an extensive series of articles strongly defending the Works Progress Administration. These were called to the attention of Harry Hopkins in Washington; he read them, and thereafter got the paper every day. From this beginning, we entered into a series of communications through his close friend Howard Hunter, who was in charge of the WPA in Chicago. Hunter was far from being a Communist and frequently criticized their views, but he thought that some Communists occasionally had good ideas—though I doubt he knew they got them ready-made from Moscow. In November 1940, after I had returned to the *Daily Worker*, I went to New Orleans to cover the American Federation of Labor convention. Returning to my hotel after one of the sessions, I found a message from Howard Hunter and learned that he was now living in the Latin Quarter there, in a recently leased house.

In accordance with his invitation, I went to his house that evening. Eventually he took me aside from the other guests and told me that he had got in touch with me because Hopkins wanted him to question me about Stalin. After talking to me, he was to telephone Hopkins in Washington, since my answers might make a difference in a policy decision concerning Soviet Russia that had to be made at once.

The questions he asked me had to do with the kind of man Stalin was and whether he would become permanently an ally of Hitler. I was astounded that these questions should be put to me—a known Communist—who under discipline could give only one kind of reply. It would have to be highly eulogistic and slanted to make Stalin appear as much of a democrat as possible and to show that his association with Hitler could not be permanent. Despite the fact that the Communists were under instructions to do everything in their power to aid Hitler, publicly they had denied that Stalin was his ally. Consequently it was easy for me to tell Hunter, citing the Reds' own documents, the things that put Stalin in the best light. When I finished, Hunter thanked me and said he would call Hopkins that evening and give him my opinion. We rejoined the other guests, and I left almost immediately.

I can also cite the case of an intellectual leader in one of our largest cities who telephoned to me regularly to learn how to interpret world events. The comrades in Thirteenth Street used to laugh about this. Here was a man who was considered a great independent thinker, especially by prominent members of the business community—and he was getting all his opinions from the Communists, through me.

The number of those in the actual pro-Red contingent among intellectuals, though large, fortunately adds up to only a tiny fraction of the total. For every professor or churchman or writer who takes the bait, there are thousands who don't. What my experience proves and what the record shows, however, is that among the educated—as among the uneducated—there are careless, bemused and confused people. It is upon them that the Communists concentrate, using their tested techniques with amazing success. The resultant committees, leagues and associations become strongly vocal, highly publicized and extremely effective.

Certain of the celebrities were so easily taken in by our schemes that they were the objects of contemptuous jests in party circles. I recall *Daily Worker* staff meetings that rocked with laughter at the expense of famous intellectuals who pretended to think for themselves yet goose-stepped on the line we drew.

One of the objects of our humor was an able scientist in the Middle West whom I had persuaded to join various Communist fronts by appealing to his hatred of Nazism. At the time he joined one of these, he had said firmly that he was, of course, as much opposed to Communist totalitarianism as to that of Hitler. This we considered amusing, especially since the professor I had sent to him as an intermediary, a common friend, was a Communist of long standing.

During the latter part of 1949, among the many rings in the intellectual circus which the Communists set going was a letter by the Reverend Eliot White, retired Episcopal minister, asking thousands of Protestant clergymen to contribute to the Red defense funds. They were requested to give one dollar a week each for a period of time. When I heard of that letter, I could not help recall the contempt with which Eliot White (whom I had got to join the party) was discussed in leading party circles. Indeed, I took my own Red reputation in my hands in mid-1945 when I chided several party leaders, among whom was Jack Stachel, for having designated White as "fit politically only to be on committee lists but not to write for the *Daily Worker*."

The Peace Congresses are but the last of a long line of organizations created by the cultural division of the Communist party. Others, many in name and number, have run all the way from the John Reed Clubs to the League of American Writers. Because of their high-sounding titles, they were usually received with respect by the American community, until their true nature was disclosed. When that happened the Reds with perfect ease would initiate a "new" organization with a different resounding title but with many of the same members and committee lists.

Out of these organizations of the intellectuals as such, there grew also groups of wider appeal which made an even more distinct impression upon American thought. Outstanding among them was the League Against War and Fascism. The original executive of that body, whom I knew well, was Dr. J. B. Matthews, who subsequently broke with the Communists. He was succeeded by Dr. Harry F. Ward, at the time the Communists first sought to infiltrate the Roosevelt camp, and the League's name was changed to the American League for Peace and Democracy. In this guise, the Politburo felt, the organization would have more influence in Washington political circles. Finally, during the Hitler-Stalin alliance, when it became necessary for the League to alter its entire approach, it became the American Peace Mobilization. Frederick

Vanderbilt Field was drawn temporarily out of the Institute of Pacific Relations to become its head.

I attended several of the Politburo meetings which set up the American Peace Mobilization and put Mr. Field in charge. He was selected primarily because of his success in cultivating officials of the State Department. He could reel off a number of distinguished names who were bosom friends of his, among them his close collaborator Alger Hiss, who was subsequently to advise the government at Yalta, Potsdam and San Francisco.

Another organization of this sort was the group first known as the Friends of Soviet Russia. Then it became the Friends of the Soviet Union. Later it was the American Committee for Friendship with the Soviet Union. After that, the National Council of American-Soviet Friendship. Throughout all these transformations, it was run by the same inner circle of faithful Reds. As it developed, it was able to snare a number of statesmen; it also became a hotbed for breeding disloyalty among some of our scientists. At the meetings of the scientific section of this body, the United States was decried as decadent and unenlightened scientifically; Russia, by contrast, was the motherland of science. The point was usually made that the Russian edition of their books sold in greater quantities than the American edition—a particularly telling argument that was always received with emphatic nods and wry smiles. One scientist, for instance, asserted that only 2,000 copies of a certain scientific work in which he was interested had been sold in America; in Russia, on the other hand, it had had a sale of 12,000 copies.

How complete was the party control of this organization is shown by an experience of my own. The chairman of the National Council of American-Soviet Friendship, when I left the party in 1945, was the Reverend William Howard Melish of Brooklyn. Mr. Melish had been placed in that post only a short time before. Prior to giving him the appointment, the Politburo had sent me out to his rectory in Brooklyn (since I had known his father in years past) to interrogate him on his attitude toward the Communist party and its leadership. After a pleasant hour, I reported back to the Politburo on the Ninth Floor that Mr. Melish's opinions were "sound from a Communist viewpoint." Shortly afterward, the Politburo sanctioned Mr. Melish's appointment to head the National Council of American-Soviet Friendship, and the Council then announced his selection.

Formed for similar wide political purposes, but again more intellectual in character, was the Independent Committee of the Arts, Sciences and Professions. This was one of the most potent of the Communist fronts, for to an almost unprecedented extent it drew in and affected people with no pro-Communist tinge at all. Born in 1944, ostensibly to support the re-election of President Roosevelt, the committee lived to follow every twist and curve in the party line, until it ended up in Henry Wallace's camp. By then, of course, the Red control had become evident, and a great many of the original members had resigned.

The committee was created in my office in the *Daily Worker*, and largely at my instigation. For several years we had been holding regular meetings of what Alexander Trachtenberg called the "cultural commission" of the *Daily Worker*. The Politburo in this country and Moscow's representatives here had become acutely aware of the party's rising influence among artists, scientists and professional people. At several National Committee meetings, the leaders had pointed out the value of these contacts to Soviet Russia in time of economic tension or war, and had stressed the desirability of strengthening them. As a matter of fact, a special secretly operating commission to direct infiltration among American scientists had been set up as early as 1939.

Our *Daily Worker* commission, created at the suggestion of Trachtenberg and the Politburo, consisted of Trachtenberg himself as chairman, Joseph Fields (whose real name is Joseph Felshin) from the staff of *The Communist*, Lionel Berman, Robert Reid (who also had another name), V. J. Jerome, and me. As a general thing, our meetings took place in my office, though occasionally we met outside the building when we were conferring with "Peter Stone," a scientist who was in charge of the infiltration work among his colleagues, and "Peter Ivy," who was engaged in similar work in the radio field.

One day in 1943, Trachtenberg reported that "amazing progress" was being made among certain American scientists; and Berman, who was section organizer for New York's artists, writers and actors, gave a glowing account of advances in Manhattan and Hollywood. It was an optimistic session. Then I proposed that we capitalize on these "gains" to strengthen the party's leadership among American intellectuals of all kinds. The best way, I suggested, would be to channel our present strength into a committee for the re-election of Mr. Roosevelt. Naturally, it would be completely under Red domination. We knew, of course, that the same Red professionals who had denounced the President as "another Hitler" in 1940 could be counted on to cheer him now, if told to.

My proposal was enthusiastically accepted, and we decided that Trachtenberg and Berman should take it to the Politburo for approval. The approval was quickly given, for the Politburo had been experimenting on a smaller scale with a somewhat similar idea. To test its possibilities, they had ordered the comrades in the Hollywood Writers Mobilization, led by John Howard Lawson, to work out a Writers Congress. Under the direction of Trachtenberg, Jerome and the Politburo, the comrades on the Coast had persuaded Dr. Robert Sproul, president of the University of California to lend them the campus for a meeting place and to let them use the University's name as a cosponsor of the event. Under its win-the-war dress, the Congress had been successful—and a marked triumph for the party.

The Politburo was therefore eager to go ahead with the suggestion of our *Daily Worker* group. We got busy at once, and week after week Berman and Trachtenberg reported on the progress of the preliminary "contacting" for the Independent Committee (as yet unborn). We had some difficulty at first in deciding upon a chairman, the choice lying between a noted and handsome motion-picture actor and the man finally selected, Jo Davidson, the sculptor. The Politburo's decision in favor of Davidson rested on his "long relationship with the Party, since the days of his friend, Lincoln Steffens."

How the Communist writers, scientists, and professionals were mobilized and how they obtained the co-operation of scores of non-Communists in this Red-controlled organization is a rather simple story. Trachtenberg and Berman carried the main responsibility; Jerome was to co-operate with them. As a start, they simply got in touch with small knots of Communist writers, artists and scientists in New York and Hollywood. These men and women immediately asked others, friends and acquaintances, to join them on the Committee. Since the idea of supporting Roosevelt was in itself a popular one, an impressive list was soon run up in these two centers. Then an order in the name of the Politburo went out through our mail-drop system to every district organizer in the country, instructing them to mobilize their local cultural workers in like fashion.

As usual, the Communist leaders made sure that they had secret control of the apparatus of the organization. That meant having enough concealed Communists on the executive committee and in the key posts of the outfit to exercise directing power. Since these are the jobs in which the actual hard and thankless work of a committee is done, few people are eager for them. Consequently it generally was easy enough for us to place our people in those spots. In addition, in this case, the names of all the office workers were carefully scanned by the Politburo itself before they were finally accepted for service.

Eventually the Independent Committee went through a couple of transformations, to end up in the Progressive Citizens of America and finally the Progressive party. But the special section of the

Arts, Sciences and Professions was continued as an auxiliary, to
be called upon for big demonstrations when necessary.

Through all the years I was in the party, similar organizations
fairly tumbled out of the Communist machine, and new ones are
still being formed today. Again and again, with noteworthy regu-
larity, the same people appear as members or sponsors. Among the
artists, for instance, Hanns Eisler was particularly helpful to Moscow in getting a number of committees started. One of the best
known was the Theatre Arts Committee, on which Eisler and
Lionel Berman joined hands with Hester Sondergaard, Mrs. Donald Ogden Stewart, Lillian Hellman and Herman Shumlin. Robert
Reid, in charge of infiltration among the actors, was a comember
with Philip Loeb of the same committee. Its legal adviser was
Harry Sacher, known for his professional services to the Communist leaders.

Many of the same people appear again as sponsors of other Communist fronts. Recently there was formed the Committee for Far
Eastern Democratic Policy, to help Red China. On that committee
we find Herman Shumlin; Donald Ogden Stewart is mentioned as
a sponsor, along with Ben Gold, Paul Robeson, Muriel Draper,
Howard Fast, Paul Draper, the dancer, and Congressman Adam
Clayton Powell.

Back in the days when the Communists wanted to win the war,
a number of the same names were associated with the Artists Front
to Win The War. There we discover Muriel Draper again and
Hanns Eisler, the main agent in the creation of the committee. With
them were associated Charles Chaplin, Rockwell Kent, Paul Robeson, Larry Adler, and such others as Albert Maltz, John Howard
Lawson, and Dalton Trumbo. It will be recalled that the last three
refused to state under oath whether or not they were members of
the Soviet fifth column.

On the People's Songs organization we find Michael Gold, the
Communist, working with Rockwell Kent, the artist; as well as
Larry Adler, Paul Robeson, Norman Corwin, the radio man,

Woody Guthrie, the songster who formerly was connected with the *Daily Worker*, and Earl Robinson, who wrote the ballad in honor of Earl Browder.

When we turn back to the American Youth for Democracy, formed from the Young Communist League, many of the same names appear again. Among them were John Howard Lawson, Dalton Trumbo, Howard Fast, and Adam Clayton Powell. To these were added on that occasion Bartley Crum, the California lawyer, and Edward Dmytryk, the moving picture director, who refused to tell Congress under oath whether or not he was a Communist.

Recently, in the Mundt-Nixon protest, we find Paul Robeson again joining hands with John Howard Lawson and Rockwell Kent. With them is V. J. Jerome, the editor of the Communist theoretical organ; Representative Vito Marcantonio, connected for years with the Communist-controlled International Labor Defense; and Paul Draper.

Let me say here that no one realizes better than I that appearance on these committees does not by any means necessarily mean that a man is a Communist. Let me also add that I am fully conscious of the dangers inherent in "guilt by association." There is another consideration, however; that is what Morris L. Ernst, the well-known lawyer and counsel for Robert Vogeler, calls "guilt by appraisal." Ernst refers to the rather famous statement by Emil Maizey, secretary of the United Automobile Workers: "So far as I know, so-and-so may not be a duck. But if he quacks like a duck, walks like a duck, consorts with other ducks, then I have a right to think he is a duck." As Ernst adds: "Then in my appraisal of him, I can only call him a duck."

What the party gave the professors, writers, editors, ministers, and Broadway and Hollywood celebrities whom it persuaded to join their fronts was a feeling that they were in the swim of "progress." It also provided them with ready-made audiences, applause and publicity. What the Communist cause got in return were their glamorous names and prestige, their time and talent, and sometimes their cash.

Most pro-Red societies formed with the aid of cultural leaders, it is interesting to note, are, like the Peace Congresses, frank extensions of similar world-wide Soviet fronts. The most important in my Communist years was the League of American Writers, formed according to detailed blueprints drawn up at the International Congress of Writers held in Paris with Soviet applause and preliminary Soviet fanfare. Besides the central apparatus in New York, the League had dozens of branches throughout the country. The most active was the Hollywood chapter, drawing on the powerful pink cocktail set in the movie capital.

How closely attuned the League of American Writers was to party wishes is to be discovered in the fate of Waldo Frank as its president. During the 1936 campaign, Frank accompanied Earl Browder on his tour as the Communist presidential candidate. He was publicized as Browder's friend as well as traveling companion. But shortly afterward, when Frank expressed doubts about the validity and veracity of the famous Moscow purge trials, he was made so uncomfortable that he resigned his post as president of the League; he was also assailed by the Communist party. His successor was Donald Ogden Stewart, veteran member of all sorts of pro-Communist fronts, who had no such qualms about the Bukharin-Trotsky trials.

Another magnetic pole for the Red intellectuals and their friends has long been the Joint Anti-Fascist Refugee Committee, set up for the specific purpose of bringing useful European Communists —useful, that is, from Moscow's point of view—to the United States. In this it has been highly successful. Several members of this front were convicted of contempt for refusing to reveal the committee's records to the House Committee on Un-American Activities. A petition for rehearing went before the Supreme Court, which rejected it. The reluctance of the group to reveal their records is understandable, for unless they have been destroyed or doctored, they would show that "anti-Fascist" is just another way of saying Communist agent. That was proved satisfactorily enough in the trials and convictions of Gerhart Eisler, one of the prize "anti-Fascists" of that committee, who made its office his hide-out and used one of its chief employes as his courier to the Ninth Floor.

In addition to the more or less permanent organizations such as I have been describing, the Communists frequently form "volunteer" committees or groups for one special occasion or campaign. These committees, bolstered with a number of prominent names favorably associated by the public with meritorious service in some field, disappear promptly after the statement they endorse has been made. There is an amazing repetition of names in these groupings, also, with a new name or two added from time to time. The Ninth Floor, in analyzing the effect of the volunteer committees, came to the conclusion that they were of the greatest help precisely because of their temporary character. The grouping did not bind the signatories for long; but on the basis of their public statement concealed party agents could extend and expand the campaign in unions, fraternal organizations, community groups and elsewhere. The statement became a text, with even more pro-Red interpretations put upon it as the campaign progressed.

How are such volunteer committees formed? That is, after all, a rather simple process, as in the case of the more permanent committees. Two or three Communists in the intellectual field—a doctor, educator, writer, let us say—get up a statement at the request of the Politburo, or it is handed to them. With that, they visit or write to a few men and women of outstanding position in American life, dividing a list of names among them. After these famous names have been obtained, or as many of them as possible, many other people not so conspicuous but nevertheless well known in their respective occupations or communities are approached, the famous signers being used as bait. The district offices of the party are enlisted in this larger endeavor, and the Red district leaders call in the concealed Reds in educational, writing and similar fields and get them busy. Often these Communists can persuade non-Communists not only to sign the statement but also to go out and obtain other signatures.

Let me offer a few specific examples. I recall one particular volunteer committee that was initiated solely to protect the party's undercover work. As I sat in on the entire discussion that led to the emergence of this group, I can give it as a striking illustration of the party's methods.

It was the group of 148 "American educators, churchmen, scientists, and civil leaders," to quote the news release describing them, who called upon Attorney General Robert H. Jackson in May, 1940, to investigate the Committee on Un-American Activities. Now there were a number of people who were not too happy about the House Committee and the way it functioned, and they had a right as citizens to say their say on the matter. But the Communists in this group of 148—and there was among its members a good bloc of persons under Communist discipline—knew that the purpose of the demand was to divert the attention of the public from the details of Earl Browder's passport violations, which had been revealed by the Committee on Un-American Activities.

The party leaders, it should be understood, were then greatly alarmed by the capture of Nicholas Dozenberg, whose name Browder had used on one of his passports and who was a Red Army spy in the United States. "We can't permit the public to know extensively that the general secretary of the party, Comrade Browder, took the name of a man who is about to expose himself as a Soviet spy," stated Gene Dennis emphatically, adding that he was also speaking for J. V. Peters and other "important comrades" who had already gone underground at that time. "Any such revelation would cause doubt in the minds of the people as to whether we are foreign agents or not; it would tie us up organizationally in the public eye with the Soviet secret service here."

Dozenberg was denounced in the pages of the *Daily Worker* as a "rat," "stool pigeon" and other uncomplimentary terms, the party having learned that he was about to co-operate with the government in the Browder case.

But many members of the group which blossomed forth to assail the Committee on Un-American Activities (and to take the heat off Browder) had no idea of the ulterior purpose they served. Such stable citizens as the late Professor Irving Fisher of Yale and Dr. Mary E. Woolley, for example, certainly would have been amazed to learn that they were helping to divert American scrutiny from the ugly features of the Browder case. Nor had they any notion that they were helping a financial agent of the Comintern—Robert William Weiner—to escape a jail term for defrauding the government. (Weiner, you will recall, had been found guilty of forging his birth certificate and misrepresenting his citizenship, having sworn that he had been born in Atlantic City and having had the City's records of vital statistics tampered with.)

Again to my knowledge, in early 1939, another committee of the character we have been discussing was initiated directly by the Soviet secret police. The octogenarian Professor John Dewey inadvertently caused the entire episode by his proposal that there be an investigation of the Moscow purge trials by hearing the testimony of Leon Trotsky on the matter. At that time I was working with the Soviet secret police, unwittingly helping to forge the murder ring that ultimately assassinated Trotsky.

Meeting me in the chain restaurant that was one of our rendezvous, Roberts, the secret police agent, showed me a list of "liberal" names. Which of them, he wanted to know, was best suited to lead the counterdrive against Professor Dewey? After some discussion we chose Corliss Lamont.

Few if any of those who eventually signed the whitewash of the trials could possibly have known that the idea was hatched by top Communist officials in conference with NKVD agents. Not even the five gentlemen who sent out the letter soliciting signatures—Robert Coates, Malcolm Cowley, Stuart Davis, Marc Blitzstein, and Paul Strand—had any inkling of the police angle. But on

April 28, 1939, the *Daily Worker* was able to announce with high glee: "Nearly 150 American artists, writers, composers, editors, movie actors, college professors and Broadway figures yesterday issued a statement in support of the verdicts of the recent Moscow trials of the Trotskyite-Bukharinist traitors."

Shortly after this, we obtained an impressive list of 400 signatures of people in the arts and professions denouncing "the fantastic falsehood that the U.S.S.R. and the totalitarian states are basically alike."

This array of names was obtained under high pressure as a counterblast to a declaration by a group of non-Communist writers and educators who had organized to fight Red infiltration. They had said, among other things, that Soviet Russia was a totalitarian regime as despotic as Nazi Germany and Fascist Italy. For that they were labeled "reactionaries" and "Fascists" by the 400.

But history played a cruel trick on the Reds' mighty list of people. Their open letter defending the Soviet paradise from all suspicion of totalitarian associations appeared on August 14, 1939. Nine days later, on August 23, Stalin announced the Moscow-Berlin Pact of friendship and nonaggression. It was a big letdown —temporarily at least—for those unwary professionals and artists.

But Red intellectuals have kept up their persistent and persuasive work and innocents have continued to be found in high places, down to the present moment. Just before I left the party, plans were laid for the creation of the Civil Rights Congress—achieved, as is so often the case, through the merger of other fronts. One of these was the International Labor Defense, which had for years been the Communist defense organization, a replica of similar groups in other lands. The other was the National Federation for Constitutional Liberties, headed by the wealthy George Marshall, one of the editors of *Soviet Russia Today*. All three groups—the two merged ones and the result of the merger—are on Attorney General Clark's list of subversive organizations.

And yet, the Civil Rights Congress was able to ensnare as its sponsors in April, 1946, when it was formally launched, such non-Communists as the Reverend Harry Emerson Fosdick, Dr. David de Sola Pool and a Wall Street lawyer, Allen Wardwell. Worse still, a conspicuous anti-Communist, Oswald Garrison Villard, was also caught. And Mr. Villard uttered an eloquent truth as he got out fast: "The trouble is that liberals are always being roped in by seeing the names of their friends."

As editor of the *Daily Worker*, in 1944 I reported the formation of the American Committee for Yugoslav Relief. Under this innocent guise, the plan was to help Marshal Tito secure control of that unhappy land. But many persons who are conspicuous as non-Communists helped it along. Mrs. Eleanor Roosevelt became honorary chairman, and among the sponsors were Senator (now President) Harry S. Truman, William Green and Philip Murray. There was also Rita Hayworth. These and other sponsors dropped out when in the course of time the Committee's domination by the Reds was learned. But the organization collected $3,000,000 before it was disbanded. The end came in July, 1948, and then it was dissolved, not because Tito no longer needed help, but because he had fallen into disgrace with the Kremlin. The new Communist line all over the world was to denounce him and to starve out his regime—and this supposedly independent organization acted immediately to choke off the flow of dollars to his bailiwick.

The clever deception practiced by the Reds is reflected in the sad comment of an eminent Republican, Senator Leverett Saltonstall of Massachusetts, who had been persuaded to become a member of the national committee of a group which, it turned out, was backing up Soviet aggression. The Senator resigned quickly. "I thought it a relief organization," he said in hurt tones, "and I felt sure it was all right when one of the respectable citizens of New England—from one of the leading and oldest families—asked me to sign."

That is the picture of an innocent who undoubtedly has learned his lesson. If more would learn—and quickly—America could rest easier.

It is obvious that not a few of the people who so unthinkingly sign some of the Red statements or petitions are independently and rightly filled with concern about abuses existing in our society. But then, from a Communist friend or acquaintance, whose true political affiliation is generally not known, they are too often given a distorted view of how to remedy these evils—and before they know it, they find themselves on lists favoring Soviet ends.

And they are constantly being cultivated. Despite the contempt which the Communists express in their own Thirteenth Street quarters for many of these intellectuals, the Comintern, or Cominform—call it what you like—keeps the Red leadership here continually aware of the high value it places on these people's services. The Red leaders, in turn, steadily drum it into the sub-leaders in the various localities. Partly as a result of this emphasis, Communists are constantly being recruited from the professional ranks and organizations. The intellectual who becomes a party member—or agrees to be placed "under Communist discipline" without possessing a card—is subject to a special course of treatment and training. It is laid down as a "must" that he be drilled regularly in Marxism-Leninism, "particularly in the scientific writings of Stalin," so that he will be devoted to the head of the Soviet State. Then he is tested repeatedly, to learn if he displays a "thorough readiness to accept party discipline." As further tests of his subservience, he is assigned tasks in his profession; he may even be given the order, when that is feasible, to write "new school textbooks and rewrite history from a Marxist viewpoint." The tests can be positive or negative, and may range through a wide list of acts, according to the decision of the Politburo or of the district organizer. As positive tests, he might be instructed by his party superiors either to recruit some colleague into the party or to take a stand in a scientific association, or in his immediate professional group, that might lead to suspicion that he is a Red. They might also propose that he allow open or concealed Communists to associate themselves with projects on which he is engaged. As a negative test, he is carefully observed to note whether he applies for party permission to remain silent on certain critical occasions or to take other measures to protect himself from being exposed as a Red.

While I heard such instructions handed out frequently on the Ninth Floor and in National Committee meetings, they are also specifically set down in print by William Z. Foster in a milestone article in party history, appearing in the September, 1938, issue of *The Communist*. This article, "The Communist Party and the Professionals," was ordered prepared and published by the Politburo after an extended report by Alexander Trachtenberg on recruitment among professionals.

Foster wrote, "our scientists must organize more effectively the battle against the idealists in every branch of science, our doctors must introduce new methods into medicine . . . our lawyers must challenge the prevalent musty legal conceptions and rewrite legal history, our writers must bring forward class-struggle themes in literature and the theater."

There was to be developed, in short, "a powerful Marxist-Leninist ideological front" in every field of intellectual and artistic endeavor.

After receiving the intensive training in "Marxism-Leninism" which Foster says is imperative, the intellectual who becomes a Communist is then committed to M. J. Olgin's fundamental statement in *Why Communism*: "We Communists say that there is only one way to abolish the capitalist state and that is to abolish it by force. To make Communism possible, the workers must take hold of the State machinery of capitalism and destroy it." The Roosevelt administration was such capitalist machinery, in Olgin's interpretation.

These Red professionals must also become familiar with J. V. Peters' famous booklet, *The Communist Party: A Manual of Or-*

ganization.* There they learn that "As the leader and organizer of the proletariat, the Communist Party of the United States leads the working class in the fight for the revolutionary overthrow of capitalism, for the establishment of the dictatorship of the proletariat, for the establishment of a Socialist Soviet Republic in the United States."

They have learned from W. Z. Foster's latest work, *The Twilight of World Capitalism,* that the director of this violent upheaval in the United States is Stalin. "The chief architect of these new developments in Communist policy," writes Foster, "was Joseph Stalin, the greatest living Marxist." Indeed, says Foster, "the working theory of Marxism has thus become Marxism-Leninism-Stalinism."

Their major loyalty is therefore to the master of Bolshevism, no matter how pre-eminent they may be in their own spheres, and they know that their obligation is to carry out the Leninist morality of lying to those regarded as enemies.

We know today, from reading how obediently the Communist party here accepts the Stalinist theories on biological science, that the Red scientist is compelled to adopt officially the Kremlin-endorsed Michurgin theory, bootlegging it to others if not publicly backing it. And Communist writers have to place themselves in step with the party line, which is "cleansing" out all bourgeois ideas among Red writers from Leningrad to our own land.

How powerful is the grip of Moscow over the Red intellectual circles in the United States and elsewhere is illustrated by two articles denouncing "an obsequious and servile attitude toward Western bourgeois culture," which appeared in *Political Affairs.* They were written in 1946 and 1948 for the scientists and writers of Soviet Russia by two of the most powerful men in the Soviet oligarchy, the late A. A. Zhdanov and Georgi M. Malenkov, and reprinted here as guides for the American Reds working in intellectual circles.

* The signature was "J. Peters." He often discarded his middle initial.

Malenkov stressed the urgency of wiping out completely "old capitalist conceptions" of cultural life and of bringing about the "triumph of a militant Soviet patriotic spirit among scientists and art workers" in order to support in cultural activities *the wise Stalin foreign policy of the Soviet Union.*"

Any intellectuals who as Reds must swallow such regimentation will with immense willingness mislead their fellows. They have acquired that peculiar spirit of self-immolation before Stalinite wisdom that marks all devoted Communists. In his article on the professionals Foster sets down first of all the following obligation, "In drawing professionals into the Party, care should be exercised to select only those individuals who show by practical work that they definitely understand the Party line, are prepared to put it into effect, and especially display a thorough readiness to accept Party discipline."

Foster paid a tribute, even then, to the work being done by the Red professionals. "Our writers, artists, and actors," wrote he, "have long since been doing effective work in their respective spheres, our doctors are playing a more and more important role in the developing struggle of the masses for adequate medical care, and our other professional groups are increasingly active."

And Foster adds: "Any tendencies in our Party to underestimate the importance of these elements [the Communist professionals] should be combated."

The question naturally arises in the mind of the average American, *Who are these "writers, artists, and actors" to whom Foster applies the term "our"?* It is vital to American defense and to the integrity of American public opinion to know who are the Red agents of a foreign and hostile dictatorship. And yet, they are nowhere to be found—as Reds. When the acts of certain men and women, the fronts they join, their repeated refusal to differentiate themselves *by deed* from the Communists, are called to public attention, an outcry invariably rises from one quarter or another against such an exposé. Seldom even is it suggested that these people are laying themselves open to this sort of suspicion by their own records. The Reds have won a tremendous battle in this respect.

As a matter of cold fact, the Red intellectuals enjoy a peculiar protection from criticism—an immunity which constitutes an injury to the American public, since by record alone each one of them could be known and properly designated. For instance, if I were permitted to, I could name more than four hundred concealed Reds functioning as editorial writers, actors, authors, educators, physicians and the like. I knew them as members of the Communist conspiracy; I was acquainted with them and their records as builders of Communist fronts and undercover workers for Communist objectives. However, our present libel laws, which make it libelous to call a man a Communist, although it is not criminal for him to be one, render it impossible for me to call this roll.

There is another reason for my silence. If I were to mention these names before a court or commission, there would be such an uproar of criticism as to vitiate any good I might do the nation's security.

There are for example two rather notable radio writers who are doing an excellent job for the Communist cause over the air waves. Both of them have been repeatedly signed up for Communist fronts; one of them particularly has belonged to almost every front declared subversive by the Department of Justice. Each time he has expressed surprise that the new front was Red in origin, and has said he was just too busy to know what he was doing. It is interesting to know, however, that he had time to persuade many other writers to join these organizations about which he claimed to know so little. Both of these men are in key positions to confuse public opinion badly.

At one of the several receptions for the so-called elite of the party which I attended at the town house of Frederick Vanderbilt Field, there were present: a man who has made a notable success in the publishing field, partly in connection with comic sheets but also in much more intellectual pursuits; a noted singer who is a kind of hero in certain professional groups; and a writer of books which have enjoyed wide popularity and who was one of the most bloodthirsty in his calls for action against the United States.

But American complacency permits the "iron curtain" to extend to this country—and to prevent the truth about these Reds being told the American people. Thus Foster's *"writers, artists, and actors"* —doing such excellent work for the Soviet cause, as he says—are enabled to carry on because they palm themselves off as "liberals" and everything else but the Reds their records prove them to be.

Just before I left the party, the Politburo's decision to permit Communist intellectuals to sue for libel if called Communists put an additional check on free speech. Before then the party had discouraged this practice since it implied that a Communist was something bad to be—otherwise the charge would not be libelous. But that point of view was changed in 1945, so far as those pretending to be non-Reds were concerned.

The Politburo did not believe for a moment that the suits would be won by the Reds suing; but as Trachtenberg pointed out, "the action in itself will tend to silence our enemies because it will be too burdensome financially even to win the case against us."

How serious the suppression of the truth about the Red intellectuals is proving to our nation can be learned from the following series of facts drawn from my own experiences. I am willing to remove each fact from its anonymity, supporting my statements before any governmental agency in executive session with names, dates and places.

I know, for instance, that thousands of dollars have been contributed by a group of exceptionally highly paid professional people to finance directly subversive work against the United States in Hawaii.

Since 1937, to my knowledge, an intellectual of some wealth and social standing has directed espionage work in Washington aimed at benefiting Soviet Russia in Asia.

I know that the Office of Strategic Services was infiltrated during the recent war under a plan worked out by Eugene Dennis and with the co-operation of a well-known writer and several government and professional workers. This work proved of much assistance to the Red cause.

I know, too, that a professor in a Pennsylvania college, a woman of culture and grace, served as a courier and information gatherer in Washington for the Ninth Floor, even entering the White House and bringing back information valuable to Stalin for the Yalta Conference. She was instrumental in getting various governmental moves made which enhanced the political position of the Communists.

I know that the influence of the Communists in various key departments in Washington has been great, and was particularly effective in causing the United States to "pull its punches" in regard to Poland and China.

I know that 80 per cent of the original list of those who backed Wallace for the Presidency were composed of concealed Communists, mostly in the professional field.

I know that the great number of those who signed for the Congress of Intellectuals in New York and Mexico City are concealed Communists, although publicly they appear as eminent professional people without political affiliations.

I know that the stealing of State Department papers (such as occurred in the *Amerasia* magazine case and as revealed by Whittaker Chambers) was only a part of the anti-American work done by organized groups, some of whom I can name, composed of professionals. I was, for instance, introduced to one of the people mentioned as prominent in espionage work at a National Committee meeting—the introduction being made by a well-known Red.

I know that a popular writer, after getting a job in Hollywood, was specifically ordered by the Politburo to obtain employment for writers who had formerly been in the *Daily Worker–New Masses* milieu. He was amazingly successful in this endeavor, securing top-flight writing jobs for a number of Communists who had previously had a mediocre literary output.

I know of many professional people in less conspicuous positions than the famous list-signers—people like Elizabeth Bentley, honor graduate at Vassar, and Judith Coplon, honor graduate at Barnard —who were drawn into the party by first being attracted to the fronts with their big and innocent-sounding names. They were then recruited quietly for special training schools for "infiltration," which later made them eligible to be drafted into espionage work.

I could go on, but I think I have said enough to suggest that America has a long way to go before the danger from Red work among the intellectuals, innocent and otherwise, is ended.

The versatility of the Communists is indicated in no better way than by their invasion of the conservative precincts of Westchester County, New York. I am not referring to the open invasion by thousands of Reds from New York City, with their security guards, which took place at the time of the Paul Robeson affair near Peekskill. What I have in mind is the quiet infiltration of Westchester County circles and communities, worked out carefully and well financed, that has been going on for a number of years.

I learned of this program in 1944 when I was requested by the State Committee of the New York Communist party to become chairman of the Westchester County Red organization.

It required financing, an obligation that was placed on the shoulders of the considerable number of Communist lawyers, doctors, and other professional people who lived in New Rochelle. Their group, the Professional Workers Club, which formerly met on North Avenue in the heart of the city, contained a number of men who were making as much as $100,000 a year. With this financial base, the party set up colonies of Red residents in various communities, where they lived as average citizens, although their first aim was to bolster the American Labor Party, which is of course completely controlled by the Communists. Lement Harris advised the party on building up a scattered Red colony in the

Pleasantville and Chappaqua areas, and other Reds were planted around Lake Mahopac. And so it went throughout the county, with a particular concentration in Mt. Vernon.

In order to direct the work of community infiltration, and to be easily accessible to the concealed Communists among the wealthy lawyers aiding him, Alexander Bittelman was induced to settle in the general area of Peekskill. His house was bought for him by Robert William Weiner. The Communist colony at Croton, which included Joseph North of the *New Masses* and Robert Minor, former American representative to the Comintern in Moscow, was given the special assignment of establishing friendly relations with men and women in government service who might live in Westchester.

The invasion of Westchester had two main objectives. The first, which was discussed in great detail in a number of Political Bureau and New York State Bureau meetings, had to do with the establishment of a series of educational camps throughout Westchester and adjoining counties. The camps were to be anchored at one end by Camp Beacon, the site of the National Training School sessions. The other terminus was at New Rochelle, which as "Tom Paine's City" was to be the home of a large Communist school. The unions under Communist control and the International Workers Order were to co-operate by setting up camps of their own, so organized that they could if necessary be turned over to complete party control. In line with this plan, the United Electrical, Radio and Machine Workers Union set up a camp just above northern Westchester in Dutchess County. The IWO could not obtain what it wanted in the county proper, but eventually, after I had left the party, did get a large estate in Ridgefield, Connecticut.

As Trachtenberg stated, these camps were established in order to make certain that Reds would have a "reservoir for educational work," and one that would be near New York City.

Another phase of this elaborate plan was the invasion of the Westchester County mind, especially in exclusive circles. People of wealth in the party, such as Louise Bransten (who was also a Soviet agent) and Mrs. Muriel Draper, were given the responsibility of working out relationships which would plant the Communists firmly in Scarsdale, Larchmont, and Bronxville. Where actual Communist converts could not be made, friendly associations were to be initiated which would permit concealed Communists to speak before community organizations as experts on foreign affairs, particularly on the satellite states and China. Pro-Communist books were to be plugged at informal dinner parties, in women's clubs, study groups, and educational institutions.

Some of the reports on the progress made were amazing and amusing. In a residential area, it is not difficult to persuade your neighbors that you are a person of culture and leadership and know a great deal about many things. By this method, concealed Reds not only succeeded in having their friends address many women's clubs and other local groups, but were able even to induce some important industrial managers and Wall Street executives to adopt attitudes helpful to the Soviet fifth column.

The Red cultural commissar for America, responsible for manipulating the intellectuals, and doing it so well, is Comrade Alexander Trachtenberg. For a quarter of a century this short, squat, dark man, with black eyes and black mustache, has been directing and co-ordinating pro-Soviet activities in our country. Standing out publicly as head of the International Publishers, the chief book-publishing company of the party, he also supervises all the other party publishing firms as well as its schools, was one of the principal founders of the Jefferson School of Social Science, and checks on all "cultural work" everywhere in the United States. After 1945, when the party had to be reorganized thoroughly along anti-American lines, he added to his manifold duties the job of chairman of the Control Commission for a period of several years.

Trachtenberg came to America from Russia in 1908, when he was twenty-three. After representing Lenin's point of view in the Socialist party here, which he promptly joined upon arrival, he was elected to the Central Committee of the underground Communist party of the United States in 1921. Chosen as a delegate to the Fourth Congress of the Communist International held in Moscow in 1922, he remained in the Soviet capital the next year to receive "enlarged revolutionary training" and to take part in the enlarged session of the Executive Committee of the Communist International. Thence he returned to America as the Red commissar of cultural activities here, which he has remained ever since, with occasional trips to Russia for indoctrination.

Soviet organs in America have paid public tribute to his work, notably on his fiftieth birthday, in 1935, when the Central Committee of the Communist party adopted a special resolution hailing him as a "stalwart Marxist-Leninist." The Committee added that he had attained a "mastery of the theory of Marxism-Leninism," the higher tribute that can be paid to the intelligence and Red integrity of a comrade.

A decade later, in the *Daily Worker* of December 8, 1944, the columnist Mike Gold wrote of Trachty: "He has organized or helped in every writers' or artists' or cultural group I have known since the John Reed Clubs." Gold adds that Trachtenberg "also publishes all the Marxist-Leninist literature in America—has issued millions of books, pamphlets, studies on that subject." That figure is no exaggeration. It also explains why he is in constant touch with the Marx-Engels-Lenin Institute in Moscow.

It was Trachtenberg who first broke the good news to me in early 1940 of the arrival of a new Stalinist agent for cultural infiltration, one who was to do much to advance the invasion of the intellectual world in this country. When I returned to New York from my Chicago post that year, Trachty was in a state of high merriment. A $20,000 fellowship by the Rockefeller Foundation to the agent in question for studies in "new musical forms" was making it possible for him to carry on his chief commission from Moscow. "Capitalist money is paying for the fight against capitalism," Trachtenberg said, chuckling.

The man involved was Hanns Eisler, composer brother of Gerhart Eisler. The Rockefeller Foundation officials, of course, were innocent victims of Communist wirepulling. Certainly they were not informed that Hanns has served since 1935 as head of the International Music Bureau, connected with the Communist International, the purpose of which was to spread pro-Soviet allegiance among musicians, musical critics and composers the world over. He came directly from that position in the Soviet capital to his labors here.

Shortly after his arrival, Comrade Hanns introduced his "new musical forms" to a secret session of 300 leading Communists and fellow travelers. When a chorus under his direction broke into one of his best-known Red songs, "We Are Ready to Take Over," composed for the Communist International, the audience exploded with enthusiasm. It is an item that assuredly did not appear in his Rockefeller Foundation thesis.

Hanns Eisler was quickly introduced to Hollywood. There he got remunerative assignments and simultaneously took over the political direction of the Reds in professional fields. That was his real goal when he landed on our shores; it had been said for some time (and Gerhart Eisler had emphasized it on more than one occasion) that a comrade who could command the political respect of the Hollywood comrades was needed there. The chief arena of activity of the Red International Music Bureau, at that time, also happened to be America. Under Hanns Eisler's direction, many new fronts blossomed in Hollywood and increased sums of money flowed into the Red coffers.

Mention of Hollywood inevitably brings us to the name of John Howard Lawson. He is undoubtedly the most important of the ten writers who preferred to appear in contempt of a Congressional Committee rather than to say "Yes" or "No" to the question concerning their Communist party membership.

Having known Lawson before I entered the party, it was no surprise to me to learn that his statements on behalf of Red institutions were used to stimulate young intellectuals in party loyalty. The manner in which this was done illustrates admirably the technique by which the party bolsters the devotion of its members. In meeting after meeting which I attended in the cultural section (or of cultural workers in various cities), Lawson's endorsements of the *Daily Worker* over the years and his services as a special correspondent for the paper in 1934 were brought forward. The organizers of the cultural section, first Robert Reid and then Lionel Berman, repeatedly called attention to what it meant for "a top-flight playwright like Lawson to lend his name and prestige to our cause."

Lawson's plea for the *Daily Worker,* published in that paper in 1935, was quoted often: *"The Daily Worker* is our bulwark against all the barbarous schemes of the oppressors of the working class, of the oppressors of culture, of the oppressors of every genuine form of intellectual and aesthetic activity." He took occasion then to assail the Roosevelt administration, "its inhuman wage scale, its intolerable 'work or starve policy.' " He denounced "Mr. Roosevelt's contribution to the Fascist war-mongering program" when the administration protested to Soviet Russia for holding the Seventh World Congress of the Communist International, in violation of Stalin's pledge to end subversive activities in America. Lawson then proclaimed the Soviet Union to be the "great toiler for peace."

Later on, when the party was following the "lesser evil" trail by allegedly backing Roosevelt, Lawson's appeals for the *Daily Worker* and his other public statements were pitched in a pro-Roosevelt tone. As is to be expected, Lawson is found today denouncing "American imperialism" and applauding "Soviet peace aims," in endorsing the Western Hemisphere Congress (of Intellectuals for Peace) held in 1949 in Mexico City.

Another and much greater writer whose name was used repeatedly, though in a slightly different way from Lawson's, was the late Theodore Dreiser. Both Lawson and Trachtenberg had great influence with him, and it was through Trachtenberg that I became personally acquainted with the famous American author.

It is not with any relish that I cite Dreiser's pro-Red record, but it is essential to do so in order to stress the slick ways in which the Communists operate. They are now manipulating Albert Einstein in much the same way; though occasionally he shows his independence, his name has frequently appeared on pro-Red lists. The latest is the very recent call for the Western Hemisphere Congress, in which Einstein joins Lawson, Richard O. Boyer, who has publicly admitted his Communist membership, and other Reds in denunciation of this country and cheers for the Soviet Union. It is obvious that such internationally known names as Dreiser and Einstein go far toward influencing lesser lights to sign up on pro-Red lists—and that they also blunt the awareness of the American people of what is afoot.

Dreiser permitted the Communist party to announce his membership in 1945, when some big move became necessary to offset the demoralization resulting from the spotlight thrown on "Browderism." To my knowledge, however, he had been a party member since the early thirties; and as far back as 1933 had publicly lent his name to the Red cause, thereby securing for the party the allegiance of many lesser writers.

One of Dreiser's famous statements (so far as party circles went) was his endorsement of the *Daily Worker,* published in that paper on January 26, 1933. I have heard his statement quoted repeatedly at party discussions, as demonstrating the agreement of great minds with the violence proposed by Marxism-Leninism. Dreiser wrote, "The *Daily Worker* is the only newspaper in the English language in America today which devotes itself whole-heartedly to the vital interests of the workers. I find in its editorial columns, as well as in its presentation of news, those things which I believe should and do develop in the American Worker of today a sense of his just dues, and the manner in which, in regard to them, he is deceived and exploited." He concluded that the paper was "a singular and most needed force."

Only a week prior to the Dreiser commendation, the Central Committee of the Communist party had published in the same

Daily Worker an appeal "against imperialist war." (January 18, 1933.) The main burden of that appeal was the primary duty of the American people *"to fight against 'our own' imperialist government"*—in other words, to turn the imperialist war into civil war. The editorial columns of the paper necessarily were in wild agreement, and harped on this theme constantly. In citing Dreiser's praise of the paper's editorials, the nature of these editorials was stressed.

It was at that period, it must be remembered, that many liberals and professional people of some note were hoodwinked into joining the League against War and Fascism, which the party viewed as its main means of carrying out the commands of the "open letter" among the intellectuals. It was, as I have said, a replica of other organizations with similar names founded at that time by pro-Soviet agencies in other countries. In the platform of the League, published on October 23 of the same year, 1933, these intellectuals solemnly pledged "to work toward the stoppage of the manufacture and transport of munitions and all other materials essential to the conduct of war through mass demonstrations, picketing and strikes." They were, in this, adopting faithfully the blueprint for violent upheaval first laid down by the Sixth World Congress at Moscow.

That was the atmosphere in "pink" circles when Dreiser wrote his endorsement of the violent tenets of the *Daily Worker*. Two years later, he was inveigled into being a founder of the League of American Writers, along with some other professional authors sprinkled in among Earl Browder, Alexander Trachtenberg and a great number of party hacks, including one or two men whom I knew later as Red espionage agents.

So when I was introduced to Dreiser by Trachtenberg in 1940 at the Hotel Commodore it seemed a matter of course that he should be as putty in Trachty's hands. Foster was with us at Dreiser's request, and Dreiser spoke of him warmly as "the most magnificent of Americans, and the most beautiful character in current American history." As though he were ordering a schoolboy around, Trachty proceeded in a businesslike way (amid his usual chuckles) to tell Dreiser what was wanted of him, by way of a public statement. I was there to write it for Dreiser's subsequent signature. Dreiser used it word for word as given to him. As a good Red in those days I performed a similar ghostwriting function for several other distinguished Americans.

This incident is interesting principally in that it illustrates how some of our best minds are moved around like pawns by the Communists, smaller people often preparing the way for the party leaders by cajolery and suggestion. Secretaries, nurses and other lower-rung professional workers are trained by party section organizers to spy on their employers, and likewise if possible to influence them. That is one of the big reasons for the party's determination to keep control of the United Office and Professional Workers Union, recently expelled from the CIO. (In addition, of course, it has a financial value as well as a nuisance value as a source of pro-Red resolutions and recruits for party picket lines.) I have heard section organizers in New York and Chicago tell secretarial workers what blandishments to use on their employers and how to take advantage of the whims and weaknesses of the particular person involved. In the case of someone important, this softening-up process is often preliminary to his being asked by a Communist friend to sign a petition or to join a certain front.

Another American of note who of late years has appeared on many Communist fronts is Dr. Harlow Shapley, the astronomer, of Harvard University. He was, for example, one of the group of 148 American educators, churchmen, scientists and civic leaders who demanded the investigation of the House Committee on Un-American Activities in 1940. More recently he endorsed the Western Hemisphere Congress of Intellectuals for Peace, although he can hardly be unaware of the fact that writers and scientists alike in Soviet Russia have just been put through a far-reaching purge to rid them of "decadent western culture."

Shapley's association with Communist fronts has been of value to the party in an insidious way. Men like Steve Nelson lost no time in making use of it to win youthful scientists to the same or similar Red fronts and then to sympathy with the party. This has been the introduction in some instances to more serious underground work for the Communist cause.

The Ninth Floor, when I was there, divided into three groups the prospective intellectuals who might be drawn into their fronts. The first, of course, was composed of "our actors, artists and writers," the trained Communist agents; the second was that peculiar type who knows he or she is dealing with Reds but rather likes it; and the third—and in some respects the most valuable—was the unwary innocents who could be reached through their alleged friends or associates. Often, as we have seen, these are people of high position.

The intellectual or professional person in America at this hour bears a grave responsibility. He can no longer sign lists without a thorough examination of the political character of all the signers and of what the real aim of the group is to be. If the name of a busy person in public life is found on one or two Red lists, it is bad enough, though one understands how it can happen. But when that name is discovered on three, four, ten or even a dozen such, America has the right to ask today: *"Can he be so innocent?"*

Should not the famous men and women whose names are placed on such lists respond as Sinclair Lewis recently did? At the first "peace" congress in Poland, Comrade Alexander Fadeev of the Soviet Writers praised Lewis highly for having written that an artist must stand against "tyranny, cruelty and mechanical obedience." Fadeev's aim clearly was to win Lewis to the Soviet side. But Lewis commented that his statement placed him "not as standing for the Soviet Union and its hysterical crusade but against it and its 'tyranny and mechanical obedience.' "

This nation's defense requires statements in similar vein from all those who bear the responsibility of being considered leaders of public opinion. They cannot play the part of pawns to advance the Soviet conquest of America.

(X)

"Cloak and Dagger"

ON AN afternoon in the late spring of 1936 J. V. Peters (then functioning under the name of Jack Roberts) gave me some valuable information on Asia and the Pacific. It is unfortunate that all America could not have listened in on that conversation on Thirteenth Street.

Had America seen and heard us that day, it would have profited by knowing much earlier the man who directed Whittaker Chambers in obtaining stolen documents from the State Department and who was such a big factor in Alger Hiss' career. His work as "the link—the liaison man—between the Soviet secret police and the Communist International apparatus here," as he told me a little later, would have been surmised.

We were in conference on the Ninth Floor, where he had summoned me to get a report on the operation of a Reuter's News Agency correspondent in China who was an alleged Trotskyite. I obtained my data on such matters from Bill Reich, a Communist agent in the Trotsky camp. When that question was settled, Peters brought up the possibility of my finding (among my friends who had championed Soviet recognition) one or two persons who could spy upon the "agents of American imperialism in the Far East."

It was in this connection that he suddenly asked me, in that abrupt, precisely worded manner of his: "Do you know the Stalinist perspectives in the Far East?"

Since I had to reply that my knowledge was only of a general

character—I had joined the party only about six months before—
he proffered this advice:

"Begin then at the beginning, and acquaint yourself with the
Resolution of the Sixth World Communist Congress on the Colonial Question and the Joint Manifesto to the Workers and Peasants of the Philippines."

Diving into his desk he brought out a printed copy of the Joint
Manifesto. I noticed from its title that it came officially from the
combined Communist parties of the United States, China and
Japan, and was an appeal to the Filipinos to take up arms against
the United States. What was more to the point, it set forth the
united determination of the Communists in the Pacific areas, under
Moscow's direction, to drive America out of the Pacific. The Reds
of China, Japan and the United States urged upon the Filipino
people the responsibility of depriving the United States of the islands as "a military base . . . for attempts to crush the ever-growing
power of the Chinese Soviets" and "for the planned war of intervention against the Soviet Union . . ."

Having thus played upon the peace sentiments of the Filipinos,
the Manifesto declared that the only way to peace was through the
inevitable war on the side of Soviet Russia. The heart of the Manifesto asserted that the road to freedom from "Yankee imperialism"
was along the following route:

"It is necessary to add that self-determination will be a fraud, and
independence will be unobtainable without the victorious armed
revolutionary struggle of the masses of workers and peasants led by
the C.P.P.I. [Communist Party of the Philippine Islands]." These
"armed masses" were the sole means by which the "imperialist op-
pressor," that is, the United States, could be defeated; the Communists in the islands (if they faithfully followed the guidance of the
Communist International) would bring about "the liberation of the
Philippine nation under the red banner of a Workers and Peasants
Soviet Republic." (Italics mine.)

With his mechanical smile, Peters reminded me that the "parties in the three largest capitalist countries in the Pacific" had made this their common call to the Filipinos. The Manifesto was no temporary spur to action; it was a permanent program, in which all Red parties joined, to "rid the Far East of imperialism and imperialists, and specifically of Yankee imperialism." This knowledge, he hoped, would underline for me the value of discovering men who could be of service in informing Soviet Russia (through him) of Yankee schemes in China and the Pacific.

In pursuance of this program, James Allen (Sol Auerbach) who later became foreign editor of the *Daily Worker*, was dispatched to the Philippines as a Comintern agent. Allen was well suited to the assignment, since he is one of the bitterest enemies that "American imperialism" has, and he was successful in establishing mail-drop contacts with many active Reds in the Philippines and adjacent territory. It was recognized even then that the Red conquest of China would provide a jumping-off place to Formosa and thus enable the Soviet Union to wrest the Philippines "from American imperialism."

On both the Eighth and Ninth floors this Manifesto calling clearly for Soviet conquest of the Pacific was an often-quoted document. One year after Peters brought it to my notice, I heard Alexander Bittelman tell the Politburo that the "unity of the parties for defense of the Soviet Union in the Pacific" was a key to the Red outlook in America. It was cited again, just on the eve of my leaving the party, in a Politburo discussion of Moscow's order to keep the United States out of China. That discussion, incidentally, later produced a "Get-out-of-China week," headed by a committee under the chairmanship of the late General Evans Carlson, to prevent the United States from taking any decisive action in the Far East.

An echo of the Manifesto is to be found in the judgment rendered by *Political Affairs* for August, 1949, on the staggering defeat of the United States in China. It says: "The defeats inflicted on American imperialism by the victories of the Chinese Liberation Armies guided by the brilliant Leninist, Mao Tse-tung, have already made a tremendous contribution to peace and democracy." It declares exultantly that "the Open Door policy is now in limbo . . . because the Chinese people are closing the door on American imperialism."

What has happened in China was all blueprinted in the Resolution and Manifesto adopted at the Sixth Congress, blueprinted and published for anyone to read—the aim itself, and the ways in which such Communist-engineered revolts among peoples can be merged with disruption within the "imperialist countries" to achieve Soviet world dictatorship.

No one, no matter how politically blind, who had read this document or heard Peters discuss it with me that day in 1936 could have had any doubt that widespread infiltration of government and political agencies was a set Soviet task. Nor should he have been surprised to hear Peters, in his precise manner, outline definite plans for obtaining information on America's military policy in the Far East by setting up a third spy ring in Washington. In addition to its espionage work, this ring was to serve as a check on the famous "Washington cell" and also on the agents penetrating the Institute of Pacific Relations. Peters asked for my help in setting it up because the young people trained in the YCL for this kind of work either were not the type he wanted at the moment or were not available. I was able to make some suggestions which he later admitted grudgingly had been useful. His third ring was set up. What it did, of course, I never learned in detail. In a conspiracy, the left hand never lets the right hand know what it is doing—and the right hand never asks questions.

I did learn, however, while I was in the party, that there were various divisions of Soviet espionage in the United States. Most of my information came from Jacob Golos, and he was an expert in Soviet espionage. The Soviet military forces conducted their own activities, frequently making arrangements with men and women in the party apparatus here to carry out specified assignments. Bluntly, this meant that certain American Communists were turned over to Soviet agents for espionage service to obtain some particular, definite piece of information. It might have to do with atomic secrets; it might have to do with the latest airplane construction. In addition, some comrades, because of their position, were permanently assigned to this kind of work. In this role, Noel Field, a Bostonian and former State Department employee, walks like a shadow through report after report to the Ninth Floor.

There was also the direct activity of the Soviet secret police, the NKVD or MVD, which was more concerned with obtaining State secrets and information on the leading figures in American public life. A third division was the Comintern apparatus, which also carried on espionage work, the value of which in many cases was to break the ground for the other two agencies.

Co-ordination of these various efforts was definitely in the hands of the Soviet secret police, who served as a clearing house for both general political and espionage activities, as well as a channel of information.

And finally, as we know from my conversation with Gebert, recounted earlier, there was being developed in 1945 a plan to make wider use of the satellite states' embassies and staffs. The thought was that both the direction of espionage and the transmission of instructions to the party here could be expedited and safeguarded by their diffusion through the diplomatic representatives of these countries.

Naturally, the activities connected with the work of these several agencies led occasionally to jurisdictional disputes among the heads of different Soviet spy rings. Everybody connected with espionage was always seeking feverishly to set up an effective apparatus to further the assignments given him. It is impossible to convey an idea of the pressure on the Soviet secret police from Moscow and in turn the pressure exerted by them on the comrades with whom they worked. Many of the secret-police agents complained of heart trouble, which was one reason they always hastened to get rid of any documents on their persons.

It was through one of these jurisdictional contests over the infiltration of the OSS in 1943 that I learned of Eugene Dennis' direction of that form of espionage in Washington. For just as the Communists made a determined effort to get as many men as possible into publicity posts affecting the soldiers, so did they make the infiltration of the OSS one of their major concerns. When you had a secret clique helping you, it was not too difficult. The conflict in this case was between Dennis' ring and one supervised by Golos. It started when Golos asked me to begin building up a number of espionage contacts in Washington. One of the men I approached was a writer who was connected with the moving-picture industry. He told me, however, that he was responsible to Dr. Martin Blumberg and to Dennis, who were directing the agents in the Office of Strategic Services. Dennis spoke to me about the matter, too, asking me not to recruit this particular writer into the group around Golos but to get other men for that purpose. It was then I also learned that Carl Aldo Marzani, known sometimes as Tony Whales in party circles, was one of the Dennis ring. Marzani is now in Federal prison for swearing falsely that he was not a Communist at the time he entered the OSS or while associated with it.

Out in Chicago, Morris Childs was also directing espionage activity, though his public position was that of district organizer for Illinois. One of Boleslaw Gebert's greatest difficulties at this time was avoiding friction with Childs while at the same time directing the espionage work of the Slav comrades in the northern Illinois and northern Indiana areas. It went so far that Gebert often slipped into Chicago without Childs' knowledge—a practice that on one occasion led to a brief but sharp altercation between them. The subject of their quarrel was a Czech comrade who was doing vital underground work for Gebert.

To the jurisdictional quarrels over particular espionage agents was sometimes added a difference of opinion concerning the degree of secret work a comrade should do. At one time, Browder had a serious clash with Golos, Peters, and others on this issue. It was re-

solved by the intervention of the secret police, who effected a compromise based upon the position of the comrade in relation to the
party.

Another dispute of this nature occurred during a National Committee meeting, and incidentally it confirmed what I had learned
previously at the *Daily Worker* of the valuable services rendered by
Noel Field to the party and the Soviet state. In the course of the
conversation, in which I took a small part, his continuous work as
an operative for the Soviet secret police was brought out clearly,
and I was not surprised when he disappeared in 1949 behind the
iron curtain. As Noel Field, at least, his services for Stalin's secret
police had ended. The immediate reference to this able State Department employee's long labors as a Red agent was made during
a small conference at the back of the hall among Bittelman, Stachel
and Dr. Martin Blumberg over the nature of the report to the meeting from the District of Columbia. For several years the question of
how much time should be spent in Soviet espionage activities and
how much in promoting domestic party objectives had been particularly acute with respect to the Communists in the national capital.
There was some concern on the Ninth Floor itself that the direct
influence of the party on certain congressmen and senators might be
dissipated if the persons making the contacts were diverted into
illegal assignments. Blumberg wished to use Field as an illustration
of the problem. Bittelman and Stachel finally agreed, provided the
allusion was a veiled one.

In addition to such frequent reminders of the undercover nature
of much of the party's work, I had at my elbow, almost every day
during my last three years at the *Daily Worker*, Felix Kuzman,
Eisler's courier to the Eighth and Ninth floors. I knew him well,
and something of his record in the Spanish Civil War. He would
come into my office quietly, always on the alert to make certain no
"outside person" was there, and then would unobtrusively and
quickly deliver his message. That he regularly visited men in scien-

tific fields I know from several references he was compelled to make
in order to render his instructions for me more understandable.

Having thus lived for ten years in the company of Soviet spies
and undercover agents, I find myself sometimes at a loss to understand the innocence and complacency of America concerning the
extent of Communist infiltration and espionage. Nothing is more
indicative of this attitude than the popular use of the phrase "cloak
and dagger" to characterize spy revelations—even after it is known
that the American code was stolen from the State Department at
Peters' orders and with Chambers' connivance; that valuable data
on China was filched from the same files under the direction of a
Soviet agent in the *Amerasia* magazine case.

It is also a well-known fact—and I know it much better than
those who have commented on it from outside the Communist ranks
—that the union among the Federal employees, formerly in the
CIO, the United Public Workers Union, was long under Red
control. One of its top officers used to come frequently to New
York, to my house, to confer with me, and I also had a number of
conferences on the Ninth Floor with Roy Hudson, then head of
the party's labor division, and another leader in this union, a woman
who visited the Red headquarters regularly for enlightenment and
instruction. It must be obvious that many secretaries and other office
workers in Washington who were members of this union were
influenced by the leadership and even persuaded to engage in anti-
government activities.

Of the many persons who I knew were penetrating or influencing
the government for the Reds, but whose names our libel laws prevent me from mentioning, this one comment can be made: It is a
matter of grave concern in this crisis that the former counsel for
such a large government agency as the National Labor Relations
Board should refuse to state under oath whether or not he is a
member of the Communist party. That is what Nathan Witt has
done. It is a further serious fact that the general secretary of the
large and vital United Electrical Workers union should likewise

refuse to swear concerning his alleged Communist allegiance. This man, Julius Emspak, is not only the head of a union so notoriously under Red control that the Atomic Energy Commission refused to permit it on any project, but he was also a member of the President's Labor Commission during the war, a most delicate position.

Much of the misunderstanding of today's realities—including the cloak-and-dagger phraseology—arises undoubtedly from the emotions and alliances of World War II. The Communists were well aware of the advantages they were gaining through the war propaganda about "our gallant ally," a propaganda which Stalin was careful not to copy concerning America. At all their wartime party meetings (and even in published articles) they pointed out that this would aid them for years to come. As Peters wrote in a memorandum to the Politburo: "The good repute which the Soviet Union and Comrade Stalin win now will not be wiped out for years. By that time, we will be in another position, an impregnable position, if we work correctly." There is also a good-natured tradition in America, rising in part from the country's long-isolated position, that one must avoid "hysterical" attitudes. This too concealed Soviet agents can cultivate successfully.

The seriousness of the cloak-and-dagger business, however, has been verified innumerable times—most recently by the conviction of Judith Coplon, by the revelations in the trial of Alger Hiss, and by the confirmation of Elizabeth Bentley's testimony by a number of people, including Henry Julian Wadleigh, who had every reason not to confirm it. It will be remembered that Miss Bentley told of extensive espionage activities as a courier between New York and Washington under the direction of Jacob Golos of the World Tourists. After Golos' death, Miss Bentley (whom I knew as Helen Johns) was assigned to work directly with the Soviet military espionage agency, and at that time became aware of the ruthlessness of their methods and aims. She went voluntarily to the FBI and even turned over to them the $2,000 she had received as "final payment" from the Russians when she asked to be relieved.

The fact of conspiracy is most eloquently supported by the inability of the Communists themselves, in trial after trial, to put up a sound defense; instead, they resort to legal technicalities. An outstanding instance is the incident in the trial of Harold R. Christoffel for perjury, when the chairman of the Communist party of Wisconsin, Fred Bassett Blair, refused to say whether he knew the defendant as a Communist or knew him at all. *His reason: that the answer would tend to incriminate him, Blair!*

By taking advantage of the minor technicalities of our judicial processes the Reds do succeed to a degree in giving the people a blurred picture of the extent of their seditious activities.

Even more damning are the lengths to which the Red will go in order to avoid trial at all. One common device of the Communists, when caught with a serious espionage or passport offense which may dramatize their connections with Moscow, is to get busy immediately with a "compromise." The late Joseph Brodsky, a Communist lawyer who was entrusted with the secret transmission of funds and information between the Communist party here and the Reds abroad, was a past master in working out these arrangements. In his office in mid-Manhattan he explained to me one day in 1945 how this was done. "Politicians don't like to have trouble," he commented in his forthright fashion, "and we have enough concealed comrades in both the Republican and Democratic parties to persuade the politicians that a compromise in these cases is the best thing." That is the way, he went on to say, that they had got Jacob Golos to plead guilty to not registering as a foreign agent for the World Tourists and to pay a small fine. And through that arrangement they had persuaded the government to drop a number of other cases which would have embarrassed the Communist party. It was, for instance, so that other charges would be dropped that Philip Jaffe pleaded guilty to stealing the *Amerasia* papers. Brodsky laughed heartily as he pointed out that if Jaffe had come into possession of the papers through a theft, someone else must have stolen them.

As the record stands, the papers came into Jaffe's hands illegally, but in some mysterious way.

Brodsky's dissertation on "compromises" was occasioned by a discussion of the need for working out a strategy of a similar nature in case of new arrests on espionage or passport-fraud charges. The whole effort had to be to reach some quiet arrangement which would continue to hide from public scrutiny the wide extent of these practices.

Where possible of course, the Communists prefer to rely on pressure tactics to get a case dropped. Not long after I went to Chicago, many returned members of the Abraham Lincoln Brigade were arrested in connection with passport frauds, for it was on false passports or through false representation that the Communist party got them into Spain. But after a while, all the cases were dropped and the entire matter was hushed up. This action was not attributable to the Attorney General, Robert H. Jackson, who on the whole proved to be more aware of the Red danger than many men in high positions at that time. The cases were dropped through a terrific back-of-the-scenes pressure campaign conducted by the Communists, largely in the Chicago area, which enmeshed a number of their newfound political friends. One of the big political bosses in Chicago was persuaded by his cousin, who was a Communist, to become an active champion of the "rights" of the Red fighters in Spain. The labor adviser to another important figure in Chicago political circles was also a Communist, well concealed, of course, and he did his share in getting that particular member of the Kelly-Nash machine to act. A woman lawyer, who is likewise a Red, and who enjoys ironically enough, the good will of the *Chicago Tribune,* also did effective work behind the scenes in the City's influential political circles. As a result of these combined pressures, added perhaps to other efforts, it was an easy matter to get the cases dropped.

As exhibits of what cloak-and-dagger Communist underground work accomplished (and bearing in mind that influence is as much a part of this endeavor as espionage) we can present the strange cases of China, Henry Agard Wallace, Wendell Willkie and Wall Street.

I have said before that to my mind one of the major hoaxes perpetrated in our generation was the legend that the Chinese Communists were not Communists at all, but merely agrarian reformers. In that role, it was said, they had little or no relation with Moscow. Authors who visited the Orient solemnly wrote books to that effect and had them solemnly and often favorably circulated. One of these authors, Harrison Forman, whose book the Communists were ordered to push in 1945, even though he was not a party member, went to the length of saying that in Red Yenan he had seen no evidences of control by Moscow of the Chinese Communists. He could have saved himself from a long trip and a bad mistake by staying right here in America and consulting (in English incidentally) the Chinese Communist official declarations of subservience to Stalin.

The Communists, fortunately, are obliged to put a lot of their thoughts into print in many languages, since that is one of the principal ways in which they send out their world-wide conspiratorial instructions. Thus we can read the official greetings of the Central Committee of the Communist party of China to the Seventh World Congress of the Communist International, held in Moscow in 1935. There the Chinese Communists express their gratitude to "the glorious Bolshevik cohorts" of the Soviet Union, and look forward to "the decisive barricade fights for the Soviet Power throughout the world," with a pledge that the Chinese Communists will not be found wanting. They also state that they will defeat "international imperialism" in China, and add: "We are certain that, under the leadership of the Communist International, this mighty creation of Lenin and Stalin, we shall achieve complete and decisive victory." In a spirit of adulation for the great leader, they conclude: "May all the work of the Seventh Congress be filled with a practical Stalinist spirit, with Stalinist wisdom, with Stalinist belief in the justice of our cause and a Stalinist will to victory! *Long live the Communist*

International! Long live our teacher and guide, Comrade Stalin!"

Our Ninth Floor discussions were often dominated by a consciousness of the tremendous potential of China's manpower and materials. That land was labeled "the key to Asia and the Pacific." When J. V. Peters took up with me plans for infiltrating Hawaii with our California undercover agents, he emphasized the relation between those islands and China.

The path that Asiatic operations would follow was traced on many occasions—by Jacob Golos in secret conferences on infiltration and by party theoreticians like Bittelman and Max Weiss in more open party "educational" discussions. Always stressed was the necessity of aiding the struggle of the China Reds as a preliminary to "the overthrow of our own *bourgeoisie.*" The two are linked up in immense detail in the Resolution of the Sixth World Congress (1928) on revolutionary activities in the colonial countries. They were constantly brought to our attention as being "hand-in-hand" operations.

The route of Soviet conquest, as mapped out more vividly by the secret agents Golos and Peters, was always the same. China first, followed by Japan and Korea, the Philippines—and then Hawaii and Alaska! The success of the Chinese Reds today makes quite real the possibilities of this program. Our military authorities have shown that they understand the parachuting potential in the Chinese manpower by suggesting even at this early date the transfer of our aircraft factories from the West Coast to the interior of America.

This grave threat to our national security is largely of America's own making. Most Americans, during World War II, were victims of the Moscow line that the Chinese Communists were not real Communists. They firmly believed that Mao Tse-tung's soldiers were nothing more than "agrarian reformers," as many of the commentators on the Orient told them. To prove that contention, they could cite T. A. Bisson in the *Far Eastern Survey,* who wrote that "by no stretch of the imagination can this be termed communism;

it is, in fact, the essence of bourgeois democracy, applied mainly to agrarian conditions."

And that is just what Moscow wanted the Americans to believe. The deception of government officials and of the public was the result of a planned campaign; its aim was to win American confidence so that the United States' foreign policy on China might be influenced to Moscow's own ends. The principal objective was a Chinese "coalition government," in which Chiang Kai-shek (or any other Chinese Nationalist leader) would accept the "agrarian reformers," at the insistence of the United States.

My own activities in this connection led me among men in high places in Washington, including a noted senator, a leading congressman, and a man whose missions for this country took him to many parts of the world. But the Asiatic consignment's chief contact man in the capital was Frederick Vanderbilt Field, who at that time concealed his Red affiliation but has since acknowledged it. Today, as a matter of fact, he is the Communists' chief policy man on the Far East.

Field's mission was to the State Department, where there were valuable channels through which to pour his propaganda that Mao Tse-tung's followers were "democratic." But once the Chinese Reds gained the upper hand Field changed his tune. In July, 1948, issue of *Political Affairs*, he wrote:

"Our Chinese comrades are destroying American imperialism in the Far East. Let us American anti-imperialists, at least accept and make use of the historic contribution which they are making toward their own welfare."

This alternate presentation of the Chinese Reds as bleating lambs and as the nemesis of the United States shifted with the devious, opportunistic course of Moscow strategy. The first twist, in my experience, came in 1937. Earl Browder, then general secretary of the party, called a "Chinese conference" on Thirteenth Street.

Grouped beneath pictures of Lenin and Stalin in the Ninth Floor office overlooking the street were ten U.S. Communist leaders. In addition to Trachtenberg and Peters, there were present: Fred Brown, tall, impressive-looking, bearded, whose real name was Ferucci Marini and who was a Communist International secret agent; the late Harry Gannes, foreign editor of the *Daily Worker* and Red expert on China; Sam Carr, national organizer of the Canadian Communists and now in prison for espionage; Carl Bristel, active in the Young Communist League which was in turn active in underground activities; Frederick Vanderbilt Field, Browder and myself.

Browder announced that he had received word that "the followers of Mao Tse-tung have to be presented in a new dress." With a sardonic grin, he said the new object was to picture them as something like "North Dakota Non-Partisan Leaguers of some time back," a mild variation of agrarian reformers. Up to that point they had been known simply as Chinese Communists; indeed many articles praised them for their Soviet aims.

We agreed that the change could not be effected immediately, since our recent emphasis had been so firmly on the "revolutionary aspects of the Chinese Soviets." Then Field outlined an alternative. We could work through legitimate Far East organizations and writers that were recognized as Oriental authorities. Field emphasized penetration of the Institute of Pacific Relations. This is not a Communist organization; but Field later succeeded in becoming secretary of its American Council, and its staff has always been weighted with Reds or pro-Reds to a painful degree. Also chosen for propaganda and contacts were the American League Against War and Fascism and the American Friends of the Chinese People, both of them Red-front organizations. Their publications *Fight* and *China Today* were to be used in this deception.

The "agrarian reformers" idea began to spread from there. It took deep root in leading Far Eastern cultural groups in the United States, spread to certain policy-making circles in the State Department and broke into a prominent position in the American press. The Reds pressed it with all the intensity and shrewdness of which they were capable; later on Browder was to state to the National Committee (of which I was a member) that the "winning of a Red China is a matter of life or death, and is the special assignment to the American party."

It was Browder who directed the new Chinese policy. Having served two years in China as a Comintern representative, he was a Red authority on that country. Ostensibly, back in 1927, he was one of a three-man International Workers Delegation to China, composed of himself, Tom Mann of England and Jacques Doriot of France (Doriot later renounced Communism). Actually, Browder's job in China had been to undermine American prestige by shouting about the evils of "the Dollar Republic" and its sins as "the exploiter of all countries."

Significantly, he had arrived in China just after Chiang Kai-shek threw out the Communists who tried to take over the Kuomintang. A raid on the Soviet embassy in Peking a short while before had revealed conclusive evidence of the Comintern plot to use the Kuomintang for its own purpose of world revolution. Then, as now, China was considered the focal point for the establishment of the world proletarian dictatorship. And one of Moscow's agents in the Kuomintang Central Executive Committee prior to the 1927 expulsions was Mao Tse-tung, the peasant leader who had helped organize the Chinese Communist party in 1921.

But ten years later—by 1937—Mao Tse-tung was just an "agrarian reformer." The Reds were seeking "coalition" with Chiang Kai-shek (coalition, of course, as in Czechoslovakia and other countries, meaning the destruction of the one foolish enough to "coalesce" with the Reds). When the Japanese invaded China, Mao proposed "national unity arrangements" to Chiang.

That show of co-operation lasted until Stalin's 1939 pact with Hitler. Immediately, the Chinese Reds branded the European conflict an "imperialist war" and broke relations with the Nationalist government. Soon after, Soviet Russia signed a nonaggression pact with Japan.

As docile tools of the Kremlin, Mao and his associates approved that act and of course went further. While wartime Red propaganda in our country made use of the "gallant fight" Mao and his armies were ostensibly continuing to make against the Japanese, no Communist apologist has been able to explain what actually happened. Ten Japanese divisions moved from Manchuria into the central China front—*through Communist-held territory*—without meeting any show of resistance. It was that Japanese force which eventually cut through east China and overran General Claire Chennault's U.S. Fourteenth Air Force bases. That development is not particularly surprising when we recall that Maurice Thorez, chairman of the French Communist party, and other French Red leaders deserted their nation's Army rather than fight against Stalin's friend Hitler.

In the midst of the Stilwell crisis in October, 1944, the Chinese Reds issued another call for "coalition" government through Chou En-lai, leading assistant to Mao Tse-tung and chief negotiator during the 1946 China mission of General Marshall. But just six months later—before Marshall went to China—the Communist duplicity in this proposal was revealed, and by none other than Mao himself. At the Seventh National Convention of the Chinese Communist party, Mao made a special report on coalition government. Coalition, he said, was merely a slogan that would lead to the destruction of Chiang Kai-shek and the defeat of "reactionary American imperialism." That revelation re-emphasized the party resolution adopted in 1944: "The cooperation of the Chinese Communist Party with the United States is a temporary strategy."

From Thirteenth Street we watched with intense interest these moves in China, constantly working like beavers to mislead the American people and their leadership. General Marshall was the particular object of secret "influences" of which he was unaware.

This game of Red deceit began the rout of Nationalist China in late 1945. Soviet Russia, permitted by us to enter Manchuria, carried on a phony war of six days with the Japanese there, disarmed

625,000 Nipponese soldiers and turned their weapons over to the Chinese Communists. That Russian-donated booty enabled the Chinese Reds to drive Chiang Kai-shek's soldiers out of north China and led to the serious collapse of today. Three months before Soviet Russia thus armed Mao Tse-tung's forces, Moscow had pledged friendship to Chiang's Nationalist government in return for China's forced agreement to the Kremlin's claims in Manchuria.

One of the devices by which the Communists impressed their views on certain key people in the American State Department was to plant articles with the proper slant in such magazines as *Far Eastern Survey, Pacific Affairs,* and *Amerasia.* The first two are both publications of the Institute of Pacific Relations.

While, as I have said, that Institute is not in itself a Communist front, party members and apologists infiltrated its most influential committees and publications, and their articles and speeches were used as reference material by the Far Eastern Division of our State Department. Communist writers like James Allen, who had been the chief Communist representative in the Philippines and who was to become foreign editor of the *Daily Worker,* were used openly as pamphlet writers for the IPR. Another writer it relied upon to inform the American public on the Pacific was Abraham Chapman, one of the editorial-board members of the Communist *Daily Freiheit.* So blatantly did the Reds take advantage of their connections in the IPR that when Frederick Vanderbilt Field, an official of the Institute, attended the opening conference of the United Nations at San Francisco, he served at the same time as a correspondent for the *Daily Worker*—a dual role that was made much of at a special Communist meeting staged at that time in San Francisco.

The Aladdin-like success of *Amerasia's* entree to at least some key circles of the State Department is a court-proven fact. Its coeditor, Philip J. Jaffe, after paying a fine of only $2500 for stealing State Department papers in 1945, entertained his codefendants (some whose indictments had been dismissed) and members of the *Daily Worker* staff at a party. Toasts were drunk that night to the "coming victory of Communism in China and the defeat of American imperialism."

Jaffe had also edited, with Field, under the names of Phillips and Spencer respectively, an openly Red magazine called *China Today*, and for several years had the offices of the magazine in the same brick building on East 52nd Street that housed the Institute of Pacific Relations, in order to be able to work more conveniently in that organization, where, of course, both he and Field were known under their own names.

Among the people with whom Jaffe rubbed shoulders in the IPR was John S. Service, now American consul in Calcutta. A champion of the Chinese Communists and an adviser to General Stilwell in China, he was one of those who urged a coalition between the Chinese Nationalists and the Communists; he also served with Owen J. Lattimore as adviser to Vice-President Henry Wallace and to our government on Chinese affairs. Mr. Service became sufficiently impressed with Jaffe to collaborate with him on *Amerasia*, the magazine through which Jaffe came into possession of the papers from the State Department files. Service was accused of being involved in this theft, but was exonerated by the Federal grand jury at the same time that Jaffe pleaded guilty.

I had first learned about Jaffe from the Soviet secret police in the United States. They said he was a "valuable friend." Later, through reports of the National Committee, I learned that *Amerasia's* main objective was to establish State Department contacts which would be helpful in stopping U.S. aid to Chiang Kai-shek.

The Reds used to laugh about the ingratiating manner Jaffe assumed at the IPR meetings. He would bustle about, passing out programs and acting as busy as if he, like Field, were a member of the staff—which he was not. This act paid off well eventually, for both men moved back and forth in the most confidential Washington circles, spreading news and information helpful to the Chinese Reds.

When America's arms and valor had tipped the war scales against

Japan, Soviet Russia immediately assailed Chiang Kai-shek. An editorial in the *Daily Worker*, for August 15, 1945, declared that *"not a single American gun, soldier, plane, or other war equipment must be placed at the disposal of the Fascist clique at Chungking."*

Less than twenty-four hours after Japan surrendered, therefore, Chiang had become a "Fascist," a term which indicated that war to the death was on. In the top stories of Thirteenth Street, we were alerted to our task; it was to raise the cry, "Hands off China!"

Two days after the first editorial in the *Daily Worker*, there appeared in its pages a paid "message" to President Truman. Its wording was substantially the same as the *Daily Worker* editorial of August 15. It was signed by "twenty-one prominent Americans." Among them: Frederick Vanderbilt Field; Lawrence Salisbury, an IPR editor; T. A. Bisson, the China expert to whom the Chinese Reds were "the essence of bourgeois democracy."

Later, the *Daily Worker* editorial was supplemented by a memorandum from the New York State office of the Communist party. The subject: Campaign of Struggle against United States Imperialist Intervention in China. I still have a photostatic copy of it.

The memo ordered picket lines, mass meetings and Congressional protest delegations "in opposition to the Truman Administration and Republican party policies of imperialist world domination . . . and imperialist intervention in China." As a means to that end, it recommended the sale and maximum distribution of Mao Tse-tung's book, *China's New Democracy*. It didn't mention, however, that the U.S. version of Mao's book had been revised by Earl Browder and other Communists back in the late 1930's to edit out embarrassing references to the "dictatorship" (in the image and likeness of Stalin's) that he planned to establish once the Reds came to power in China.

The memo also suggested books by two American authors as reading material: Harrison Forman's *Report from Red China* and Gunther Stein's *Challenge of Red China*. Both had pictured the Reds as agrarian reformers.

Almost at the same time Mao Tse-tung openly declared that he stood with Russia and against the United States, telling the Chinese Communist Convention of 1945 that "coalition government" was a temporary expedient, one that would lead to the destruction of Chiang Kai-shek and American imperialism. Mao's attack on America was made while U.S. and Russian troops were still celebrating their link-up at the Elbe River.

Thus the conquest of China by Soviet Russia was assured, owing in considerable degree to the influence exerted on agencies and organs of public opinion by the Soviet fifth column, often acting through people who were not even Communists. At Yalta in February, 1945, while the Chinese Reds were preparing their anti-American crusade, the United States gave to Soviet Russia the Japanese arms and arsenals. Our State Department placed an embargo—or what amounted to one—on assistance to Nationalist China. As far back as the late spring of 1945 the comrades were holding small celebrations among the top-circle people, congratulating themselves on their success in blinding America to its own interests in China.

It is a fact that for weeks prior to the Yalta Conference, Communist agents in Washington had been instructed to gather every reliable bit of data available on President Roosevelt's hopes, plans, and fears in the war. All this information was garnered by the Ninth Floor and forwarded to Moscow. Since Stalin could check this information against that coming in from other agents, it can be appreciated how well prepared the Soviet dictator was for his meeting with Roosevelt and Churchill.

The Ninth Floor had remarkably accurate knowledge of exactly when the conference was to take place. Jack Stachel told me that it was about to occur long before the news agencies sent out secret advance information to their affiliated editors to that effect. It was also a foregone conclusion at Communist headquarters that Stalin would get all he went after, and that the meeting would represent a great Soviet victory.

About this time, Stachel showed me a map of how Europe was to be divided which was quite prophetic. It placed Poland, Hungary, Czechoslovakia, Bulgaria, Rumania, and Yugoslavia in Soviet hands. He even pointed out that this would accord more closely with the longitudinal division of Europe.

"It does not mean that this division is static from the Soviet viewpoint," Stachel explained with a smile. "The Soviet democratic wave will undoubtedly move beyond these lines. When it hits Greece, or crosses Austria or western Germany, which are tentatively set in the Western Powers' zone, there will be an anti-Soviet outcry. That has to be prepared for, but we will be able to call upon the spirit of Yalta in standing by Soviet demands."

The case of Henry Wallace, whom the Kremlin favored openly for the Presidency of the United States, is less complicated than that of China. But it follows the same pattern.

Wallace, though not a Communist, has the unique distinction of having been directly chosen by the Kremlin to lead the "progressive" political forces in this country. Not even the top men of the American Communist party know what, if anything, happened during Wallace's visit to Siberia to cause the Kremlin to send urgent directives to this country that his political ambitions were to be supported.

Wallace went on his mission to China and to Soviet Siberia in the fateful year of 1945. The American people never knew much about Wallace's adventures in Siberia except what they read in the newspapers and what was disclosed in his book, *Soviet Asia Mission*. Perhaps there was nothing more to know. In Soviet Asia Wallace praised conditions. Speaking in the slave-labor region at Irkutsk, he proclaimed that "men born in wide, free spaces will not brook injustice and tyranny. They will not even temporarily live in slavery." This speech was made soon after Wallace had posed for a photograph with Ivan Nikishov, chief of the NKVD (secret police) and dictator of Russia's slave empire. Wallace described Nikishov as an "industrial boss."

It was while Wallace was on his Siberia-China trip that the order to support him came through from the Kremlin.

The Communist campaign to take Wallace "into custody" had begun long before—to be exact, in late June of 1944. On a hot night in that month I was busy at my desk in the office of the *Daily Worker* when Jack Stachel burst into the room. He was greatly excited, and told me to come upstairs at once for a special meeting of the National Board. Urgent orders from Moscow had just been received through Gerhart Eisler that Henry Wallace was to be supported for the Vice-Presidential nomination at the forthcoming Democratic National Convention. Only Stachel did not say "from Moscow"; the Communists seldom mention the Soviet capital. With characteristic indirectness they say that a message has been received "from across the sea" or "from the east" or even, sometimes, simply "from there."

When the meeting convened, six or eight top-flight Communist leaders were present, including Earl Browder, Eugene Dennis, Robert Minor, Jim Ford and Alexander Bittelman. And, of course, Jack Stachel. Alexander Trachtenberg was there, too, though technically not a member of the Board. Eisler was not present. He had gone underground and was not appearing at such conclaves. However, full reports were made to him by Stachel and Bittelman for transmission to Moscow.

The instructions from the Kremlin had caught the members of the Board by surprise. Only a month before, Adam Lapin, Washington correspondent of the *Daily Worker*, had surprisingly been ordered to write that Wallace was too intemperate in his criticism of big business, and that if he was defeated for the Vice-Presidential nomination it would be largely his own fault. Bear in mind that this was at the time when the Communist party had been officially "dissolved" and transformed into the Communist Political Association, and during the period when the line was to concede graciously that capitalism had a place in the world.

Stachel raised the question of whether Wallace was to be backed "at all costs." He argued that further clarification was essential, and that action should be postponed until the orders from Moscow could be more clearly interpreted. The comrades were also concerned about Wallace's reported association with Nicholas Roerich, the so-called Guru. The Guru letters were already being talked about in Washington, and we had received complete reports of Wallace's mystical adventures from our excellent sources of information at the capital. The Communist leaders, to my knowledge, had had certain underground relationships with Nicholas Roerich, and they were of the opinion that any admiration of his occult powers was a sign of irresponsibility.

After a few hours this worried group of comrades adjourned, and another meeting was called for three days later. Meanwhile Stachel and Bittelman were to obtain from Eisler a clarification of the Kremlin directive.

At this second meeting, held in a hall near the Thirteenth Street headquarters, there were present all who had attended the earlier session. In addition, there were Gil Green, then head of the New York State Communist organization, and Roy Hudson. Stachel and Bittelman reported that the party need have no further doubts about Wallace; that Eisler had said that he was to be supported to the limit and at all costs. It was at this meeting that Bittelman made the statement that the Soviet Union would support Wallace. "For us," he said, "this is decisive."

Bittelman's statement settled everything. Immediately every man present became an enthusiastic Wallaceite. Earl Browder led off with a brief speech urging full and unrestrained support for the Iowan. He was followed by Robert Minor in a similar vein. Minor, who had always said that he would stand or fall with Browder, and who finally fell with him when Browder was deposed as party secretary, took occasion to hail Browder as "the greatest Marxist in the Western Hemisphere," a description that Bittelman greeted with a sly and prophetic smile. Other speakers pointed out that Wallace had "ever been a sincere friend of the Soviet Union."

As far as I know, Wallace was not told that he had been adopted as the darling of the comrades. There is no doubt, however, that the Communists did all in their power to see that Moscow's wishes were carried out. Nearly all the public sentiment which developed in favor of Wallace during the few weeks prior to the Democratic Convention of 1944 was fomented and organized by the Communists.

Both before the Hitler-Stalin pact and in the period which followed Pearl Harbor, when the Russians were greeting the capitalistic Americans as brothers-in-arms, the party had been busy. We had strengthened our position in many labor unions, and had gained a controlling voice in several. We had formed a large number of front organizations, and had infiltrated law and other professional groups and community associations. We had gained a foothold in Democratic party organizations in almost every state, and were particularly strong in Ohio and New York, and in California, too, where yeoman service had been performed by the Hollywood party unit of movie actors, writers, producers and directors.

From all of these organizations came a flood of demands to the Democrats, inspired by the Communist members, for Wallace as Roosevelt's running mate. The *Daily Worker* gave impetus to the drive. Earl Browder told me that one editorial alone, published on July 12, 1944, had caused 20,000 letters to be written in two days to Democratic politicians, all demanding the nomination of Wallace.

Every Communist in the country recognized this editorial directive as an urgent order to get to work. They immediately began to stimulate their neighbors, associates and fellow workers to write or wire on Wallace's behalf. Nor were the farmers and the people of the small towns neglected. The rural campaign was placed under the direction of A. W. Mills, the underground agent of the Soviet Union who had been ordered deported in 1936, but was still here eight years later because Russia, where he was born, had refused to accept him. They did not work or write as Communists, mind you. Just as Americans—loyal Americans.

The Communists explained away Wallace's failure to get the nomination by stating that they had been mainly interested in Roosevelt's re-election, but they were not dissatisfied with what they had accomplished. And they at once let Wallace know that they had supported him to the limit of their strength. This they did by editorials and articles in the *Daily Worker* and other publications. These were called to Wallace's attention by Communists and fellow travelers close to him. None reported that he showed any displeasure.

When the confirmation of Wallace as Secretary of Commerce was before the Senate early in 1945, the Communist organization went all out for him to an even greater extent than it had before.

It was during this campaign that Alexander Trachtenberg told a meeting of the National Board that "we are taking Wallace into custody." A few days after Trachtenberg made this statement, two comrades who held important posts in Washington told us that good progress was being made in winning Wallace's confidence.

Twice during the year that followed Wallace's confirmation as Secretary of Commerce, the Soviet Union gave evidence of its high regard for him. In April, 1945, Jacques Duclos, general secretary of the French Communist party and known in secret Communist circles as the "voice of Moscow to the West," published his famous article attacking Earl Browder, which resulted in Browder's losing his job as general secretary of the American party.

In denouncing Browder for taking a too-complacent view of "the trusts," Duclos praised Wallace thus: "It is known that the former Vice-President of the United States, Henry Wallace, has denounced their evil doings and their antinational policy."

The second public assurance that Moscow had not changed its mind about Wallace was in the nature of a rebuke to the American comrades. In September, 1946, during a speech at Madison Square Garden, Wallace remarked that he thought the Soviet Union should try to "understand" the United States. He was promptly booed, to his great bewilderment.

In its issue of September 15, the *Daily Worker* sharply criticized Wallace. But the next day, September 16, the Russian newspaper *Pravda* praised Wallace for having detected and opposed America's "imperialistic designs." On September 17, several Soviet leaders eulogized Wallace over the radio.

On the nineteenth of September, William Z. Foster spoke highly of Wallace at a meeting in Madison Square Garden, and the Communist audience became wildly enthusiastic. Throughout the evening every mention of Wallace's name was wildly cheered. And at the plenum of the National Committee, held in December, American Communist leaders beat their breasts in groveling apology for the "incorrect and harmful" editorial in the *Daily Worker*. Eugene Dennis said with great feeling that it was "a serious error" and "an unpardonable mistake."

This was the nearest that Wallace ever came to having trouble with the Communists; since then there have been no serious signs of a rift.

The first official mention of a third party was made by William Z. Foster at a secret meeting of the National Committee on June 18-20, 1945. At that time Foster said the party's goal was a Farmer-Labor party, although the expression was deleted from his published remarks.

Soon after the Potsdam Conference, the Communists came into the open with their plans, and Wallace's ambitions and Communist schemes began gradually to coincide. In December, 1946, an editorial in *Political Affairs* urged the creation of "a people's party which will include the Communists." This editorial singled out Wallace as one who had "contributed a great deal toward checking the G.O.P. advance."

On December 29, 1947, Wallace announced that he would run for President as an independent candidate.

Another voice from the Soviet Union now began to be heard in behalf of Wallace. In the *New Times*, in the issue of January 21, 1948, a leading article praised Wallace, advocated his election as President and proclaimed the Progressive Citizens of America to be the sole remaining "progressive political organization in the United States."

The Progressive Citizens of America—which initiated the Communist line for Mr. Wallace and the Progressive party—was Communist-controlled from the beginning, and several prominent citizens who had been induced to join resigned as soon as they found what they had got into. I have described earlier how the National Citizens Political Action Committee and the Independent Committee of the Arts, Sciences and Professions, had been merged to form the P. C. A.

At the Progressive party convention held at Philadelphia in July, 1948, Wallace found his machinery in the hands of those who have always been pro-Soviet and can be designated definitely as Communist-minded. Among these prominent figures were Lee Pressman, former national counsel for the Congress of Industrial Organizations, and John Abt, former counsel for Sidney Hillman's Amalgamated Garment Workers. Championing the Progressive party likewise was Nathan Witt, former national counsel for the early National Labor Relations Board. Each one of these men refused to state to the Committee on Un-American Activities whether they were or were not members of the Communist party. The partial record of my own acquaintance, as a Red, with these gentlemen and their activities is covered in testimony before Congressional Committees.

It is little wonder that the Communists, in their enunciation of the splitting program within the Labor movement, placed such confidence in the Progressive party. In Sid Stein's directive to the comrades in the August, 1949, issue of *Political Affairs* the building of Mr. Wallace's party as a front for Communist infiltration of the unions occupies a conspicuous position. Nor can we be surprised that in September, 1949, in dealing with the thirtieth anniversary of the Communist party, the Red leadership makes "the building of this independent political party" its final and urgent order to the Communists (*Political Affairs*, September, 1949, page 96).

From my knowledge of the political loyalties of the overwhelming majority of those controlling the Progressive party, the Reds can speak of their plans for it with perfect confidence. Mr. Wallace cannot move to the right or left within that party except by their consent. Should there be any friction of a serious character between him and them, they could easily discard him.

The slogan under which Mr. Wallace's party is now to operate, according to Red decision as stated in these documents, is the winning of a "people's government." Since that term, people's government, is the great battle cry under which Soviet satellite status was foisted on Poland, Bulgaria, China, Hungary and the other dictatorships now advertised as "People's Democracies," it is clear that Henry Wallace is a prisoner of the Communists, whether he is aware of it or not. He reached that spot because the Communists continually planted around him men and women who would lead him in the pro-Red direction.

Then there is the case of Wendell Willkie, to prove that the Reds were not partial. Their leaders worked both sides of the political street assiduously, trying to penetrate each of the old political parties. That they concentrated on the Democratic party more intensively was merely because it was the party in power. But in 1940, when the Red leaders began to attack Roosevelt bitterly in an attempt to keep him from helping Britain, the emphasis shifted. Then the Politburo, proctored by Moscow, decided to aid Willkie in a left-handed way, in order to hamper Roosevelt. I sat in on several Politburo meetings and small conferences with Browder in which this decision was arrived at and its execution worked out.

For a long time the party had "one of its own" among the lawyers high in Willkie's political confidence. Secret conferences between Browder and this man, who has always asserted that he is a non-

Communist, led to the much-talked-about advertisement in the *Daily Worker* favoring Willkie's candidacy. Browder brought the original copy of the ad from one of these conferences, and we went over it together.

"It will be valuable to have roots in the Republican camp, too," Browder remarked dryly as he handed the ad to me.

Events soon bore out the wisdom of Browder's observation. The One World camp of Wendell Willkie proved to be a fine springboard into the Republican party, and there were as many comings and goings connected with the penetration of that party as there had been with the original infiltration of the New Deal groups.

One newspaper, close to the Willkie views, was so successfully infiltrated that it came to be known around Red headquarters as the "Republican edition of the *Daily Worker*." When Browder went off to jail at Atlanta Penitentiary, he ordered that paper as the one he wanted sent to him. "It represents our present line closer than any other capitalist voice," he told me.

The envelopment of Mr. Willkie became as large an item in Politburo sessions as the infiltration of the Roosevelt camp. The Ninth Floor was so satisfied with the progress made that in 1942 it took up the matter of persuading Mr. Willkie to represent William Schneiderman, California Communist district leader, in his deportation case then coming up before the United States Supreme Court. A cousin of Carol Weiss King, the shrewd lawyer for the Reds, was drawn into the discussions, and added invaluable support to the influence on Willkie of the lawyer previously mentioned.

I am sure it would have surprised the former Republican presidential candidate to know that some of his most private conversations were known and repeated on the Ninth Floor. It made the process of "softening him up" a comparatively easy one, and by the spring of 1943 Mr. Willkie was before the Supreme Court pleading the legality of the Communist fifth column in America.

Had he been aware of the discussions in the Politburo, he might have considered the matter in a different light. As Bittelman said, the expectation was that Justice Frank Murphy would take a strong stand for the Communists' view in the court, and that one or two other justices would be with him. Willkie's appearance for the defense would give these justices a certain added strength with the whole court. The Politburo therefore looked upon Willkie more or less as a front for their campaign to establish the legality of the Communist party.

The Reds, in their plans for penetration, have not overlooked Wall Street and some of the lawyers who advise Big Business. As a Communist official, I had more access to law offices serving large corporations than I have had since leaving the Communist party. This does not indicate that a great number of these gentlemen are pro-Red; it does show that too many of them are either pro-Soviet or have been led by false conceptions of how to make easy profits out of Soviet trade. Undoubtedly, the welfare of the United States did not enter too strongly into their profit calculations.

It was through a lawyer in Wall Street that I was introduced to an important United States senator, during the period when the Reds were spreading the "agrarian reformer" idea in regard to the Chinese Communists. It was a Wall Street lawyer who admitted to me that many in Big Business were convinced that the United States should co-operate in making all Europe Communist, on the grounds that the United States could trade peacefully with such an entity. This man has wide business relations and political friendships, and he spoke for others beside himself in expressing that view. I do not mean to imply that all Wall Street is going pro-Communist; but I do mean to say quite definitely that in my experience many men connected with Wall Street look upon Soviet Russia more as a market than as a menace to American independence. Only recently, in 1949, a witness before the Congressional Committee investigating Red espionage declared that

Lammot du Pont of the great financial house had expressed skepticism of any Red danger.

In my experience, one force relied on by the Communists in China was the representatives of large American industries residing in Shanghai. This estimate was not incorrect. At the height of the Red advance against Nationalist China, the American business representatives in Shanghai issued statement after statement complaining about Chiang Kai-shek's determination to resist the Communists. Dispatches to that effect appeared in both the *New York Times* and *New York Herald Tribune*. And immediately after the fall of Shanghai, in early June, 1949, American businessmen in that city got out propaganda for a loan to the Chinese Reds. The excuse given—which was scarcely a patriotic one—was that a failure by the United States to lend money to the Communist setup would cause the followers of Mao Tse-tung to abandon any policy of moderation. (Note specifically Walter Sullivan's dispatch to the *New York Times* of June 13, 1949.)

This attitude was partially the result of the constant contacts with American business interests in China established by such Communist agents as Frederick Vanderbilt Field and Philip Jaffe, with the corps of other and more concealed Reds working with them and under their direction.

The work of these pro-Soviet activities—as the Communists call them—was favored by the atmosphere of appeasement developed in America. One of the voices in business circles expressing complacency about Soviet advances is David Lawrence, editor of the *United States News*. In the May 13, 1949, issue of that interesting weekly information source for American business it is stated, "There are signs that outsiders—including Americans—can continue to do business inside a Communist China." And it is strongly hinted that if we don't learn how to be nice to the Chinese Communists, the British will get all the trade. It is unfortunate that the editors of the *United States News* do not know that this is precisely the propaganda recommended to the

American Communists even while I was in the party—to create conflict in business circles between American and British interests. And in 1949, the expected conflict was counted upon publicly, in the various organs dealing with directives coming from Moscow, to weaken the whole western world.

Again, as another instance, in its issue of May 20, 1949, the *United States News* stated in a summary of a more extensive piece:

"Real reason for Russia's shift in tactics is that the U. S. future looks brighter than Stalin once thought it would.

"Idea that U. S. might not crack up after all is catching on in Moscow. . . .

"Russian leaders are deciding they must live with capitalism, or drift to war. So a softer policy is given a trial now."

Such statements certainly did not jibe with what the Communist publications were saying. In the same month that this optimistic view of Russia appeared, *Political Affairs* published an English translation of an outstanding article by I. Kuzminov, which had appeared in *The Bolshevik* of December 15, 1948. The article was entitled, "The Crisis Character of the Economic Development of the U. S. in the Postwar Period." Its theme is clear. It called the comrades to understand that the United States was about to go into an economic tailspin—and they were to do all in their power to hasten it.

This was an order to do everything possible to injure the American economy. The decision of the World Federation of Trade Unions at Milan, a few months later, to create disruptive movements through its trade department was evidence of this. For informed Americans to have had a different idea constituted one more victory for Soviet propaganda.

The Kuzminov article was followed immediately by two significant articles entitled, "The Beginnings of the Economic Crisis in the United States," by Alexander Bittelman. His conclusions were, of course, that the comrades should work to create disorder and uproar on the American scene.

The background of appeasement in certain Big Business circles
—reminiscent of the selling of scrap iron to Japan—is fostered
and taken advantage of by the concealed Communists. I have heard
discussions on the Ninth Floor, in which the leaders of the United
Electrical, Radio and Machine Workers have been credited with
successfully pulling the wool over the eyes of officials in the General Electric Company and the General Motors Corporation. The
public acts of these corporations seemed to confirm this Red claim.
In the entire struggle that has gone forward in the UE against
the Communists, these large concerns have made no move which
can be construed as anti-Red. Indeed, in the agreement by the
General Motors Corporation in 1947, made with the UE through
James Lustig, organizer for the union's GM division, terms were
set which for a while definitely weakened the hand of Walter
Reuther, leading anti-Communist in the large CIO auto workers'
organization. Lustig is one of the men whom I met back in 1936
in the Red caucuses on the third floor of Thirteenth Street.

This judgment is not changed by the recent victory of the CIO's
union over the UE in General Motors.

So far have some corporations gone in their complacency toward
the Red control of certain unions that they have discharged
workers for anti-Communist activities. One case that can be cited
is that of Bart Enright, who was let out of a New Jersey plant at
the specific request of Communists because he was opposed to
their antipatriotic program in the union.

The bait offered Big Business by the Reds for co-operation of
this kind is sometimes a pledge of industrial peace within a plant
and sometimes trade with Soviet Russia. In either case, it is a
snare as well as a delusion, since Red trade-union policy fluctuates
with the Moscow line and Soviet trade is merely a war weapon
in the hands of the most intense of all war economies.

The Communist agent, in his cloak-and-dagger act, is therefore
playing for big stakes. He knows it is a serious business, even
though many "informed" Americans do not. Through it the fate

of peoples is decided, as in China or Poland, and America is persuaded to betray herself.

Those are fruits of the underground work by way of influence. To it we do have to add the evil results of espionage. No one is better qualified to testify on this subject than Marshal Tito, who as Josip Broz was one of Stalin's chief secret agents in Europe. In arresting a number of Cominform men in Yugoslavia, he accused them of setting up spy nets endangering the security of the Yugoslav state.

If that is done in this thieves' quarrel between Stalin and his ex-henchman, American should know without the Coplon, Bentley, Hiss-Chambers, Steve Nelson and other cases that persistent espionage goes on here. The Communist party, as that evidence shows, is the recruiting ground for this treacherous work against the United States.

The Soviet atom blast was the triumph of the Red underground. It told the world of Soviet success in filching the atom bomb know-how from the United States. The uncovering of Klaus Fuchs, British atomic scientist, as a Soviet espionage agent, again reminded America sharply of how serious subversive infiltration can be. The cloak-and-dagger business is paying huge dividends in further guarantees of Soviet world conquest.

(XI)

Clear and Present Danger

IN ALL the Soviet publications today which give directives to the Communists there is a faster beat in the commands to forward the "World Proletarian Dictatorship."

"Today," the *New Times* of May 4, 1949, tells the comrades, "the camp of democracy and socialism represents a mighty power, capable of thwarting the perfidious and blood-thirsty designs of the imperialists." The Soviet reply, the reply of the victorious Chinese Communists and of the "People's Democracies" is to smash the American imperialists and set up the proletarian dictatorship. And on August 24, the same Moscow paper promises Soviet succor to the peoples of the western countries "still languishing in capitalist slavery." With the same seditious battle cries that were echoed by the *Daily Worker* and the Reds in general before 1935, it calls upon the western peoples to "refuse to be cannon fodder." It urges them to say, "Never shall we make war on the Soviet Union, the mainstay of world peace!"

By September 7 it was proclaiming "The Collapse of the Myth of West-European Economic Recovery," the title heading an article which forecast complete chaos out of the "Marshallization" of Europe.

In confident words, Moscow reminds its followers that "the Soviet Union no longer faces the imperialists alone"; it emphasizes that in the Soviet camp there are now "five hundred millions of China, who are shaking off the fetters of imperialism." They are attracting to the Soviet banner "the peoples of the other Asiatic countries that are devotedly fighting for their national liberation."

Repeatedly we are told that Stalin's promise that "the war-mongers will be defeated" is on the eve of being fulfilled. And that end can be achieved only by applying "the Leninist science of victory," winning world Soviet rule.

Thus does the 1949 and 1950 world Communist press foretell in the name of peace the early success of war upon America.

In the House on Thirteenth Street, it is this expectation that keeps alive the fiery devotion of the comrades. The Soviet conquest of America, prophesies William Z. Foster in his new book, *The Twilight of World Capitalism*, will come to pass in less than a generation. In his dedication he dates this occurrence by stating that his great-grandson shall see a Communist America. From this, every Communist knows that the plan is to set up the Soviet dictatorship within the comparatively near future, since according to Red theory the Communist Society can emerge only *after* Soviet rule has been established by force and violence—and after mankind has been "perfected" by the whiplash of the dictatorship.

As Foster sums up the case: "The forward march of socialism is irresistible. For the world capitalist system the handwriting is on the wall." In the language of the Communists that is a declaration of the invincible onward march of Soviet conquest.

Many other important articles by leading Communists last year had the same theme, particularly in assessing the results of Red advances in China.

In strange contrast, too many of the leading people in America seem to think the Communist problem was disposed of with the inauguration of the Marshall Plan. There is considerable talk of the "containment of Soviet aggression."

America seems seriously obliged, in view of these diametrically opposed conclusions, to examine its present position. It must ask soberly: "Is this period the beginning of the end of Communist attacks upon the other nations, or is this the beginning of the end of the United States as an independent nation?"

The initiative in the contest still remains in the hands of the Soviet dictatorship. The Marshall Plan (now supported by the Military Aid Program) has momentarily slowed down the march of Soviet success in Europe. But meanwhile, millions of Chinese have fallen under Soviet slavery. The new government's adherence to Russia, openly stated in its constitution and recently underlined by the signing of the Sino-Soviet pact, is a measure of how extensive has been the defeat of the United States in this area. That Mao Tse-tung would place himself completely at the disposal of Stalin was a foregone conclusion, and it will be a long time in history before America can repair the damage done by the organized chicanery that led her to believe otherwise.

The United States, the most powerful nation on earth, has been unable to prevent Soviet Russia's seizure of 700,000,000 people since 1945 and great land areas and resources which split the world in two. On the floor of the United Nations, there is no strong presentation on behalf of the Polish people, to whom we made a solemn pledge of free elections. The Chinese issue comes belatedly there, a tragedy brought about largely by our own self-deception.

There has been some rejoicing over Tito's break with Stalin, which was caused in large part by the Yugoslav dictator's inability to Russify the Croats and Serbs. But it is uncertain whether the real lesson of the Tito incident has been learned—that *a firm moral stand would cause many cracks in the Soviet façade.*

The inability to deal effectively with either the Soviet dictatorship or its agents here arises, in my opinion, from a lack of understanding that Communism is based on the same ideology that creates capitalist excesses. Historical materialism, the basis of the Soviet state and the philosophy from which the Soviet dictatorship acquires its ruthless determination to overthrow all the countries on the globe, is of the same nature as the philosophy that bred capitalist crimes against the workers in the name of The Economic

Man. It is from this philosophy that Communists draw their conviction that Stalin and his cohorts of the Bolshevik parties "will be victorious throughout the world under the militant banner of Marx-Engels-Lenin-Stalin."

From my own knowledge of the strength of the Communist forces, and from my experience within the Communist movement, it seems clear to me that America is more than powerful enough materially to check Soviet advances in other countries and here, but that she has not yet developed the necessary moral weapons and techniques.

In recognizing this fact, no partisan consideration can be involved in the sense of Republican or Democratic contests. Within both parties, appeasement tendencies have been strong and the issue has been clouded. In neither party do we hear any call for the Four Freedoms as clearly as during the war.

There is an awakening, but it is too slow. Confronted with overwhelming evidence that the Communist party is Stalin's agency, changing its program always in accordance with Stalin's plans, America hides this fact from itself and refuses to act upon it. The Communist party has no hesitancy in saying where its allegiance lies. In 1928 the Communist International let all the world know it controls the Communist party here by its "open letter" driving Jay Lovestone from leadership and membership. Behind that action was the determination to maintain the American party as an agency of the proletarian dictatorship guided by Stalin.

Today the Communists say that their chief aim must be "deepening and further developing our Marxist-Leninist theory as Stalin has taught us." That is the instruction given to the comrades by Alexander Bittelman in the September, 1949, issue of *Political Affairs*. Now Marxism-Leninism—that golden Aesopian word—means, as it is important to keep in mind, a dedication to the violent overthrow of the democratic bourgeois governments by force and violence. When Communists "return to Leninist prin-

ciples" or to Marxism-Leninism, they steel themselves anew to a
program and plans which will bring about the early and violent
shattering of the government of the country in which they are
operating. They say to themselves, in other words, that they will
do everything from then on to prepare for the violent destruction
of their "own" government within the shortest realizable period
of time.

William Z. Foster emphasized Bittelman's instructions when on
the same occasion he stressed the fact that the party was based
on "the classical works of Marx, Engels, Lenin and Stalin." And
complete subservience to Stalin was the theme of the *New Times'*
special supplement on "The U.S.S.R. Conference for Peace,"
which contains at least twenty speeches devoted to the glorification
of Stalin as the leader of all peoples.

The American Communist party, in a special resolution by the
National Committee on December 21, 1949, reiterated its own
fealty to Stalin. At the same time it feverishly prepared for extending "the United Front from below," the tactic used during the
days of the Red trade unions by which it hopes to create endless
confusion in the American economic scene. The loud talk of
"peace" and of a "peace pact" between the United States and Soviet
Russia in which the Communists are indulging cannot be taken at
its face value. It was under the cloak of talk of peace that Soviet
Russia was able to win American acquiescence to its entry into
Manchuria and to what Arthur Bliss Lane, our former ambassador
to Poland, has called the betrayal of that country. If the American
people were aware of the real meaning of Communist documents,
they would know that the only peace that Soviet Russia will ever
agree to is the "peace" of complete Soviet conquest of the United
States.

To sum up the current events that mark the Communist party as
Soviet Russia's fifth column would be too repetitious. Numerous
publications label it a fifth column; every intelligent American

knows it to be such. Yet few effective measures have been taken to deal with it according to its true character.

The Communists have been much more alert than patriotic Americans in bringing pressure on Congress. Any step to deal effectively with Soviet subversion has been the object of an immediate organized attack. Hundreds of thousands of letters flooded the House and Senate against the Mundt-Nixon Bill and successfully smothered this anti-Communist legislation. Some of this opposition is obviously not Communist—for there are some people who persist in the illusion that the Communist party is not what it is. The campaign itself, however, was entirely the product of the Communists, working through other sectors of American life and opinion.

The Communist technique of "stirring up" or "mobilizing" the people is one of the most effective methods of minority control of public opinion ever developed. Just before I left the party in 1945, Eugene Dennis could state proudly that "our campaigns have defeated over and over again the entire anti-Communist efforts of all the veterans' organizations." That happens to be the truth.

Under the persuasion of Communist agents, thousands of American men and women raised their voices in behalf of issues to which, if they knew the truth, they would be opposed. During the three years I worked for the party in Chicago, we used this technique constantly. I saw clearly how it operated to deceive the American people and, as Foster said, "to frighten cowardly politicians."

Every Communist district leader in the United States receives the *Daily Worker* by air mail. He reads it with great care and attention. If he finds an editorial which embodies a command, such as the defeat of the Mundt-Nixon Bill, he immediately calls his staff together, including the comrades in charge of trade unions, professions, and so on. Forthwith they flood Washington with wires and letters. Postcards are prepared on mimeographing machines for people who do not write easily.

Many of these letters are decidedly synthetic. A Communist who is secretary of an organization, or an officer or member of some subcommittee, with access to the organization's stationery, will not hesitate to write a supposedly official communication without authority. If he feels that the organization will not support the view the party has ordered him to voice, he will frequently send in a communication on his own account, pledging the organization to that stand.

In contrast to this fanatical campaigning patriotic Americans have been laggard, and consequently not clearly heard in Congress. Again, this phenomenon cuts across political party lines; it is a common weakness of the American people as a whole.

America has found particular difficulty in dealing with the Soviet fifth-column activities that feed on domestic abuses. One of the great tactics of the Communists is to play up certain weaknesses in the non-Soviet nations. Though these weaknesses may exist in a much more repulsive form under Soviet rule itself, native Reds nevertheless carry on a systematic campaign to stress them in their own countries, simply in order to foster sedition and disorder.

For example, when it served Soviet Russia's purpose to ignore the Negro, the party, as we have seen, left him severely alone. But now that incitation of the colonial peoples is again the order of the day, the attention of the Communists has turned once more to the Negro as a potential tool of their anti-American activities. They are exploiting the harsh lot of the Mexican-Americans with the same cynical attitude.

America must be more alert to these strategems of the Communists. To genuine regard for Negro rights and the protection of Mexican-Americans will have to be added a keen understanding of the Communists' misuse of some of these just causes for Soviet ends. It is not a hopeless undertaking.

Another weapon America must develop for its own protection is a technique for coping with concealed Communists. Actually there is no reason today why any man should be falsely accused of being a Red. Nor is there any longer any excuse for not knowing when

Communist work is involved. The Committee on Un-American Activities in Washington has a research bureau which can help. Agencies like Counter-Attack, at 55 East 42nd Street, New York, can provide valuable information on the degree of co-operation or the extent of affiliation existing between the Communists and certain individuals and organizations.

The ease with which the Communists are able to form organizations adorned with prominent names is another defeat for the ordinary American. He is living in an unreal world as far as knowing anything about actual Red operations is concerned. Consequently, either he or his neighbor is constantly being taken in. Almost everybody is against Communism in America today—but many, out of misinformation, are aiding the Communist cause. If Communism were to present its case openly, it could not rally any more people than it gets into the party. But as things are, it moves thousands without their knowing it. In a democracy it is high time that there be enough public knowledge at least to locate the enemy or those aiding the enemy.

When we speak of the Communist party as a conspiracy directed by Moscow, we cannot realistically accuse every individual rank-and-file Communist of being consciously in that conspiracy. Few of the rank-and-filers know anything at all about Gerhart Eisler or J. V. Peters. They do what they are ordered to do. Many of them, attracted by Communist cries against social injustices, find themselves as Reds promoting the greatest injustice of all—the advance of the Slave State. Even some of these people come to understand in time that monopoly capitalism and Communist monopoly are brothers under the skin, with Red rule the more ruthless. This belated realization is the reason why there are thousands of ex-Communists in America today, and why the turnover in Red membership is so high.

So, too, every man or woman who appears on a list engineered by a Communist front is not consciously aiding Stalin. It is an occasion for much concern, however, that so often men and women in outstanding positions get caught in these fronts. One case recently at hand was the so-called Bill of Rights Conference held in New York on July 16-17, 1949. This was the biggest Red-front gathering since the Congress of Intellectuals held at the Waldorf-Astoria in March of the same year.

The main feature of the affair was the presence of seven of the eleven members of the Politburo on trial at that time, three of the others being in jail on contempt charges. And yet to this thoroughly Communist-run front such a known non-Communist as Senator Warren G. Magnuson of Washington was induced to lend his name. At least it appeared on the list of sponsors. Other people connected with the meeting included men like Prof. Thomas I. Emerson of Yale Law School, Robert W. Kenny, former Attorney General of California, and Prof. Linus Pauling of the California Institute of Technology, who is also president of the American Chemical Society. Prominent among the speakers was the Hollywood director, Herbert Biberman, now under indictment for refusing to tell Congress whether he is a CP member or not. Sidney Roger, party-line commentator on the American Broadcasting Company's San Francisco radio station KGO, told in his speech how he had contributed to the defeat of anti-Communist legislation in the California legislature. There were seven professors on the list from one university alone, the University of Chicago.

The serious thing about this business is that these people were induced to lend their names to what will be turned into a big propaganda drive—to assail the Federal Bureau of Investigation, to disguise the character of the CP, to frighten liberals, and to attempt to influence Supreme Court justices. Paul Robeson announced to the cheering audience that a new "nonpartisan committee" would be created to defend the eleven Communist party leaders. The *Daily Worker* opened the campaign by denouncing the FBI as "Public Enemy No. 1." In this manner, under cover of outstanding names, the active comrades doing the real work will create confusion in public opinion, as they have done on a number of other occasions.

The American people have been persuaded that much has been

done to check the Soviet fifth column in this country; that the various Communist trials and the expulsion of the Communist unions from the CIO have had a real effect. It is a matter of cold fact, however, that the Communist party, with some rearrangements, is just as destructively placed as it has been for some time. From my own knowledge and observations I can say flatly that in the professional, intellectual and creative fields particularly, it is more strongly entrenched than it was when I left the party in 1945. Infiltration of certain government agencies and opinion-making organizations has reached such a new high that the scene begins to resemble the early days of the People's Front, when Communists worked their way into important posts on the National Labor Relations Board, were high in the Department of Agriculture, and were extensively employed on the Federal payrolls. Small indications of this are the facts that the National Lawyers Guild is one of the agencies consulted by the Senate Judiciary Committee on appointments to the Federal bench, and that even the Economic Cooperation Administration in charge of the Marshall Plan is being infiltrated with friends of the Communists. Particularly has the party made headway in the radio field, which is such a potent force in shaping public opinion today. Indeed, some weeks it has looked as though a special effort had been made to put Reds on the airways. Again, not until early in 1950, *for the first time,* did the unit of the American Newspaper Guild in one of the largest of our national news magazines succeed in electing a non-Communist slate of officers. That this occurred only after five years of the cold war is indicative of the grip the Communists had on the staff of that publication. It was considered for years the pride of the party. My knowledge of this fact is based on my own role in directing the infiltration of similar publications.

In all these fields, I repeat, the Red contingent is a distinct minority. However, more serious in many ways than the possession of the materials of war by the Soviet Union is the continued misapprehension of the American people of how the Communists measure their strength. One Communist placed on a key radio chain, for instance, can create endless confusion in grass-roots opinion. Similarly, though the greatest advances against the Communists have been made in labor, they count on their small cells in the basic industries, which can expand rapidly in time of crisis. And those cells are being maintained.

All this—the insinuation of pro-Communist views in certain national radio programs, the creation of new Communist-front organizations under distinguished sponsorship, and the many other devices to tint American public opinion in favor of the Communists —forms a disturbing current pattern. There are, however, some encouraging signs. A substantial victory against Communism was won in June, 1949, when the leading educational organizations in the country officially recognized reality. The Educational Policies Commission of the National Education Association said then in its report that members of the Communist party should not be allowed to hold jobs as teachers. The Committee included President Dwight D. Eisenhower of Columbia University and President James B. Conant of Harvard. This is decidedly to the good, since it was only a short time ago that President Raymond B. Allen of the University of Washington was assailed on many campuses throughout the country for having discharged three professors, two of whom belatedly admitted that they were Communist party members. Despite Allen's generally liberal views, the Reds and their friends denounced him as a modern ogre.

It will also be helpful in smoking out concealed Communist agents that Judge Bennett Champ Clark in the United States Circuit Court of Appeals has found against the Hollywood writers who refused to state to Congress whether or not they had been members of the Communist party. While this decision will probably be reviewed by the United States Supreme Court, it offers hope that the investigation of others who have worked for the Communist cause consistently can be forwarded more effectively in the future.

In no way does America weaken its defenses more surely than in its hesitancy to raise the moral issues arising from Soviet aggression and Soviet tactics.

This has to be repeated time and again, because it is apparently not fully realized. The Communists steep themselves in a carefully worked out, preconceived point of view under which they become entitled, in their own eyes, to fit their propaganda to the ends they are seeking to attain. Thus America can be represented as wanting to conquer the world, whereas that is the Soviet aim. (Indeed, it is a common Communist practice to accuse others of doing what they intend to do themselves.)

Americans may be experts in mechanical know-how, as is so often said, but they are babes in the woods when it comes to conspiratorial know-how. There is little appreciation of the fact that the basic philosophy of Communism makes for the ruthlessness and determination to achieve world conquest—the "World October"—that mark the Soviet dictatorship. This book cannot analyze this Communist philosophy, for that is not its purpose. A few moments' thought could show, however, that historical materialism, with its conception of a dialectical movement produced by force and violence, leads to those characteristics. The Soviet dictatorship will not and cannot discard them. Every Marxist prophet—Marx, Engels, Lenin, and Stalin—has made that premise the cardinal point of the Red world view.

During my last days at the *Daily Worker*—just before my departure from the party—there came into the House on Thirteenth Street an article in the *New Times* of June 1, 1945, which received some attention in the trial of the eleven Communists. It should attain still more fame. Its title was "Patriotism" and its author one N. Baltisky, unknown even to the Ninth Floor. But the importance of his message was known there, for orders were given to reproduce the piece in the October, 1945, issue of *Political Affairs*.

The Baltisky piece clearly prepared the Communists fully for the cold war; its burden was that patriotism to one's country could best be expressed through patriotism to the Soviet Union. Among other things in this remarkable document, Baltisky told the comrades of the world: "When the workers of Russia became the complete masters of their country, the intelligent workers of other countries naturally conceived a deep attachment for our Soviet country and began to call it the motherland of the workers of all countries. But at the same time their attachment for our country aroused in them a deeper attachment for their own country. The inspiring example of the Soviet people led them to believe in a brighter future for their own people."

A "proletarian patriotism" arises, then, "born of the reflection of Soviet patriotism in the hearts of the workers of other countries."

The solidarity of these "Soviet patriots"—that is, the Reds in every land—with the Soviet dictatorship is the highest patriotism to their own nation, writes Baltisky. This is so because the Soviet Union is a socialist state, he argues, one which cannot by its nature injure another nation.

By that article, which says much more to the same effect, the Kremlin established a theory which justifies quislingism in every nation, betrayal of any and every non-Soviet country into the hands of Soviet aggression in the name of "patriotism."

Having accepted that premise, it is easy for the devoted Red to spread far and wide any fabrication that bears the Soviet label.

The Communist is prepared to defend Soviet aggression from the following self-established base: "By its very nature, the land of Socialism cannot wage aggressive war." The reason is clear, states Maurice Thorez. A country in which the capitalist regime, the regime of the exploitation of man by man, no longer exists, naturally cannot pursue imperialist aims. That is why the foreign policy of the Soviet Union enjoys such confidence among the working people of the world; "that is why they look toward the Kremlin walls with such love" (*For a Lasting Peace, for a People's Democracy!*—Organ of the Information Bureau of the Communist and Workers Parties, March 15, 1949).

Consequently, when the Soviet Red armies entered the Baltic

countries, in violation of pacts solemnly made, that was not conquest; it was "liberation." And so "liberation" has moved on—into
Poland, Bulgaria, Albania, Rumania, Yugoslavia and now China.
And if Marshal Tito were to be overthrown, very possibly by assassination within his own Red household, the Soviet empire would
"liberate" Yugoslavia a second time.

By such reasoning, if you dare to call it that, a man is forbidden
to reason at all. He must accept the premise laid down by Moscow
and carried out by force. It is this closely knit and fanatically committed drive that has carried Soviet aggression to its heights of
present conquest.

Only a strong moral stand internationally at every point and a
firm position internally can successfully meet such a ruthless foe.
Such measures are vital to this country's life. The danger becomes
greater and more immediate with each day that Soviet Russia is
allowed to tighten its control of the satellites. It increases with each
failure to halt the activities of the Communist party, and today a
factual report would show that they have not been halted at all.

Such a foe, working assiduously within the nation to destroy it,
constitutes a clear and present danger to the American republic.
There is much discussion in many quarters whether Russia will
launch a military conflict against the United States. The real answer
is that World War III is already on. It has not reached the shooting
stage so far as the United States is concerned, but thousands of
other casualties have taken place in this war. The Communists are
taught constantly the dictum of General Clausewitz that war is
merely the extension of politics by other means. They know too, as
I learned when a Communist, that the converse is true. Politics can
be war.

When we consider the question of clear and present danger, we
have to note what has happened in a very short time. Soviet Russia
is waging a two-front war upon this country—the "creeping blitzkrieg" I predicted some years ago. It has met with such startling
success that within five years Stalin's empire has grown from

190,000,000 people to more than 900,000,000. This was the proud boast of Georgi M. Malenkov on November 7, 1949—the anniversary of the Bolshevist Revolution.

Since the expendability of human beings in order to attain a goal is accepted as the master tactic of Soviet warfare, it must be plain that American security is in a defensive position today.

I am not seeking here to present a program of the measures America should take. I am merely reporting what I know and what I saw, hoping from that to tell the nation of the immediate danger with which it is confronted. Further self-deception about the intention of the Soviet dictatorship will prove fatal to this country.

The moral initiative which the situation requires would end all pretense regarding the realities. It would recognize that Soviet spies do operate here on a large scale and that the Communist party is their recruiting ground, as it was proved to be in Canada. What could be more eloquent testimony than the conviction of the national organizer of the Canadian Communist party and of the chief Communist member of Parliament for direct participation in the Soviet military espionage machine? It was nondebatable documentary evidence, taken from the Soviet embassy in Ottawa, upon which they were convicted.

A firm initiative would lay upon all Americans, learning humility in this new world-wide moral crisis, the obligation to engage in the democratic processes of the country. They must let Washington know how they feel about these matters and what they want done. They must wrest the offensive from the apologists of the Stalinist regime with petitions and communications to Congress and the President.

Americans will have to proceed on this course with calmness but with determination, knowing that a firm stand for our pledges and against Soviet slavery on a moral basis will inspire and enlighten the peoples everywhere.

Within America, our citizens must protect civil liberties but present the truth on this issue and not the falsehoods and fabrications of the Communists. A true defense of civil liberties recognizes that the Communists mean to destroy such liberties. To safeguard American freedom the fifth column which menaces that freedom will have to be dealt with as a fifth column and not as something else— a legitimate political party, for example, which is pure fiction.

We must not be guilty of convicting people by association, but we will be required realistically to judge men and women in public life by their deeds. There is every reason, in the name of national security, that those who constantly give aid and comfort to the Kremlin be called to strict account in a court of public opinion for their acts against the country of their citizenship.

God grant that America may have the alertness to distinguish fact from fancy, the wisdom to understand the true nature of her Soviet opponent, and the courage to stand firm for her own defense and that of all mankind.

INDEX

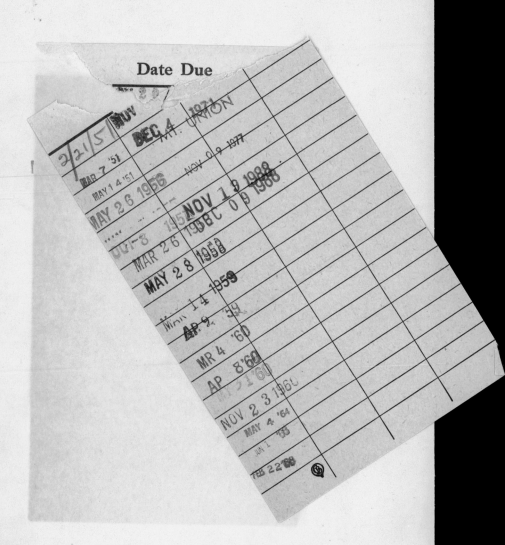

Date Due

3/21/51	NUV	DEC 4 1971 MT. UNION		
MAR 7 '51		NOV 0 9 1977		
MAY 1 4 '51				
MAY 2 6 1966		NOV 1 9 1988		
		NOV 1 9 1988		
OCT 3 195	MAR 2 6 '58	BEC 0 9 1988		
MAY 2 8 1958				
MAR 1 4 1959				
AP 9 '59				
MR 4 '60				
AP 8 '60				
NOV 2 3 1960				
MAY 4 '64				
JUN 1 '65				
FEB 2 2 '66				